YORKSHIRE'S CRICKETING LEGENDS
Yorkshire-born Test Cricketers

YORKSHIRE'S CRICKETING LEGENDS
Yorkshire-born Test Cricketers

GRENVILLE FIRTH

breedon **books**
PUBLISHING

First published in Great Britain in 2009 by
The Breedon Books Publishing Company Limited,
3 The Parker Centre, Derby, DE21 4SZ.

ISBN 978-1-85983-726-9
Printed and bound in TJ International Ltd,
Padstow, Cornwall.

CONTENTS

ACKNOWLEDGEMENTS

I wish to thank Breedon Books, Michelle Harrison and Steve Caron in particular, for ensuring this book has come to publication and to the following for assistance in the furnishing of information or illustrative material and images: Arthur Bower, Mick Pope (www.adelphiarchive.co.uk), Richard Holdridge (Hon Archivist) Leicestershire County Cricket Club and Rebecca Trbojevich, Communications Manager of Lancashire County Cricket Club, Rick Smith, Tasmania, Ron Foley (Walton Caster Ltd) and Neil Leach (Scotland Historian).

Last, but by no means least, my thanks go to Raymond Illingworth for readily agreeing to contribute the foreword. Always a favourite cricketer of mine, Ray, along with Wilfred Rhodes, is the only Yorkshire-born Test cricketer to have scored over 1,000 runs and taken in excess of 100 wickets for England. He is also the only captain to have set off without the Ashes and not only come back with them, but also retained them in England as well. In my humble opinion, he was the best tactical captain that I have seen walk out onto a cricket field. Ray also sets an example to all former Test and first-class cricketers in that he has never forgotten his cricket roots and is still actively involved in all aspects of his beloved Farsley Cricket Club.

Grenville Firth

2009

INTRODUCTION

Of all the 18 first-class cricket counties, there are none with a richer and more illustrious history than Yorkshire County Cricket Club.

Many have walked onto the field of play to represent the White Rose County, but not all have worn the famous cap and sweater, while some have gone no further than a brief appearance or a second XI match, but it is certain that none will ever forget the day they did.

There are only 78 cricketers that have gone on to represent their country, and some have become household names in every cricket-playing country in the world, thus becoming the true legends of Yorkshire and England cricket.

Of course, not all Yorkshire-born cricketers who played for their country have played for their native county, in fact 15 of them did not. Some moved to distant lands early in their career, while others could not break into the Yorkshire team for one reason or another, but all have a connection to the county because of their birth. It is, I think, fair to assume that all who did not would have played, given the chance, and this book will allow the reader to see who those players are and why this select band of 95 cricketers have got something very special in common.

Jim Laker and Derek Shackleton, to name but two, are players that slipped the Yorkshire net, each because of different circumstances, and imagine what a Yorkshire bowling attack it would have been in the 1950s and 60s with Laker and Shackleton joining Trueman, Wardle, Appleyard and Illingworth. Indeed, would Surrey have won the County Championship seven times in the 1950s if those two in particular had worn the White Rose of Yorkshire? In addition, three others, Hanson Carter, George Glover and Dr George Thornton, played Test cricket for Australia and South Africa respectively.

The intriguing question is who will be the 96th Yorkshire-born cricketer to represent his country? My guess is that if he continues to progress as we all hope, both for Yorkshire's and England's sake, not only will Adil Rashid become that player but he will also be the first Asian-born Yorkshireman to wear the three lions on his sweater.

FOREWORD

When Grenville asked me to write a few words as a foreword to his book *Yorkshire's Cricketing Legends: Yorkshire-born Test Cricketers* I was more than interested in the list myself, not only for those players who have played for Yorkshire, but also for the great cricketers like Jim Laker and Derek Shackleton who never played for the county of their birth. Looking at the full list, I am sure that no other county can come up with a list of names to compare with Yorkshire's, and a few of the players such as George Hirst and Wilfred Rhodes hold records that will never be beaten.

Unfortunately, a lot of the traditions I grew up with no longer apply within the game, such as having to be born in Yorkshire to play for them. Many a wife had to make the dash back to the Broad Acres to make sure the offspring was born inside the county, indeed my own daughter made the trip from Buckinghamshire to Leeds.

One name missing from the list is a man who had a lot to do with Yorkshire's fortunes in the early days and is one of its most famous names: Lord Hawke. However, he was born in Lincolnshire.

Looking at the list of 78 players who played for Yorkshire it is amazing how many left for one reason or another to play for other counties – myself included. I certainly think that this had something to do with the way the club was run at one time. I can assure those people who think that the players these days are pampered, this was not the case until the 1970s. At certain grounds the wives of players had to find a seat wherever they could, even at the far end of the ground, and they had to listen to some not always nice comments about their husbands. However, I am pleased to say that today things are much improved for the players and their families.

To finish, I am sure a lot of people will get great pleasure from reading this book and from some of the amazing feats of the players. I am certainly proud to have my name on the list and I know that players of my era would have given their right arm to play for the County of the White Rose. I hope that feeling still applies.

Ray Illingworth
2009

Robert Appleyard

RHB & ROB, 1950–58

Born: 27 June 1924, Wibsey, Bradford.
Played for: Yorkshire.
Test Matches: (9) 1954–56 Cap No. 373

Batting Career for England

I	NO	HS	Runs
9	6	19*	51
AV	100	50	Catches
17.00	-	-	4

Bowling for England

Balls	Runs	Wkts	Av
1,596	554	31	17.87
Best	5wl	10wl	Sr/Rate
5–51	1	-	51.48

First-Class Career: (152 matches) 1950–58

Batting

I	NO	HS	Runs
149	54	63	776
AV	100	50	Catches
8.52	-	1	80

Bowling

Balls	Runs	Wkts	Av
30,026	10,965	708	15.48
Best	5wl	10wl	Sr/Rate
8–76	57	17	15.48

Bob Appleyard was a promising schoolboy cricketer, and in 1938, at the age of 14, he took 5–5 in the Yorkshire Schools Cricket Association Cup Final. He then joined Manningham Mills in the Bradford League and later joined Undercliffe.

Upon leaving the Royal Navy he joined Bowling Old Lane and after a successful spell with Yorkshire Seconds was given his first-team debut against Scotland in Edinburgh in 1950 at the late age of 26. Appleyard played three matches that first season and took 11 wickets, but the following year, 1951, he struck gold when he claimed an astonishing 200 wickets at 14.14 in what was his first full season. His haul of wickets included 12 for 94 against Somerset at Taunton (5 for 36 and 7 for 57), 12 for 93 against Leicestershire at Grace Road (5 for 72 and 7 for 16) and 12 for 43 against Essex at Bradford Park Avenue (6 for 17 and 6 for 26). It was the most wickets ever taken by a bowler in his first full season and he also headed the national bowling averages. During the season he achieved his best bowling figures of 8 for 76 against the MCC at Scarborough and was selected as one of *Wisden's* five cricketers of the year.

Bob Appleyard was the ultimate multi-purpose bowler. Tall with a high, easy action, he could bowl medium fast in-swingers and off-breaks, with subtle variations of pace. In addition he could bowl leg-cutters and off-cutters, which made him as lethal as he was unique. Remarkably accurate, he seemed to gain unusual bounce and this, together with a deceptive flight, made him a difficult prospect at any time but completely devastating on drying pitches.

The following spring, after just one game, he was diagnosed with tuberculosis and missed the next two seasons, before he made a spectacular return in 1954. He took 154 wickets at 14.42, including 12 for 88 (5 for 72 and 7 for 16) against Somerset at Taunton and 12 for 124 (7 for 44 and 5 for 80) against MCC at Scarborough, and he came second in the national averages and won his first England cap against Pakistan at Nottingham, taking a wicket with his second ball. He also returned figures of 5 for 51 in that match, his best in Test cricket.

This brought about selection for Len Hutton's party for the 1954–55 tour to Australia, where he played an important part in England successfully retaining the Ashes, taking 11 wickets at 20.36 and providing magnificent support for Frank Tyson and Brian Statham. On the New Zealand leg of the tour he took nine wickets at an average of 8.88 in the two tests, returning 4 for 7 in the second innings at Auckland when New Zealand were bowled out for 26.

In 1955, now almost exclusively bowling spinners, Appleyard was almost unplayable on the early season wet wickets, but unfortunately a knee injury wiped out almost all of his cricket after the middle of June. However, he recovered well enough to capture 110 wickets for Yorkshire in the following summer, which included his last 12 wicket haul, 12 for 106 (6 for 37 and 6 for 69) against Derbyshire at Chesterfield, and he made the last of his nine Test appearances against Australia at Trent Bridge, Nottingham.

Sadly, tuberculosis returned once again and his form suffered so badly that he decided to retire at the end of 1958, unable to fulfil what many had predicted – that he would become one of the best bowlers of all time.

For Yorkshire he played 133 matches, taking 642 wickets at 15.42, scored 679 runs at 8.59 and he held 70 catches.

After his retirement Appleyard became a very successful businessman and founded the Yorkshire Cricket Academy at Bradford Park Avenue, working with the Sir Leonard Hutton Foundation Scheme for young cricketers. The proceeds from his book *No Coward Soul* was donated to this fund. He was also involved in a High Court case with the late Robert Maxwell over pension funds and won quite a large settlement. In 1997 he was awarded an honorary doctorate by the University of Bradford.

As a reward for his services to the county, he was made President of Yorkshire County Cricket Club.

Thomas Armitage

RHB & RM, LOBS, 1872–79

Born: 25 April 1848, Walkley, Sheffield.
Died: 21 September 1922, Pullman, Chicago.
Played for: Yorkshire.

Test Matches: (2) 1876–77 Cap No. 1
Batting Career for England

I	NO	HS	Runs
3	-	21	33
AV	**100**	**50**	**Catches**
11.00	-	-	-

Bowling for England

Balls	Runs	Wkts	Av
12	15	-	-
Best	**5wl**	**10wl**	**Sr/Rate**
-	-	-	-

First-Class Career: (56 Matches) 1872–79
Batting

I	NO	HS	Runs
56	8	92	1,122
AV	**100**	**50**	**Catches**
13.35	-	3	23

Bowling

Balls	Runs	Wkts	Av
4,197	1,699	119	14.27
Best	**5wl**	**10wl**	**Sr/Rate**
7–26	12	3	35.26

Born in Walkley, Sheffield, Tom Armitage was an excellent opening or middle-order batsman and a straight round-arm medium-pace bowler who also bowled underhand high lobs. He was also a good fielder.

In 1870, Armitage, a mason by trade, played as a professional for Keighley and two years later took 18 wickets against Wakefield, 8 in the first innings and all 10 in the second. Later that season he made his debut for Yorkshire against Nottinghamshire at Trent Bridge, opening the batting in the first innings, but he failed to make an impression, scoring 0 and 1, and failed to take a wicket from eight overs.

His next appearance for the county was against a United South of England XI in 1874, but it was another 12 months before he made his mark for Yorkshire, scoring the first of four half-centuries for the county with 68 not out against Surrey, and he also took 5 for 8 in 4.1 overs against

Nottinghamshire, who were declared County Champions for that year. In addition he played for the United North of England against a Derbyshire XI, snaring 12 for 61 in the match (7 for 27 and 5 for 34) and bowling unchanged throughout both completed innings with his Yorkshire colleague Allen Hill.

The following season he scored his highest first-class score, 95, against Middlesex and was the outstanding player in the game against Surrey at Bramall Lane. He top scored with 47 out of a total of 173 and then proceeded to destroy the Southerners' batting attack with his lob bowling, taking 13 wickets for 46 runs (6 for 20 and 7 for 26) and he finished the season with 45 wickets at 14.86.

His successful season brought him an invitation, along with four of his Yorkshire colleagues, Tom Emmett, Andrew Greenwood, Allen Hill and George Ulyett, to join James Lillywhite's tour of Australia in the winter of 1876–77. All five played in the Test match at Melbourne in March 1877, which was later officially recorded as the very first Test match. While Armitage did nothing of note in the match, scoring 9 and 3 runs respectively, and failing to take a wicket in 3 overs, he did manage to make history by being credited, due to alphabetical order, as the first player to represent England in Test cricket and is therefore number one in the order of Test caps. He played in the second Test again at the MCG, scored a Test best of 21 but did not get to bowl in what was his last Test appearance.

In the summer of 1877 he had his best of five seasons with the White Rose County, taking 42 wickets at 11.66 apiece, which included 6 for 32 against Lancashire in the Roses match at Old Trafford as well as contributing 72 with the bat. In addition, he took 7 for 58 against Surrey at Bramall Lane and 6 for 43 in the return match at the Oval, and he took 10 for 74 versus Nottinghamshire at Sheffield (5 for 39 and 5 for 35).

The following year, 1878, proved to be his last for Yorkshire, and once again he distinguished himself at Bramall Lane, scoring 45 against the Australians (in a Yorkshire victory by 9 wickets) and 71 versus Surrey, notching up over 300 runs for the county.

For Yorkshire he played in 52 matches, scored 1,053 runs at 13.67, took 107 wickets at 15.03 and held 20 catches.

His last first-class game in England was for the United North of England against London United in 1879, before he emigrated to the United States to become groundsman and coach at the Pullman Cricket Club in Chicago. He played one more First-Class-match for the Players of United States of America against the Gentlemen of Philadelphia, scoring 58 and taking 2 for 25. He died in Pullman, Chicago, at the age of 74.

Charles William Jeffrey Athey

RHB & OB, 1976–97

Born: 27 September 1957, Middlesbrough.
Played for: Yorkshire, Gloucestershire and
Sussex.
Test Matches: (23) 1980–88 Cap No. 487
Batting Career for England

I	NO	HS	Runs
41	1	123	919
AV	**100**	**50**	**Catches**
22.97	1	4	13

First-Class Career: (467 Matches) 1976–97
Batting

I	NO	HS	Runs
784	71	184	25,453
AV	**100**	**50**	**Ct/St**
35.69	55	126	429/2

Bowling

Balls	Runs	Wkts	Av
4,810	2,673	48	55.68
Best	**5wl**	**10wl**	**Sr/Rate**
3–3	-	-	100.20

One of a number of Middlesbrough-born players to play for Yorkshire, Bill Athey was for a long time seen as a natural successor to Geoff Boycott. Unfortunately, a lack of consistency at vital periods in his career meant he never really fulfilled his potential at Test level.

A talented schoolboy cricketer and a product of Acklam Hall Grammer School, he made his first-class debut for Yorkshire against Northamptonshire at Northampton in May 1976, scoring 10 and 37 respectively. In the same summer and in only his fifth match he notched up his maiden first-class century, 131 not out, against Sussex at Headingley.

Athey received his county cap in 1980 after scoring 1,113 runs at 34.78 with two hundreds and eight fifties, and he was voted the Young Cricketer of the Year by the Cricket Writers' Club. He also made his one-day international debut for England against Australia at the Oval and his Test debut in the centenary Test at Lord's, scoring 9 and 1 against the Old Enemy.

In the winter of 1980–81 Athey was selected for the tour to the West Indies but only played in the fourth and fifth Tests at St Johns and Kingston respectively, scoring only 7 runs in 4 innings, and he disappeared from the England scene for six years soon after.

At county level he had his best season for Yorkshire in 1982, amassing 1,339 runs at 43.19 and scoring four centuries, with scores of 100 against Glamorgan and Kent, 114 not out against Surrey, and his highest score for the White Rose County, 134 against Derbyshire at Derby. However, the troubles surrounding the Boycott controversy had an affect on him and after a further summer with Yorkshire he departed to Gloucestershire in readiness for the 1984 season, with 6,320 first-class runs at 28.08, 21 wickets at 47.76 and 144 held catches and two stumpings for his native county.

The change certainly did him good, for in his first season with the Cotswold county he enjoyed a fruitful season, scoring 1,812 runs at an average of 37, which included 114 not out against his former county at Bradford Park Avenue. It also kick-started his England career, as he was selected for the England B tour to Sri Lanka in the winter of 1985 and he hit a career best of 184 at Galle. Despite a poor Test series against the Kiwis and India, in which he scored only 249 runs in 18 innings, the selectors stood by him for the winter tour to Australia. He repaid their faith with 76 at Brisbane and 96 at Perth, where he and Chris Broad added 223 for the first wicket. The partnership is still England's highest for any wicket at Perth.

Fortunately, that elusive first Test century was not far away for the following summer he registered his one and only Test ton for his country when he scored 123 versus Pakistan at Lord's. However, continual inconsistencies against Pakistan and New Zealand in 1987 and 1988, when he failed to score a single half-century in 15 Test innings, meant an end to his Test career, with a somewhat disappointing average of only 22.97 in 41 innings. In one-day international cricket he did slightly better, averaging 31.40 in 31 matches with two centuries and a best of 142 not out versus New Zealand at Old Trafford in 1986. For a player with a sound and stylish technique, he was capable of a lot better.

Athey accepted the Gloucestershire captaincy in 1989, but it did nothing for his batting and he relinquished the position at the end of the season.

In 1992 he returned to form when he recorded his highest score for Gloucestershire, notching up 181 against Sussex at Cheltenham. However, 12 months later he was on the move again, this time joining the south coast county Sussex.

At Sussex he played some of the best cricket of his career, scoring several big hundreds, such as his 169 not out against Kent, 163 against Durham and 163 not out against his former county, Gloucestershire.

In four years at Sussex he totalled over 5,000 runs at an average of 39, before retiring in 1997 to become coach of Worcestershire. Athey took up a further coaching appointment at Dulwich College in 2001 and ended his playing days with Suffolk in the Minor Counties.

David Leslie Bairstow

RHB & WK, 1970–90

Born: 1 September 1951, Horton, Bradford.
Died: 5 January 1998, Marton-cum-
      Grafton, Boroughbridge.
Played for: Yorkshire and Griqualand West.
Test Matches: (4) 1979–81 Cap No. 481

Batting Career for England

I	NO	HS	Runs
7	1	59	125
AV	**100**	**50**	**Ct/St**
20.83	-	1	12/1

First-Class Career: (459 Matches) 1970–90

Batting

I	NO	HS	Runs
647	119	145	13,961
AV	**100**	**50**	**Ct/St**
26.44	10	73	961/138

Bowling

Balls	Runs	Wkts	Av
582	308	9	34.22
Best	**5wl**	**10wl**	**Sr/Rate**
3–25	-	-	64.60

One of the most popular cricketers ever to play for Yorkshire, the world of cricket was stunned by the news on 5 January 1998 that David (Bluey) Bairstow had been found hanged at his house at Marton-cum-Grafton. Reports suggested he had been suffering from depression and financial troubles, but he was by nature a fighter, one you would never have envisaged would take his own life. In doing so he joined a long list of cricketers, such as Albert Trott and Andrew Stoddart to name but two, who had done so.

Following in his father's footsteps, he had joined Bradford League Club Laisterdyke, before moving to nearby Undercliffe at the age of 14. A member of the Yorkshire Federation Team, he was coached by Laurie Bennett at Hanson Grammer School, and was still at school when Yorkshire selected him for his first-class debut at the age of 18. Indeed, he arrived in county cricket in a blaze of publicity as he had to sit a school examination on the morning of his debut against Gloucestershire at Park Avenue, Bradford, in 1970. He failed his exam but caught out five batsmen in his debut match.

For the next 20 years his voice behind the timbers could be heard by all, and the red-haired wicket-keeper batsman was as tough and unyielding as any to wear the Yorkshire cap.

Bairstow spent his early days under the captaincy of Brian Close, and in May 1971 in the Roses Whitsuntide match at Old Trafford he took nine catches in the match, six in the first innings and three in the second, to equal the previous Yorkshire record held by Joseph Hunter in 1887 and Arthur Dolphin in 1919.

In the summer of 1973 he was awarded his county cap, which he wore with great pride. As a wicket-keeper standing back he was as good as any of his contempories and was unfortunate to have to compete with two of the best ever, Alan Knott and Bob Taylor, in his early days.

In the winters of 1976–77 and 1977–78 he played in South Africa with Griqualand West and captained the side in his second season with them. The following summer he played against the West Indies at Headingley, in the centenary Test versus Australia at Lord's and gained the last of his four caps the following winter against the West Indies in the third Test at Bridgetown. In addition, he played 21 one-day internationals, which included the memorable match at the Sydney Cricket Ground in 1980 when, along with his Yorkshire colleague Graham Stevenson, he smashed 35 off the last 30 balls to win the match.

In 1981 he took 11 catches against Derbyshire at Scarborough to equal the world record, and in the same year, against the same opponents at Derby in a Benson and Hedges Cup tie, he snatched victory from what looked like certain defeat. With 80 runs still needed for victory he was joined by the number 11, Mark Johnson. Bairstow proceeded to smash the Derbyshire bowlers all around the County Ground, hitting 103 not out, which included nine sixes and three fours, with Johnson contributing a mere 4 runs.

As a middle-order batsman, he was aggressive with a never-say-die spirit and loved nothing more than to smash a fast bowler back over his head to the boundary.

In 1984 he was awarded the Yorkshire captaincy, which he held for three years. For most of his captaincy he had a very average team, but he always led from the front.

His county career ended rather sadly in 1990 when Yorkshire dropped him in his testimonial year. Behind the stumps he took 1,038 first-class dismissals (907 caught and 131 stumped) for Yorkshire, only Jimmy Binks and David Hunter took more. With the bat he notched up 12,985 runs at 26.60 (with nine centuries) and as a wicket-keeper only Richard Blakey with 12 scored more, both in total and individually. Bairstow's highest score for Yorkshire was 145 against Middlesex at Scarborough in 1980, and in 1985 he scored 1,163 runs at 50.56.

Apart from being a very fine cricketer, in his younger days he was a useful football player, representing Bradford City in midfield.

John Christopher Balderstone

RMB & SLA, 1961–86

Born: 16 November 1940, Huddersfield.
Died: 16 March 2000, Carlisle.
Played for: Yorkshire and Leicestershire.
Test Matches: (2) 1976 Cap No. 467
Batting Career for England

I	NO	HS	Runs
4	-	35	39
AV	100	50	Catches
9.75 -	-	1	-

Bowling for England

Balls	Runs	Wkts	Av
96	80	1	80.00
Best	5wl	10wl	Sr/Rate
1–80	-	-	96.00

First-Class Career: (390 Matches) 1961 to 1986

Batting

I	NO	HS	Runs
619	61	181*	19,034
AV	100	50	Catches
34.11	32	103	210

Bowling

Balls	Runs	Wkts	Av
19,338	8,160	310	26.32
Best	5wl	10wl	Sr/Rate
6–25	5	-	62.38

Chris Balderstone epitomised the all-round sportsman, playing professional football in conjunction with his commitments as a first-class cricketer. Born in Longwood, Huddersfield, he played in the Paddock team, which competed in the Huddersfield League, at the age of 14. After playing second XI cricket he made his Yorkshire debut in 1961 against Glamorgan at Headingley but made just 23 runs in his only appearance that summer. However, his football commitments, early and late season, meant that Yorkshire often gave precedence to other young players on their staff. Eventually, Balderstone decided to venture south and in 1971 joined Leicestershire, teaming up with other Yorkshire imports Ray Illingworth and Jack Birkenshaw. His career at Yorkshire had lasted from 1961 to 1969, a period in which he played 68 first-class matches, scoring 1,332 runs at 17.76, with a top score of 82, took 37 wickets at 21.35 and held 24 catches.

The move to Leicestershire proved to be very successful for Balderstone, even though he played on a irregular basis for the first two summers. However, in 1972, under Ray Illingworth's captaincy, he took the honours in the Benson and Hedges Final against his native county Yorkshire, when his 41 not out steered Leicestershire to victory and earned him the Gold Award for Man of the Match.

In 1975 he had an outstanding season, which coincided with Leicestershire's double, the County Championship Title (for the first time) and the Benson and Hedges Cup, the first time any county had won both in the same year. Balderstone made 1,222 runs with five hundreds, including a top score of 168 not out against Nottinghamshire at Grace Road, and in the process sharing a third-wicket partnership of 305 with Brian Davison. He also confirmed his all-round status by taking 43 wickets with his slow bowling. He won another Gold Award in the Benson and Hedges Cup semi-final against Hampshire after he reached 101 not out in the penultimate over, with victory coming off the last ball of the final over from Andy Roberts.

In the same year he created sporting history by being the first player to play first-class cricket and football on the same day. In the County Championship match against Derbyshire at Queen's Park, Chesterfield, on the second evening, 15 September, he was 51 not out at the close of play, after which he dashed straight to Doncaster to play for the Rovers against Brentford in a League match, returning the next day to finish his cricket innings with 116 runs. He also claimed 3 for 28 with the ball.

His football career began at Huddersfield Town, where he made 117 appearances at wing-half or inside-forward. He then moved to Carlisle United, where he played 369 games and scored 68 goals and was a member of the team which gained promotion to the First Division in the 1974–75 season. In addition to Doncaster Rovers he also played for Queen of the South in Scotland.

Balderstone's consistent batting eventually earned him an England call-up and he was picked for the fourth and fifth Test matches against the West Indies at Headingley and the Oval in 1976. The West Indies pace attack was a little more potent than county-level attacks, however, and 35 and 0 followed by a pair meant he was never selected again.

Between 1976 and 1985, with the exception of 1978, he exceeded 1,000 runs a season, and in 1981 he was opening the innings. During the season he shared a record second-wicket unbeaten partnership with David Gower of 289 against Essex at Grace Road.

In 1984 he registered his highest first-class score of 181 not out against Gloucestershire at Grace Road, carrying his bat in a total of 456. He did this on two other occasions, with 114 not out versus Essex at Colchester (total 246) in 1982 and 100 not out against Worcestershire at Hereford (total 198) in 1983. His best bowling for the Foxes was 6 for 25 against Hampshire in 1978. In all first-class matches for the county he scored 17,627 runs at 36.95 and took 271 wickets at 26.71.

In 1988 he joined the first-class umpires list and stood in two limited over internationals, and he was the first official to be used as the third umpire. He was still on the list when he died suddenly at his home in Carlisle in March 2000 at the age of 59; he had been suffering from cancer.

Wilfred Barber

RHB & RFM, 1926–47

Born: 18 April 1901, Cleckeaton.
Died: 10 September 1968, Bradford.
Played for: Yorkshire.
Test Matches: (2) 1935 Cap No. 284

Batting Career for England

I	NO	HS	Runs
4	-	44	83
AV	**100**	**50**	**Catches**
20.75	-	-	1

Bowling for England

Balls	Runs	Wkts	Av
2	-	1	0.00
Best	**5wl**	**10wl**	**Sr/Rate**
1–0	-	-	2.00

First-Class Career: (373 Matches) 1926–47

Batting

I	NO	HS	Runs
526	49	255	16,402
AV	**100**	**50**	**Catches**
34.38	29	78	182

Bowling

Balls	Runs	Wkts	Av
657	419	16	26.18
Best	**5wl**	**10wl**	**Sr/Rate**
2–1	-	-	41.06

A native of Cleckheaton, Bradford, but raised in nearby Gomersall, Wilf Barber first came to prominence when, as a 20-year-old, he top scored for Gomersall in the 1921 Heavy Woollen Cup Final.

In 1926 he made his debut for the Yorkshire Second XI and scored 600 runs at an average of 40, with a top score of 108 against Northumberland at Jesmond. Later that season he was given his County Championship debut against Worcestershire at Bradford, but did not get the chance to bat.

Barber was a textbook right-hand opening or middle-order batsman, with a solid defence and a preference for the off-side, being an excellent driver of the ball. Indeed, Len Hutton said of him that no one picked the bat up straighter then he did. An occasional right-arm fast-medium bowler, he was also a brilliant outfielder with a safe pair of hands.

Barber had few opportunities in the late 1920s due to the strong Yorkshire team, but did register two centuries in 1929, making a maiden hundred (108) against South Africa and then 114 against Glamorgan at Hull, sharing a third-wicket partnership of 213 with Eddie Oldroyd (168).

In 1932 he finally established himself in the side and notched up 162 against Middlesex at Bramall Lane, Sheffield, and in the process shared a still record second-wicket partnership of 346 with Maurice Leyland (189). He also scored 102 in the return match against Middlesex at Lord's and scored 1,000 runs for the season, the first of eight occasions that he did so for the county.

The following season he registered 1,595 runs with four centuries and a best of 124 against Warwickshire. In 1934 he improved on that figure with 1,930 runs, which included the first of two double hundreds (248) against Kent at Headingley, when he shared a first wicket stand of 267 with Len Hutton (70). He also scored 191 against Sussex.

In 1935 he had his best season for Yorkshire, notching up 2,147 runs in total at an average of 42.00, which included his highest first-class score, 255 against Surrey at Bramall Lane. He was also selected for England against H.T. Wade's touring South Africans, making his debut in the third Test at Headingley, in which he scored 24 and 14 respectively. Though failing to play a major innings, and with the game destined for a draw, he was tossed the ball and took a wicket with his second ball in Test cricket, that of South African wicket-keeper Horace Cameron, stumped by Les Ames. The game was then abandoned, leaving him with the remarkable Test bowling figures of 2 balls, 1 wicket and no runs conceded. Retained for the next Test at Old Trafford he notched up 44 in the second innings, which was his highest Test score.

In the winter of 1935–36 he was the senior professional with the MCC's 'goodwill' party which

toured Australasia, scoring 797 runs at 41.94, with a top score of 91 against Queensland at Brisbane. On the New Zealand leg he found his best form with innings of 173, 93 and 60 in four representative games, and in addition he managed a knock of 116 against Canterbury.

He continued to score runs consistently for Yorkshire, notching up over 1,000 runs a season and in 1939 scored 1,501, which included 141 against Surrey and 128 not out against Northamptonshire.

After the war he played two further seasons, 1946 and 1947, and in the former had a joint benefit with Cyril Turner from which he received £2,958. He also registered 113 against Somerset, which was the last of his 27 centuries for the county.

For Yorkshire he played 354 matches, scored 15,315 runs at 34.26, took 14 wickets at 28.85 and held 169 catches.

After retirement he became a professional with league clubs Lidgett Green, Kings Cross and Mirfield and was a coach with the North Riding Education Authority. He was later school coach and groundsman at Ashville College in Harrogate. After a short illness he died in hospital in Bradford in September 1968 at the age of 67.

Willie 'Billy' Bates

RHB & OB, 1877–87

Born: 19 November 1855, Lascelles Hall, Huddersfield.

Died: 8 January 1900, Lepton, Huddersfield.

Played for: Yorkshire.

Test Matches: (15) 1881–87 Cap No. 30

Batting Career for England

I	NO	HS	Runs
26	2	64	656
AV	**100**	**50**	**Catches**
27.33	-	5	9

Bowling for England

Balls	Runs	Wkts	Av
2364	821	50	16.42
Best	**5wl**	**10wl**	**Sr/Rate**
7–28	4	1	47.28

First-Class Career: (299 Matches) 1877–87

Batting

I	NO	HS	Runs
495	20	144*	10,249
AV	**100**	**50**	**Catches**
21.57	10	47	328

Bowling

Balls	Runs	Wkts	Av
61,033	14,980	874	17.13
Best	**5wl**	**10wl**	**Sr/Rate**
8–21	52	10	68.83

Willie Bates, born to a humble family in Lascelles Hall, Huddersfield, was only 17 years of age when, in 1873, he became a professional cricketer with Rochdale in the Lancashire League.

Four years later he took all 10 wickets for 21 runs with his off-spinners for Yorkshire Seconds against Nottinghamshire Seconds and was given his Yorkshire debut against Middlesex at Lord's. In his debut season he hit his first century for the county, scoring 102 against Nottinghamshire.

The following summer 'The Duke', as he became known due to his smart appearance, headed the county bowling averages with 94 wickets at 11.13, which included 8 for 45 against Lancashire in the Roses's battle at Huddersfield, 7 for 19 against Sussex at Hove and 7 for 38 against Gloucestershire at Bramall Lane. In addition, he also took five wickets for only one run in just four overs against Surrey at the Oval.

Bates was a fine off-break bowler of some skill, with great accuracy and flight, and a brilliant hard-hitting batsman, who Lord Hawke thought the best professional batsman until the arrival of Jack

Hobbs. W.G. Grace also thought he would have been considered the best all-round cricketer of his generation had his fielding matched his batting and bowling skills.

In 1879 he once again routed Surrey with 8 for 21 at the Oval, the best bowling performance of his career, and he made a dashing 118 against Lancashire. At the end of the season he was a member of Richard Daft's tour to North America, which was not considered first-class.

Two years later Billy topped the 100-wickets mark for the only time (with 121), but he passed 80 in a season on another four occasions. He toured Australia in the winter of 1881–82 with the Shaw and Shrewsbury team, the first of five visits to the southern hemisphere. Interestingly, Bates was also a fine vocalist and his rendering of *The Bonny Yorkshire Lass* fascinated the king of the Sandwich Islands so much that he asked him to sing it time and again on the voyage to Australia. On that first tour he made his Test debut at Melbourne, scoring 58 and 47 and took 4 for 86 off 54 overs in the match. In the second Test at Sydney he bowled 72 overs, 43 maidens and took 4 wickets for only 52 runs in the Australian first innings.

In the summer of 1882 he scored his highest first-class score, 144 not out for the Under-30s versus the Over-30s at Lord's, and in the following winter, as a member of Ivor Bligh's party to Australia, he etched his mark on the game, setting four Test records. In the second Test at the MCG he scored 55 in England's only innings of 294, before taking 7 for 28 (including a hat-trick), which included the wickets of McDonnell, Giffen and Bonner. He then claimed 7 for 74 in their second innings to clinch an England victory by an innings and 27 runs, which was the first innings victory in Test cricket. In addition, he became the first bowler to take a hat-trick in Test cricket, his 7 for 28 was a record return for an innings, and no Englishman had previously taken 14 wickets in a Test match. He was also the first player to score more than 50 in an innings and take 10 or more wickets in the same match, only four other Englishmen have: Frank Woolley, Tony Greig, John Lever and Ian Botham.

He toured Australia on three further occasions, but unfortunately on his last trip in 1887–88, a non-Test tour with G.F. Vernon's XI, he was bowling in the nets at Melbourne when he was hit in the eye by a ball struck by a teammate. His eyesight was sufficiently impaired that he never played first-class cricket again. As a result he suffered severe depression and indeed attempted suicide on the voyage back from Australia.

For Yorkshire he scored 6,499 runs at 20.37, with eight centuries (a best of 136 against Sussex in 1886) and took 637 wickets at 16.78, taking five or more wickets in an innings on 36 occasions and held 163 catches.

In 1891 he was the professional at Haslingden in Lancashire, before taking a coaching position for £300 in Johannesburg, South Africa. He then moved to Leek as a professional in 1892.

In December 1899, and already not a well man, he insisted on attending the funeral of former Yorkshire player and relative John Thewliss, but he caught a cold and his condition deteriorated such that a few days later he died in Huddersfield at just 44 years of age and was buried alongside Thewliss.

His son William Bates played first-class cricket for Yorkshire and Glamorgan and his grandson Ted Bates was the former Southampton inside-forward, who later became their manager.

John Gareth Batty

RHB & OB, 1997–to date

Born: 13 October 1977, Bradford.
Played for: Yorkshire, Surrey and
Worcestershire.
Test Matches: (7) 2003–05 Cap No. 619
Batting Career for England

I	NO	HS	Runs
8	1	38	144
AV	**100**	**50**	**Catches**
20.57	-	-	3

Bowling for England

Balls	Runs	Wkts	Av
1,394	733	11	66.63
Best	**5wl**	**10wl**	**Sr/Rate**
3–55	-	-	126.72

First-Class Career: (122) 1997–to date
Batting

I	NO	HS	Runs
186	36	133	4,061
AV	**100**	**50**	**Catches**
27.07	2	21	81

Bowling

Balls	Runs	Wkts	Av
23,750	11,452	352	32.53
Best	**5wl**	**10wl**	**Sr/Rate**
7–52	15	1	67.40

Gareth Batty was born in Bradford and became a right-arm off-spin bowler and a more than useful middle-order batsman. He comes from a family steeped in cricket, his father David played League cricket with Bingley Cricket Club and was at one time the academy coach at Yorkshire. His elder brother Jeremy also played 26 matches for Yorkshire before moving to Somerset.

Batty was an ex-Yorkshire Schoolboy and a member of the England Under-15 team which toured South Africa in 1993 and the England Under-19 team which toured Zimbabwe in 1995–96 and Pakistan in 1996–97.

In 1997 he played 15 games for Yorkshire Seconds, scoring 377 runs at 31.41 and took 37 wickets at 27.97, but he played only one first-class game, against Lancashire at Headingley (a non-Championship match), scoring 18 runs and taking 2 for 76.

He left the White Rose County at the end of the season, feeling that there were limited opportunities for him and joined Surrey. But, although he won the Surrey supporters' club Most Improved Player award and the Young Player of the Year award in 2001, he was released by the county at the end of the season.

While at the Oval he was used mainly as a one-day player and he hit his highest one-day score, 83 not out, against his native county at the Oval in the Norwich Union League.

Batty was given a contract by Worcestershire for the start of the 2002 season and in his first season at New Road he realised some of his early potential, taking 56 wickets at 30.94 with his off-spin, with 6 for 71 against Essex at Southend the best and scored 491 runs at 21.34, with a highest score of 74 against Derbyshire at Worcester.

His performances earned him a spot with the England academy in Adelaide in the winter of 2002–03, and with England touring Australia that winter and the team suffering injury problems, Gareth was called-up to play in two one-day internationals, making his debut at Sydney.

In 2003 he took 60 wickets at 26.25 and scored 529 runs at 22.04, which earned him selection for the tours of Bangladesh and Sri Lanka in 2003–04, making his debut at Dhaka. He played in four Tests, including two against Sri Lanka, scoring 38 and 25 not out at Kandy and taking 3 for 55 at Galle, taking a wicket with his third ball in Test cricket and in particular helped save both back-to-back Tests with his batting. However, he was largely the second spinner to Ashley Giles and although he was given his chances with the ball he was not overly affective.

The selectors continued to show faith in him, selecting him for the tour to the West Indies in 2004, and he was the bowler when Brian Lara scored his 400th run in the fourth Test in Antigua, the only Test he played on tour. He again toured as second spinner to South Africa in the winter of 2004–05 but failed to play a Test. His last Test appearance was against Bangladesh at Chester-Le-Street in June 2005, and he later dropped down the pecking order due to the arrival of Monty Panesar and the revival of Graeme Swann.

However, at the time of writing, Gareth continues to perform consistently for Worcestershire, both with bat and ball, and he can only hope that further chances will come his way in the future.

Jimmy Binks

RHB & WK, 1955–69

Born: 5 October 1935, Hull.
Played for: Yorkshire.
Test Matches: (2) 1963–64 Cap No. 419
Batting Career for England

I	NO	HS	Runs
4	0	55	91
AV	**100**	**50**	**Ct/St**
22.75	-	1	8

First-Class Career: (502 Matches) 1955–69
Batting

I	NO	HS	Runs
598	129	95	6,910
AV	**100**	**50**	**Ct/St**
14.73	-	18	895/176

Bowling

Balls	Runs	Wkts	Av
84	82	0	-
Best	**5wl**	**10wl**	**Sr/Rate**
-	-	-	-

Jimmy Binks was one of the best ever wicket-keepers on glove work alone, and if he had been a better batsman he would have played more than the two Test matches that he did.

Born in Hull, he joined Hull Town Cricket Club on leaving school and was coached by ex-Hull wicket-keeper Charlie Flood. He initially played for J & S Rhodes in the Leeds League before joining Leeds in the Yorkshire League for the 1954 and 1955 seasons.

When Don Brennan retired there was a fight between Roy Booth and Binks for the wicket-keeping position at Leeds. Jimmy won, and Booth departed to begin his long career at Worcestershire.

Binks made his Yorkshire debut in 1955 against Nottinghamshire at Trent Bridge, taking the first three dismissals in Nottinghamshire's second innings. From number 11 he gradually worked his way up the batting order and in the return fixture at Scarborough he scored 41 and then 8 not out in the second innings, batting first wicket down in Yorkshire's nine-wicket win.

However, it was as wicket-keeper that he was to make a name for himself with Yorkshire, and he was a key player in the teams of the 1950s and 1960s. During this period he kept wicket for some great Yorkshire bowlers, from the extreme pace of Freddie Trueman and the swing and seam of medium-fast Tony Nicholson, where he mostly stood up to the wicket, to the wily orthodox and back-of-the-hand wrist spin bowling of Johnny Wardle and the off-spin of Ray Illingworth. As with all great 'keepers you hardly noticed him, and any dropped catch or missed stumping was headline news the next day. During his career he suffered only one injury, a broken finger in 1966, but he kept wicket in the next match with it strapped up. When he retired in 1969 his hands were unscathed, unlike most of his contempories'.

On the first day of the Yorkshire match against Kent at Tunbridge Wells in June 1957 he was awarded his county cap, and a year later scored his first 50 for the county, with a score of 59 against Scotland at Acklam Park, Middlesbrough.

In 1960 Binks had his best season in terms of dismissals with 107, which included 96 catches and 11 stumpings – still a county record. His 96 catches is still a season record in English first-class cricket. The following year he had 94 dismissals and was selected for the MCC tour to Ceylon (Sri Lanka), India and Pakistan. In seasons 1962 and 1963 he had 88 and 86 dismissals respectively and in the latter season scored over 400 runs for the first time.

In terms of England selection the theory of a 'keeper having to be a good middle-order batsman weighed against him, hence the two 'keepers who were in possession of the England gloves were John Murray and Jim Parks. However, while neither were in his class as a wicket-keeper, he did eventually get his chance on the tour to India in the winter of 1963–64. He took his chance well, and because of illness in the squad he was asked to open the batting in the second innings of the second Test with fellow Yorkshireman Brian Bolus. He made a sound and patient 55 and opened in both innings in the following Test at Calcutta. However, he was left out of the next Test as Parks, who had played in the two Tests purely as a batsman, returned behind the stumps and so Jimmy's short Test career was over. It was a sad end for a true craftsman.

Ironically, in the following summer he hit his highest score for the county, 95 against Middlesex at Lord's, when he was run out five runs short of a maiden century. He also scored 826 first-class runs at 29.50, his best season with the bat.

He continued to give outstanding service to Yorkshire and acted as a vital cog in a team which won seven County Championship titles and two Gillette Cup Finals.

In 1967 he had a well-deserved benefit which raised £6,093, a fitting reward for a player who played 412 consecutive County Championship games from his debut in 1995 to his last game in 1969, a phenomenal record that will surely never be beaten. Indeed, he missed only two other games during this period: June 1957 when Eddie Legard deputised against Northumberland (a non first-class match) and May 1964 against Oxford University in the Parks, Geoffrey Hodgson from Huddersfield deputising as Binks was playing for the MCC against Surrey at Lord's.

In 1969 he played his last game for Yorkshire against Middlesex at Harrogate, a match spoiled by rain, and after retirement from the county played minor county cricket for Lincolnshire from 1971 to 1973.

For Yorkshire he scored 6.745 runs at 14.69, took 872 catches and made 172 stumpings.

His last first-class match was for an international XI against Yorkshire at Scarborough at the end of 1975, in which he scored 15 and 12 not out. Jimmy's last dismissal was Yorkshire's Colin Johnson, who was caught off the bowling of Middlesex and England spinner Fred Titmus.

In 1978 he went to work in the United States, before eventually moving to Canada.

Jack Birkenshaw

LHB & OB, 1958–81

Born: 13 November 1940, Rothwell, Leeds.
Played for: Yorkshire, Leicestershire and
Worcestershire.
Test Matches: (5) 1972–74 Cap No. 456
Batting Career for England

I	NO	HS	Runs
7	0	64	148
AV	100	50	Catches
21.14	-	1	3

Bowling for England

Balls	Runs	Wkts	Av
1,017	469	13	36.07
Best	5wl	10wl	Sr/Rate
5–57	1	-	78.23

First-Class Career: (490 Matches) 1958–81
Batting

I	NO	HS	Runs
665	123	131	12,780
AV	100	50	Catches
23.57	4	53	318

Bowling

Balls	Runs	Wkts	Av
69,193	29,276	1,073	27.28
Best	5wl	10wl	Sr/Rate
8–94	44	4	64.48

A product of Rothwell near Leeds, Jack Birkenshaw began his cricket career in the Bradford League with Farsley and first appeared for Yorkshire Seconds in 1957 as an off-spinner and middle-order batsman. He made his Yorkshire debut a year later against Sussex at Worthing, failing to trouble the scorers in his first knock and scoring 10 in the second.

In three seasons of first-team cricket at Yorkshire he played 30 first-class games and scored 588 runs at 16.80, with a best score of 42 against Nottinghamshire at Worksop, and he took 69 wickets at 26.36, with 7 for 76 against Middlesex at Headingley in 1960 his best figures, but he was well behind Ray Illingworth in the pecking order. He also represented the Minor Counties on two occasions, against India in 1959 and South Africa in 1960.

He then sought his release and signed for Leicestershire as a special registration in readiness for the 1961 season. In his first game at Northampton he returned figures of 4 for 14 off 12 overs and a long career at Grace Road beckoned.

Birkenshaw was also a useful left-hand batsman, whose main strengths were a solid defence and determination, and in 1964 he scored 930 runs for the Foxes. A year later he was awarded his county cap.

While his batting improved, his bowling remained static and he took only 102 wickets in his first six years at Grace Road. However, in 1967 his bowling kicked on and he took 111 wickets at 21.41, with five wickets in an innings on five occasions and a best of 7 for 86 against Sussex at Hastings. He also took 10 for 146 against Gloucestershire at Cheltenham College and a hat-trick against Worcestershire at Worcester. His all-round ability was confirmed with 840 runs at 24.00 and he also gained selection for the international XI that toured Pakistan that winter.

The following summer he took 92 wickets, including another hat-trick against Cambridge University at Fenners, and he also scored his maiden century, scoring 101 not out against Sussex at Grace Road. In 1969 he made his highest first-class score of 131 against Surrey at Guildford, alongside his batting partner Barry Dudleston in a seventh-wicket stand of 148. For a player who passed 50 on 53 occasions in first-class cricket, it is perhaps surprising that he only added two more centuries to his figures, with 100 not out against Nottinghamshire in 1969 and 108 against Northamptonshire in 1975. His bowling, however, was consistent and reliable, and in the years between 1969 and 1972 he took 311 wickets and in 1972 achieved his career best bowling of 8 for 94 (12 for 143 in the match) against Somerset at Taunton. Other major returns were 7 for 65 against Glamorgan and 7 for 56 against his native Yorkshire, both at Leicester in 1973.

In the winter of 1972–73 he was selected for the tour to India and Pakistan, and he made 64 on his debut in the fourth Test against India at Kanpur. Birkenshaw also took 3 wickets for 108 runs and claimed Sunil Gavasker as his first victim. He retained his place for the fifth Test at Bombay and opened the batting in the second innings, but only made 12. On the Pakistan leg of the tour he played in only the third Test at Karachi, but took 5 for 57 in the second innings of the drawn match.

He missed out in the 1973 home series against New Zealand and the West Indies but returned for the tour to the Caribbean in the winter of 1973–74. Unfortunately, a total return of 2 for 96 and 15 runs in three innings meant the end to his international opportunities. He was awarded a benefit in 1974, which realised £13,100 – then a Leicestershire record.

Birkenshaw was a fine one-day cricketer, and in 1976 he made an unbeaten 101 against Hampshire in the Gillette Cup which won him the Man of the Match award.

His last season at Leicestershire was in 1980, and after playing 420 matches for the Foxes he joined Worcestershire on a one-year contract in 1981, playing 10 matches, the last of which was against Northamptonshire in July of that year.

After retirement Birkenshaw became a first-class umpire, standing in over 250 matches from 1982 to 1988, including two Tests and six one-day internationals, four of which were at the World Cup in 1983.

He was cricket manager at Somerset from 1989 to 1991, but returned to Leicestershire in the same capacity in 1992, where, in partnership with James Whitaker, he led the Foxes to two County Championship titles in 1996 and 1998.

Richard Blakey

RHB & WK, 1985–2003

Born: 15 January 1967, Huddersfield.
Played for: Yorkshire.
Test Matches: (2) 1992–93 Cap No. 558
Batting Career for England

I	NO	HS	Runs
4	0	6	7
AV	**100**	**50**	**Ct/St**
1.75	-	-	2/0

First-Class Career: (1985–2003)
Batting

I	NO	HS	Runs
554	87	223*	14,674
AV	**100**	**50**	**Ct/St**
31.42	13	86	778/57

Bowling

Balls	Runs	Wkts	Av
63	68	1	68.00
Best	**5wl**	**10wl**	**Sr/Rate**
1–68	-	-	63.00

Richard Blakey was one of the most exciting young batsmen to appear for the county since the war. A member of Huddersfield League club Elland, and a right-hand opening batsman with a vast array of shots, he scored consistently for the Yorkshire Colts in 1983 and 1984. In the winter of 1984–85 he was a member of the England Young Cricketers team which toured the West Indies, before making his first-class debut at the age of 18 against Middlesex at Leeds in 1985, scoring 32 and 4. His season's tally of 518 runs at 25.90 with a top score of 90 against Somerset at Headingley in only his third first-class match promised much for the future. He also played overseas, playing club cricket in Sydney, Australia and later Zimbabwe.

However, in 1986 he fell behind in the pecking order of Geoff Boycott, Martin Moxon and Ashley Metcalfe, playing only four first-class matches, but in the second XI he notched up 1,168 runs at 83.42 with four hundreds, which included a massive 273 not out against Northamptonshire at Wantage Road.

The volume of runs that he had scored forced the selectors' hands and he started the following season at number three behind Moxon and Metcalf. He repaid their faith with a magnificent season in which he scored 1,361 runs at 41.24 and finished second only to Moxon in the batting averages. He started the season in great style with 99 against Somerset, 101 not out versus Glamorgan at Sophia Gardens, Cardiff, 108 versus Northamptonshire and a superb 204 not out against Gloucestershire at Headingley, which made him the youngest-ever batsman to score a double hundred for the county. Blakey was also a member of the team which won the Benson and Hedges Cup, and was awarded his county cap. In addition he was awarded the Cricket Writers' Club Young Cricketer of the Year award.

In the winter of 1989–90 he was selected for the England A tour to Zimbabwe, scoring a magnificent 221 at Bulawayo, with his innings lasting 10 hours. He was also voted Yorkshire's Young Player of the Year.

With the retirement of David Bairstow in 1990, Yorkshire turned to Blakey to fill the void, and it was no coincidence that his batting form slumped somewhat in the 1990 and 1991 seasons. With hindsight Yorkshire ought perhaps to have looked elsewhere, for there were many who felt that if he had continued his career as a batsman only he would have been one of England's best during the 1990s.

As it was he had a dual role and England picked him for two one-day internationals against Pakistan in 1992 and then controversially ahead of Jack Russell for the winter tours of India and Sri Lanka. In his first Test in Madras, India amassed a mammoth 560 for 6 and he did not concede a bye in the innings. However, he had great difficulty picking the spin of Anil Kumble and after two Tests and 7 runs in four innings he sadly disappeared into the wilderness.

With Yorkshire he continued to do a dual role admirably and in 1998 he topped the national wicket-keeping list with 71 victims and took a well-deserved benefit of £122,438.

Indeed, from 2 August 1992, the Roses match at Old Trafford, to 31 July 2000, a Roses match at Headingley, he did not miss a County Championship match, a consecutive run of 132 matches. In the same year he produced his autobiography *Taking it from Behind*, a publication which certainly produced a few chuckles.

Yorkshire decided they needed to bring on a wicket-keeper for the future and gradually replaced him for a while, first with Simon Guy, who never looked like taking his place, and then Gerard Brophy, a signing from Northamptonshire in 2006.

He continued with the gloves until 2002 and produced his highest first-class score, a magnificent 223 not out against Northamptonshire at Headingley, the first game of the season. He occasionally played as a batsman only and as a regular for the second XI, which was a somewhat puzzling decision as he was still the best batsman/wicket-keeper available.

Blakey's last Championship match was in September 2003 against Glamorgan at Headingley, and it ended a first-class career for Yorkshire that had produced 14,150 runs at 30.96 in 339 matches, with 12 centuries, the most ever by a Yorkshire batsman/wicket-keeper for the county. He also held 768 catches and took 56 stumpings.

In one-day cricket he played 371 games, scored 7,355 runs at 31.43 with three hundreds, the best of which was 130 against Kent at Scarborough in 1991. He also took 366 catches with 60 stumpings, and is arguably Yorkshire's best batsman/wicket-keeper throughout the club's long history.

John Brian Bolus

RHB & LM, 1956–75

Born: 31 January 1934, Whitkirk, Leeds.
Played for: Yorkshire, Nottinghamshire and Derbyshire.
Test Matches: (7) 1963–64 Cap No. 417

Batting Career for England

I	NO	HS	Runs
12	0	88	496
AV	**100**	**50**	**Catches**
41.33	-	4	2

Bowling for England

Balls	Runs	Wkts	Av
18	16	0	-
Best	**5wl**	**10wl**	**Sr/Rate**
-	-	-	-

First-Class Career: (469) Matches 1956–75

Batting

I	NO	HS	Runs
833	81	202*	25,598
AV	**100**	**50**	**Catches**
34.03	39	142	201

Bowling

Balls	Runs	Wkts	Av
1,736	886	24	36.91
Best	**5wl**	**10wl**	**Sr/Rate**
4–40	-	-	72.33

Born in Whitkirk, Leeds, Brian Bolus first played for the Yorkshire Second XI in 1956, scoring 696 runs at 36.63, and was given his first-class debut against the MCC in the same year.

An attacking opening batsman who cut and drove well, he was also an occasional left-arm medium-pace bowler, and he continued to be on the perimeter of the first team until 1960. In that season he notched up 885 runs at 26.81, which included his maiden first-class century, 146 not out against Hampshire at Portsmouth, that, incidentally, was his highest score for the White Rose County. He followed this by scoring 77 and 103 not out against the Rest of England at the Oval in the last game of the summer.

The following year he topped the Yorkshire batting averages with 1,596 runs at 36.27 including three hundreds, 133 against Surrey at the Oval, 117 against Sussex at Hove and 100 against Hampshire at Dean Park, Bournemouth.

In 1962 he took 4 for 40 against Pakistan at Bradford, his best figures for the county, but after only 107 matches in seven years he decided to join Nottinghamshire in readiness for the 1963 season, fired with determination to prove his native county wrong. For Yorkshire he scored 4,712 runs at 29.26 with seven centuries, took 13 wickets at 31.30 and held 45 catches.

At Trent Bridge he had a superb first season and in his first meeting against his old county in the new 65 overs Gillette Cup competition at Middlesbrough he scored an unbeaten 100 out of 159, winning the Man of the Match award. He then hit 77 against Yorkshire at Trent Bridge and followed this with 114 at Bradford Park Avenue, a game in which he received a standing ovation. He ended the season with 2,190 runs at an average of 41.32, the most runs by any batsman in the country, with only three having a better average. In addition he scored five centuries, with a career best of 202 not out against Glamorgan at Trent Bridge, which included five sixes and 21 fours. He also carried his bat through the innings against Derbyshire at Trent Bridge, making 136 not out.

A few weeks later he was selected for his Test debut against the West Indies in the fourth Test at Headingley, making 14 and 43, and then 15 in the fifth Test at the Oval. He also had the satisfaction of driving his first ball in Test cricket for four off the bowling of Charlie Griffiths. He was then selected for the winter tour to India, where in the five-Test series he scored 391 runs at 48.87, with a top score of 88 in the first Test at Madras.

He was not selected for England again and returned to Nottinghamshire to carve out a consistent county career for the next eight years. He also reined in his attacking style somewhat and became a slightly more cautious, but nevertheless successful, batsman.

In 1969 he scored a century in each innings against Northamptonshire at Trent Bridge, with scores of 147 and 101, and a year later he joined a select group of batsmen to score 2,000 runs in a season for Nottinghamshire alone. In his 10 years at Trent Bridge he made well over 1,000 runs per season and altogether scored 15,093 first-class runs at 34.69, with 25 centuries.

He was, however, released by Nottinghamshire at the end of the 1972 season and joined Derbyshire, where he had three successful years, scoring 3,279 runs at 31.83, with four centuries, the highest being 151 against Oxford University at Burton-on-Trent in 1975. Bolus was also the first player to captain two different counties in successive seasons and the third player after Bob Berry and Roy Swetman to captain three.

It was at Derbyshire that he sent off one of his own players, fast bowler Alan Ward (who played five Test matches for England). It was only the third time that this had happened in first-class cricket. Ward had bowled very fast but erratically and had gone for 56 runs off 9 overs, including 19 in one over, in the match against Yorkshire at Chesterfield on 18 June 1973. Bolus wanted to bring him back to the bowling attack after tea, but Ward declined, saying he had lost his confidence after bowling a number of no-balls. Bolus then dismissed him from the field.

After leaving Derbyshire at the end of 1975, Brian went back to playing cricket in Yorkshire with Bradford, Cleckheaton, Brighouse and Farsley, with whom he won the Priestley Cup in 1983. He also became a member of the England selection committee in the 1990s.

Major William Booth

RHB & RMF, 1908–14

Born: 10 December 1886, Pudsey.
Died: 1 July 1916, La Cigny, Serre, France.
Played for: Yorkshire.
Test Matches: (2) 1913–14 Cap No. 179
Batting Career for England

I	NO	HS	Runs
2	0	32	46
AV	**100**	**50**	**Catches**
23.00	-	-	-

Bowling for England

Balls	Runs	Wkts	Av
312	130	7	18.57
Best	**5wl**	**10wl**	**Sr/Rate**
4–49	-	-	44.57

First-Class Career: (162 Matches) 1908–14
Batting

I	NO	HS	Runs
243	39	210	4,753
AV	**100**	**50**	**Catches**
23.29	2	21	120

Bowling

Balls	Runs	Wkts	Av
25,189	11,953	603	19.82
Best	**5wl**	**10wl**	**Sr/Rate**
8–47	43	9	41.77

Major William Booth (Major being a given name, not a military rank) was born in Pudsey and attended Fulneck School. Although he lived close to the Pudsey Brittannia ground (now Pudsey Congs), he played his early League cricket with Pudsey St Lawrence.

He first appeared for the Yorkshire Second XI in 1907 and made his first-class debut against Somerset at Dewsbury in 1908. However, it was not until 1910 that he secured a regular place in the team, taking 7 for 30 against Warwickshire at Edgbaston, and he finished the season with 51 wickets at 21.37. In the meantime, in the winter of 1908–09 he had obtained work as an electrician in the South Yorkshire coalfields and captained Wath Athletic successfully in the Mexborough League.

In 1911 he came of age as an outstanding all-round cricketer when he took 78 wickets at 27.06, including the first of two hat-tricks for the county against Worcestershire at Bradford (6 for 51).

In the earlier county fixture at New Road he compiled a brilliant maiden century, which was his highest first-class score of 210, adding 233 for the sixth wicket with George Hirst, who scored 100.

Booth was a powerful right-hand batsman who favoured the off-drive and square-cut shots. As a right arm, medium-fast bowler he had a very high action and he not only moved the ball late away from the batsman, but also extracted considerable bounce off the pitch, surprising many of the leading batsmen of the day.

The following summer, in 1912, he took 104 wickets for Yorkshire, which included 7 for 50 against Essex at Leyton (including a hat-trick), 8 for 52 against Leicestershire at Bramall Lane and then a career best of 8 for 47 against Middlesex at Headingley.

In 1913 he had a magnificent season. Not only did he snare 181 first-class wickets at an average of 13.46, but he also scored 1,228 runs at 27.28, and he not only completed the double but was also the leading all-rounder in the country. He scored his second century for the county that year, a brilliant 107 not out against Middlesex at Lord's, and took 5 for 72 with the ball. In the return match at Bramall Lane, Sheffield, he took 8 for 86. In addition, he took 7 for 46 against Northamptonshire, 7 for 77 against Lancashire, both at Headingley, and 6 for 84 against Warwickshire at Bramall Lane. Not surprisingly, he was named one of *Wisden's* Five Cricketers of the Year.

In the winter he was a member of Johnny Douglas's MCC party which toured South Africa, making his Test debut at Dublin in the first Test. He was left out of the following three Tests but played in the fifth and final Test at Port Elizabeth, where he scored 32 and took 4 for 49 in South Africa's second innings.

The following summer he was once again the leading wicket taker in the country with 155 wickets for Yorkshire, and in two consecutive matches in August, he and colleague Alonzo Drake bowled unchanged throughout both games. In the Gloucestershire match at Bristol, the home county were bowled out for 99 and 84, Booth taking 12 for 89 (6 for 48 and 6 for 41), but at Weston-Super-Mare against Somerset it was Drake who took centrestage, taking all 10 wickets for 35 runs in the second innings, while in the first Booth took 5 for 27 and Drake 5 for 16.

In World War One Booth joined the British Army alongside his Yorkshire colleagues Arthur Dolphin and Roy Kilner and was commissioned as a Second Lieutenant. He first served in Egypt in 1915, before being shipped to the Western Front. On 1 July 1916 he went 'over the top' near La Cigny, France, on the opening day of the Somme offensive while serving with the 15th (S) Battalion West Yorkshire Regiment, which were known as the 'Leeds Pals'. He was followed into no-man's-land by another Yorkshire cricketer, Abe Waddington, and while both were shot, Booth's wound was fatal and he died in Waddington's arms. His body remained unidentified until the spring of 1917 when an MCC cigarette case was found in his pocket. He was buried at Serre Road No. 1 cemetery. He was only 30 years old and but for the war may well have been remembered as one of the game's greatest all-rounder cricketers. He was also a very popular man and Yorkshire player Roy Kilner named his young son after him.

In 144 matches for Yorkshire he scored 4,244 runs at 22.69 and took 557 wickets at 19.17, with 41 five wicket hauls, and he held 114 catches.

William Eric Bowes

RHB & RFM, 1928–47

Born: 25 July 1908, Elland.
Died: 5 September 1987, Menston.
Played for: Yorkshire.
Test Matches: (15) 1932–46 Cap No. 264

Batting Career for England

I	NO	HS	Runs
11	5	10*	28
AV	**100**	**50**	**Catches**
4.66	-	-	2

Bowling for England

Balls	Runs	Wkts	Av
3,655	1,519	68	22.33
Best	**5wl**	**10wl**	**Sr/Rate**
6–33	6	-	53.75

First-Class Career: (372 Matches) 1928–47

Batting

I	NO	HS	Runs
326	148	43*	1,528
AV	**100**	**50**	**Catches**
8.58	-	-	138

Bowling

Balls	Runs	Wkts	Av
74,124	27,470	1,639	16.76
Best	**5wl**	**10wl**	**Sr/Rate**
9–121	116	27	45.22

William Eric Bowes is one of only a few cricketers who have taken more wickets than they have scored runs. In 372 matches he took 1,639 wickets but scored only 1,528 runs.

Few cricketers have looked less like one than Bowes. Standing 6ft 4in with spectacles, he was clumsily built and a poor mover around the field. Indeed, he looked more like a university professor and often batted and fielded like one. Unfortunately, it was this inferior batting and fielding which robbed him of more England caps.

For Yorkshire, however, he was a magnificent bowler throughout the 1930s, a period in which his county won the Championship seven times. Bill was the leading pace bowler during the decade and in that period he was only once below 10th place in the national bowling averages.

No man worked harder at his craft and throughout his career Bowes remained content with the 10 yard run-up which his coach at Lord's, the great Lancashire fast-bowler Walter Brearley, had persuaded him to use. A natural in-swing bowler, it took him several years to master the art of producing the away-swinger, but when he did it made him the dangerous bowler he became in the late 1930s.

As a youngster he played League cricket, but was unable to break into the Yorkshire team and so he wrote to Lord's for a trial. He was taken on and in 1928 made his First-Class debut for the MCC against Wales, taking 5 for 69. In his second game against Cambridge University he did the hat-trick. Yorkshire, alerted to his progress, agreed a deal with the MCC which allowed him to be free to play for the county when not required at headquarters.

In 1929 he took 65 wickets at 19 runs each and 12 months later had figures of 8 for 69 against Middlesex at Sheffield, when he was awarded his county cap. In 1931 he took 117 wickets for Yorkshire, and in June 1932 he was selected for his first Test match against India at Lord's. In his first game for England he took 4 for 49 and 2 for 30. He also took 168 wickets for Yorkshire, including a career best of 9 for 121 against Essex, and was named as one of *Wisden's* Five Cricketers of the Year.

He was selected for the bodyline tour of Australia in 1932–33, though he only received his invitation three days before the party sailed. Unfortunately, he played only one Test at Melbourne, where his single wicket was that of Don Bradman. The skipper, Jardine, preferred the pace of Larwood, Voce and Allen.

In 1934 he played in only three of the five Tests in the home series against Australia but still took 19 wickets at 25.42, which included 5 for 55 at the Oval. Four years later, in England's biggest ever win against the Aussies, he took another 'five-for', with figures of 5 for 49.

His total number of Tests (15) was a poor reward for a bowler who took 68 Test wickets at 22.33, even though his fielding and batting was inferior to his rivals. He took five wickets in an innings on six occasions, with a best of 6 for 33 against the West Indies at the Oval in 1939.

Bowes' best first-class season for Yorkshire was in 1935, when he took 193 wickets at 15.44, and on five occasions he took seven or more wickets in an innings, with a best of 8 for 17 against Northamptonshire at Kettering. In 1938 he topped the national averages with 121 wickets at 15.23, which confirmed him as one of England's best fast bowlers of the 1930s.

During World War Two he was captured at Tobruk in 1942 and spent three years as a prisoner of war. By the time he returned home he had lost over four stone in weight, and, quite understandably, for the last two years of his first-class career he bowled at a much reduced pace.

In 1946 he took 61 wickets at 14.16, with a best of 5 for 32 against Kent at Canterbury, and in his last season (1947) he still bowled well for the county, taking 73 first-class wickets at 17.49. He was also awarded a benefit match against Middlesex at Headingley, in which he took 4 for 34, and the total sum of £8,083 raised during the season was a just reward for a player who always wore his Yorkshire cap with pride.

For Yorkshire he played 301 matches, took 1,351 wickets at 15.71, with 103 five-wicket hauls, scored 1,251 runs at 8.93 and held 118 catches.

When Bowes' career finished he became a successful cricket writer with the *Yorkshire Evening News* and later with the *Evening Post*. His cricket autobiography *Express Deliveries* is one of the finest books on cricket ever written by a professional.

Geoffrey Boycott

RHB & RM, 1962–86

Born: 21 October 1940, Fitzwilliam.

Played for: Yorkshire.

Test Matches: (108) 1964–82 Cap No. 422

Batting Career for England

I	NO	HS	Runs
193	23	246*	8,114
AV	**100**	**50**	**Catches**
47.72	22	42	33

Bowling for England

Balls	Runs	Wkts	Av
944	382	7	54.57
Best	**5wl**	**10wl**	**Sr/Rate**
3–47	-	-	134.85

First-Class Career: (609 Matches) 1962–86

Batting

I	NO	HS	Runs
1,014	162	261*	48,426
AV	**100**	**50**	**Catches**
56.83	151	238	264

Bowling

Balls	Runs	Wkts	Av
3,641	1,459	45	32.42
Best	**5wl**	**10wl**	**Sr/Rate**
4–14	-	-	80.91

Boycott was not the most naturally talented batsman of his era, but hard work and dedication honed arguably the best defensive technique of all time and made him one of the game's most effective batsman. His most productive strokes, off the back foot through the covers and the on-drive, were majestic in both power and placement, and he had enough strokes to satisfy even his most severe critic.

Boycott, a product of Hemsworth Grammer School, played local cricket for Ackworth and Barnsley in the leagues, before making his Yorkshire debut in 1962 against Pakistan. In his first full season for Yorkshire in 1963 he scored 1,628 Championship runs, with three centuries, which included one in each of the Roses matches against Lancashire. He was awarded his county cap and was later elected the Young Cricketer of the Year.

He made his Test debut in 1964 against Australia at Trent Bridge, scoring 48, and in 1964 in the final Test of the summer at the Oval he scored 113, the first of his 22 Test centuries. *Wisden* voted him one of their Five Cricketers of the Year.

A year later he won the Man of the Match award at Lord's in the Gillette one-day Final against Surrey, scoring a magnificent 146 which contributed to Yorkshire's victory.

At Headingley in 1967 he scored 246 not out against India, his highest Test score, but after only scoring 108 on the first day he was dropped for the next Test for his slow scoring rate.

A successful home series in 1969 against the West Indies with two hundreds and an average of 54 was followed by a brilliant tour to Australia in the winter of 1970–71, a series in which he was key in bringing home the Ashes. At Perth he scored 70 and 50, 77 and 142 not out at Sydney, 12 and 76 at Melbourne and 58 and 119 not out at Adelaide, and he recorded a series aggregate of 657 runs at 93.85. It was a Test average only beaten once before in Australia by Wally Hammond (with 113.12) in 1928–29. In the next home series against Pakistan, 121 not out at Lord's and 112 at Headingley gave him three successive Test hundreds. He completed a marvellous summer by scoring 2,503 first-class runs at an average of 100.12, thus becoming the first Englishman to average over 100 in a season, which included 13 hundreds.

Upon the appointment of Mike Denness as England captain in 1974, Boycott began a three-year period of self-imposed exile from the Test arena. He was by then the Yorkshire captain, and even though the county won nothing during his period of captaincy from 1971 to 1978, without his batting skills one can only guess what a predicament the side would have been in.

In 1977 he returned to the Test scene against Australia at Trent Bridge and predictably scored a century (107) and 80 not out. Two weeks later, before an adoring Headingley crowd, he scored his 100th first-class century, the first batsman to do so in a Test match, and the stroke he did it with was the customary Boycott on-drive for four. His first innings score of 191 helped England win the Test by an innings and 185 runs.

The following winter, on the tour to Pakistan, an injury to Mike Brearley gave him the chance to captain his country, something he had always wanted to do, but a drawn series in New Zealand did not help his cause.

In 1979 he became the only player ever to average over a hundred in a season twice, by repeating his performance in 1971 in scoring 1,538 runs, with six hundreds at an average of 102.53.

At Delhi on 23 December 1981 Boycott passed Garfield Sober's record of 8,032 Test runs when he scored his 22nd and last Test century. That was not the only record that Geoffrey broke, as he took part in the most century opening partnerships (48) in Tests, and his value to England was shown by the fact that only 20 of his 108 matches ended in defeat – and most of them were when he failed himself. Had he not missed the three years of Test cricket and gone on the rebel tour of South Africa, he most certainly would have been the first batsman to score over 10,000 runs in Test cricket.

For Yorkshire he scored a century against every other first-class county and on every Test ground in England. His highest First-Class score was 261 not out in a tour game at Bridgetown in 1973–74, and he scored a record of 151 centuries, the most ever by a Yorkshire batsman at an average of 56.84. It is the highest aggregate of any batsman whose career started after World War Two, and of all the batsmen to have scored in excess of 20,000 runs, only Don Bradman with 28,067 runs at 95.14 has a better average than Boycott. For Yorkshire alone he scored 32,570 runs at 57.85, with 103 centuries, took 28 wickets at 23.75 and held 200 catches.

Of all the opening batsmen to have represented England, only Hobbs, Sutcliffe and Hutton have comparable records. Had Boycott adopted a more traditional approach to being a team player he may have received the admiration from his contemporaries that his talent and dedication deserved and the acknowledgement of the truly great player that he undoubtedly was.

Donald Vincent Brennan

RHB & WK, 1947–53

Born: 10 February 1920, Eccleshill, Bradford.
Died: 9 January 1985, Ilkley.
Played for: Yorkshire.
Test Matches: (2) 1951 Cap No. 359
Batting Career for England

I	NO	HS	Runs
2	0	16	16
AV	**100**	**50**	**Ct/St**
8.00	-	-	0/1

First-Class Career: (232 Matches) 1947–53
Batting

I	NO	HS	Runs
258	74	67*	1,937
AV	**100**	**50**	**Ct/St**
10.52	-	-	318/122

Born in Eccleshill, Bradford, and educated at Downside School, Don Brennan was originally a fast bowler before he turned his hand to wicket-keeping. During the war he played cricket for the army in Egypt and developed his 'keeping skills. After the war he played for Eccleshill in the Bradford League, before making his debut for Yorkshire in 1947 against the MCC at Lord's, and he established himself as the first choice wicket-keeper that season.

Tall for a 'keeper, he became particularly adept at standing up to the wicket and earned a reputation as a technician of the highest class, with fast leg-side stumpings his speciality.

During Brennan's career with Yorkshire, which spanned 1947 to 1953, he had plenty of time to practise his skills at standing to the wickets, for in the Yorkshire team were Johnny Wardle (left-arm finger and wrist spinner), Bob Appleyard (off-spin) and Eddie Leadbeater (leg-break). He was regarded by his colleagues as the best in the country at standing up to the stumps.

As a batsman he was determined and resolute, but he generally never moved any higher than 10th in the batting order. However, his best performance for Yorkshire was in 1948 when he went in as the last man against Worcestershire at New Road, sharing a last-wicket partnership of 106 with captain Brian Sellers; Sellers made 79 and Brennan 30 not out.

In seven seasons with Yorkshire his highest aggregate of runs was in 1951 when he scored 395 runs at an average of 17.17, with a top score of 47 against Middlesex at Bradford Park Avenue.

In the summer of 1951 Brennan was chosen over Godfrey Evans for the last two Tests of the series against South Africa, although there was no comparison between the two as far as batting was concerned, Evans was way out in front.

In his debut Test at Headingley against South Africa in the fourth match of the series he was joined by his Yorkshire colleague Frank Lowson and Surrey's Peter May, both of whom were also playing in their first Test match. Brennan scored 16 in the first innings, his top score in Test cricket, and conceded only one bye. In the fifth Test at the Oval, his last for England, he made his solitary dismissal in an England cap, ironically a stumping.

He later toured with the MCC to India, Pakistan and Ceylon in the winter of 1951–52, and he scored his only half century in first-class cricket, with 67 not out against Maharashtra at Poone.

However, he decided to retire from the game after the 1953 season due to the demands of his family's textile business.

For Yorkshire he played in 204 games, scored 1,653 runs at an average of 10.66 and took 280 catches and made 100 stumpings, a very large percentage of his dismissals, which underlines his outstanding skill at standing close to the stumps.

His last first-class game was for the MCC against Yorkshire in the festival week at Scarborough in September 1964. After retirement he joined the board of Bradford Northern Rugby League Club, and was also elected to the Yorkshire Committee as a member for Bradford in 1971 and continued until 1984. He was known to be a fierce critic of the Boycott group in the early 1980s. He died in 1985 in Ilkley at the age of 64.

Timothy Thomas Bresnan

RHB & RMF, 2003 – to date

Born: 28 February 1985, Pontefract.

Test Matches: (1) 2009 Cap No. 643

Batting Career For England

I	NO	HS	Runs
1	0	9	9
AV	**100**	**50**	**Catches**
9	-	-	1

Bowling for England

Balls	Runs	Wkts	Av
186	97	3	32.33
Best	**5wl**	**10wl**	**Sr/Rate**
3–45	-	-	62

First Class Career: (73 Matches) 2003 to date

Batting

I	NO	HS	Runs
99	19	126*	2,177
AV	**100**	**50**	**Catches**
27.21	3	10	31

Bowling

Balls	Runs	Wkts	Av
11,131	6,008	190	31.62
Best	**5wl**	**10wl**	**Sr/Rate**
5–42	3	0	58.58

The talented Pontefract-born youngster seemed destined from an early age to eventually represent his country at Test level. In the year 2000 Tim Bresnan first represented England at Under-15 level, followed by the Under-17s, and two years later played in the Under-19 World Cup against India and Uganda, when he won the Man of the Match award after snaring 4 for 7 off only nine overs. Indeed, he was England's outstanding bowler in the competition which was held in Bangladesh, and overall he played seven Youth Internationals, culminating with a best of 5 for 81 against South Africa at Headingley.

Meanwhile, the young Bresnan had already made his Yorkshire first-team debut against Kent in the Sunday League competition in 2001, and at the age of only 16 was the youngest player since Paul Jarvis 20 years previously to represent the county. In the process he also won the NBC Denis Compton award for the most promising Yorkshire player.

A genuine all-round cricketer, Bresnan swings the ball from a pace of fast-medium, and his hard-hitting batting from the middle-order will, I am sure, change the course of many matches in the future.

In 2003 he made his first-class debut for Yorkshire against Northamptonshire at Headingley, and he demonstrated his batting potential with 61 off just 51 balls against Leicestershire. However, it was not until 2004 that he gained a regular place in the White Rose team, playing 10 first-class games.

A year later, in 15 Championship matches he scored 339 runs with an highest score of 74 and was Yorkshire's second highest wicket taker with 47 wickets at 33.42, which included 4 for 101 off 30.5 overs against Durham and a best to date of 5 for 42 against Worcestershire at Worcester.

The season of 2006 saw him come of age as an all-round cricketer, and he kicked-off in fine form with 3 for 60 and his highest score up to then of 94, playing for the MCC against the previous year's champion county Nottinghamshire at Lord's. In addition he notched 91 and took 4 for 36 against Hampshire at Leeds, 5 for 85 against Durham and passed 100 wickets in first-class cricket against Warwickshire at Scarborough. He was also named in the England One Day International squad to play Ireland and Sri Lanka, making his Twenty20 debut against the latter at the Rose Bowl on 15 June 2006. Two days later he appeared in his first One Day International against the same opposition at Lord's, taking 1 for 44 off nine overs as England fell to a 20-run defeat. A month later he was awarded his county cap against Warwickshire at Scarborough, a fitting reward for his advancement as a Yorkshire cricketer.

In the first Championship game of 2007 he hit his first century (116) in first-class cricket against Surrey at the Oval and in doing so, alongside Jason Gillespie, set a record ninth-wicket partnership for Yorkshire. The partnership recorded 246 before Bresnan departed stumped, and in the process he passed 1,000 first-class runs. Indeed, it was a season in which Bresnan's batting really blossomed and he notched his second hundred (126) for the England Lions against a touring Indian team at Chelmsford, which included the likes of Sachin Tendulker, Ramesh Power and Shanthakumaran Sreesanth. Bresnan scored 116 from 156 balls on the first day and shared a partnership of 129 for the eighth wicket with Stuart Broad, who registered 50.

With the ball he snared 4 for 65 against Hampshire and against Worcestershire he had the outstanding bowling figures of 4 for 10 off 10 overs. He finished the season in fine style with his third first-class century (101) against Warwickshire, again at Scarborough.

Although he had been part of Yorkshire's first team for seven years he was still only 23 years of age at the start of the 2008 season, and once again he was quickly off the mark, recording 4 for 51 against Nottinghamshire at Headingley, and he followed this with 4 for 73 against Durham at Chester-Le-Street. In June he took his third five-wicket haul (5 for 91) in the return fixture against Durham at Headingley and confirmed yet again his all-round capabilities with scores of 84 not out and 64 not out against Surrey and Lancashire respectively.

Another good start to the 2009 season saw him called into the England squad for the first Test against the West Indies at Lord's, becoming the 95th Yorkshire-born player to represent England. In his second Test at Durham he took 3–45, his best Test figures to date. For Yorkshire alone, to the end of the 2008 season he had played 68 games, scored 1,871 runs at 24.94, with 31 catches and taken 177 wickets at 31.54.

Dennis Brookes

RHB & RM, 1934–59

Born: 29 October 1915, Kippax, Leeds.
Died: 9 March 2006, Northampton.
Played for: Northamptonshire.
Test Matches: (1) 1947–48 Cap No. 327
Batting Career For England

I	NO	HS	Runs
2	0	10	17
AV	**100**	**50**	**Ct/St**
8.50	-	-	1

First-Class Career: (525 Matches) 1934–59
Batting

I	NO	HS	Runs
925	70	257	30,874
AV	**100**	**50**	**Ct/St**
36.10	71	152	205

Bowling

Balls	Runs	Wkts	Av
158	127	3	42.33
Best	**5wl**	**10wl**	**Sr/Rate**
1–7	-	-	52.66

There have been certain cricketers down the years who have played for unfashionable counties, which, for one reason or another, have seemingly been unfairly treated by the England selectors. Dennis Brookes can arguably be classed as one of these players, and if he had been born in another era he may well have received the recognition he deserved.

Born in Kippax, east of Leeds, he was spotted playing club cricket and joined Northamptonshire as a teenager, playing for the club and ground team and also for the Northamptonshire Amateurs.

He made his first-class Championship debut against his native Yorkshire in 1934 at Bradford Park Avenue, but Hedley Verity trapped him lbw for a single. However, he continued to progress and in 1937 he scored his maiden century against New Zealand, runs that contributed to 1,000 for the season, a feat he would repeat in each of the next 16 seasons, even exceeding 2,000 in 1946, 1949 and 1952.

On the resumption of County Championship cricket in 1946 after the war, Dennis notched up 2,022 runs at an average of 54.64, the first time that a Northamptonshire batsman had exceeded

2,000 runs in a season. In addition, he scored a century in both innings (112 and 154 not out) against Sussex at Eastbourne and carried his bat, notching up 80 not out from of a total of 170 against Leicestershire at Northampton.

The following summer he scored 210 against Leicestershire at Grace Road, 145 against Combined Universities at Wantage Road and carried his bat for the second time with 111 not out and 196 against Lancashire at Old Trafford.

In the winter of 1947–48 he was selected for the tour of the West Indies, and made his Test debut in the first Test at Bridgetown, scoring 17 runs in the match. Unfortunately, he fractured a finger during the match, an injury which prematurely ended his only overseas tour, and amazingly he was never selected for England again.

In 1952 he scored the largest number of runs ever by a Northamptonshire player in a single season, grabbing an incredible 2,198 at an average of 51.11, which included 156 against West Indies at Northampton, a shared fifth-wicket partnership of 347 with Des Barrick against Essex and 102 not out (out of a total of 185) against Kent. This was the fourth time he had carried his bat and Brookes said that it was his best innings for the county as it was made against Doug Wright on a turning wicket at Wantage Road.

In 1954 he was appointed captain of Northamptonshire and was the first professional to skipper the county. He was also part of a second-wicket partnership of 282 against Kent with Jack Livingstone.

Three years later, in his last year in charge, he captained Northamptonshire to a runners-up spot to Surrey and was also fittingly named one of *Wisden's* Five Cricketers of the Year. Unfortunately for him, behind the scene activity in the committee room eased him out of the captaincy in favour of Ramon Subba Row, who had been promised the position two years earlier. It was reported that Subba Row had made it known he would quit the county if the promise was not honoured.

Brookes, being the kind of person he was, played on loyally and a year later he had a second benefit with Northamptonshire. He also carried his bat for the fifth and last time, when he scored 113 not out and 252 against Glamorgan at Ebbw Vale.

He retired at the end of 1959 but led the second XI until 1968, after which he worked as assistant secretary, was elected onto the cricket committee and was finally honoured with the presidency of Northamptonshire County Cricket Club from 1982 to 1985.

He will always be remembered as one of the great legends of Northamptonshire cricket, and his records are unlikely to be beaten: most runs (28,980 at 36.13), most appearances (492), most hundreds (67), most runs in a season (2,198) and most 1,000 runs in a season (17). In addition he also took three wickets at 42.33. Brookes also had the distinction of scoring a century against each of the 16 counties in the Championship.

John Thomas Brown

RHB & LB, 1889–1904

Born: 20 August 1869, Driffield.
Died: 4 November 1904, Pimlico, Westminster,
    London.
Played for: Yorkshire.
Test Matches: (8) 1894–99 Cap No. 89
Batting Career for England

I	NO	HS	Runs
16	3	140	470
AV	100	50	Catches
36.15	1	1	7

Bowling for England

Balls	Runs	Wkts	Av
35	22	0	-
Best	5wl	10wl	Sr/Rate
-	-	-	-

First-Class Career: (382 Matches) 1889–1904
Batting

I	NO	HS	Runs
633	47	311	17,582
AV	100	50	Catches
30.46	29	76	229

Bowling

Balls	Runs	Wkts	Av
9,391	5,627	190	29.61
Best	5wl	10wl	Sr/Rate
6–52	4	-	49.42

J.T, as he was generally known, was a native of Driffield and is believed to have first played for Driffield Town as an 11-year-old. In any event, he topped both their batting and bowling averages aged 14. Four years later he headed north to Scotland to play for Perth in 1888 and 1889, but ill health from a bout of the flu restricted his cricket during the next few years. During this period he made his debut for Yorkshire against Gloucestershire at Bradford Park Avenue in 1889, and also played as a professional for Brighouse in 1892 and Halifax from 1893 to 1895.

He eventually became a regular with Yorkshire in 1894, scoring 1,196 runs for the county, which included his maiden first-class century with a score of 141 against Liverpool and District. His performances during the season were noted by the England selectors, and when Bobby Abel withdrew from Andrew Stoddart's MCC team to tour Australia, Brown was named as his replacement. In the opening Test at Sydney he scored 53 in the second innings, assisting his country to a 10-run victory, but he reserved his greatest moment for the final Test at Melbourne. With the series tied at two victories each, England, having bowled Australia out for 267 in their second innings, needed to score 297 to win and retain the Ashes. With the first ball of the fifth day, captain Stoddart was out lbw and England was perilously placed at 28 for 2. But Brown, together with fellow Yorkshireman Albert Ward (who played for Lancashire), shared a magnificent third-wicket partnership of 210 in only 145 minutes which enabled England to win by six wickets and retain the Ashes. Ward made a valuable 93, but Brown was the hero of the day with a brilliant 140, which included 16 fours and was described at the time as 'an immortal innings'. His first 50 came in only 28 minutes, still the second fastest in Test cricket in terms of time, and his 100 came up in only 95 minutes, another record at the time. J.T. returned home a hero, with 825 runs on tour at an average of 43.42, including four centuries, and he also topped England's Test averages with 343 runs at 42.88. The Test, incidentally, was the first time that more than 100,000 people had attended a cricket match in Australia.

He was naturally selected for the return series in England in the summer of 1895 and was named one of *Wisden's* Five Cricketers of the Year. Unfortunately, he did not do himself justice, scoring only 127 runs at 25.4 and sadly he was never selected again.

A forceful right-handed batsman, who loved to score his runs quickly, the short but sturdy Brown was a superb cutter, either late or square and a compulsive hooker of the ball, a shot which occasionally led to his downfall. In addition he was a brilliant out-field fielder and a useful leg-break bowler, who was good enough to take 190 first-class wickets, including four five-wicket hauls for Yorkshire, with a best of 6 for 52 against Sussex in 1898. He also snared a hat-trick against Derbyshire at Derby in 1896.

However, it was as an opening batsman for Yorkshire that he was best known and in the early 1890s he formed a magnificent opening partnership with John Tunnicliffe. His best aggregate of runs for a season was in 1896 when he scored 1,873 first-class runs at 35.33 and which included his first double century, a score of 203 against Middlesex at Lord's.

The following season saw Brown and Tunnicliffe create a new first-wicket record partnership of 378 against Sussex at Bramall Lane. Tunnicliffe was out for 147, but J.T. went on to make the first of two triple centuries for the county, registering 311, his highest first-class score; it took him six and a quarter hours. Not content with that, the pair did even better the following season with an improved first-wicket record stand of 554 against Derbyshire at Queen's Park, Chesterfield, the highest for any wicket in first-class cricket at the time. Tunnicliffe batted for five hours and five minutes for 243, while Brown batted five minutes longer for his second triple century (300). His popularity could be seen when, in the summer of 1901, 40,000 people attended his benefit match, from which he received £2,282.

A single-minded individual, he had an insatiable appetite for scoring runs and in 345 games he scored 15,694 at an average of 29.83 for Yorkshire (this may have been much higher if health problems had not affected him in his last few years). He also scored 23 centuries, took 177 wickets at 29.28 with four five-wicket hauls and held 188 catches.

Unfortunately, he was a heavy-smoking asthmatic and had to resign from Yorkshire cricket in the summer of 1904 due to heart trouble. The county sent him to London to try to recuperate, but in November of that year he died due to 'congestion of the brain and heart failure'. He was only 35 years old, but he will always be remembered as one of Yorkshire's favourite batsmen of the late 19th century.

Hanson 'Sammy' Carter

RHB & WK, 1897–1925

Born: 15 March 1878, Northowram, Halifax.
Died: 8 June 1948, Bellevue Hill, Sydney, N.S.W.
Played for: New South Wales.
Test Matches: (28) 1907–22 Cap No. 88
Batting Career For Australia

I	NO	HS	Runs
47	9	72	873
AV	**100**	**50**	**Ct/St**
22.97	0	4	44/21

First Class Career: (128 matches) 1897–1925
Batting

I	NO	HS	Runs
175	31	149	2,897
AV	**100**	**50**	**Ct/St**
20.11	2	13	181/89

Hanson 'Sammy' Carter was born in Halifax, Yorkshire, and emigrated to Australia with his family at the age of five in 1883. The family first settled in the suburbs of Ultimo, New South Wales, before moving to Woollahra in 1884. Walter Carter, Hanson's father, was a carpenter/cabinet maker and he established a funeral business in Woollahra in 1887 and later became the Mayor of Waverley, a suburb of Sydney.

Hanson eventually joined the Sydney district club Waverley at the age of 20 in 1898, and during his first season at the club he was selected for New South Wales against South Australia at Adelaide, scoring 6 not out and 15 and holding two catches behind the wickets. After only three first-class matches he was selected for the tour to England in 1902 as the understudy to James Kelly and gave many excellent displays in matches against the English Counties. The tour saw a rapid improvement in his skill behind the stumps and he was the first Australian wicket-keeper to squat on his haunches as the bowler began his run-up. Standing only 5ft 5in tall, he moved with dramatic steps as he changed ends between the overs. He refused to stand back to any but the fastest of bowlers and his usual position was about a metre behind the stumps. This gave him slightly longer to pick up the snicks than if he had been on top of the wickets, but also meant that he had to stalk the batsman for his stumpings. He became quite adept at it, for he had marvellous powers of anticipation. His squatting style caused widespread comment and was adopted by several county 'keepers.

In 1904 he notched the first of two first-class centuries, scoring 149 against Queensland at the Sydney Cricket Ground. Three years later, also at the SCG, he scored his second ton (125) versus South Australia. Against Arthur Jones' English team in Australia in 1907–08 Carter established himself as Australia's leading wicket-keeper. His glove work had become immaculate and his consistent scoring gave the Australian tail an added strength. Already he was being acclaimed as a more accomplished 'keeper than his predecessor, the tough, workmanlike Kelly.

In the first Test match against England at Sydney in December 1907 he made an immediate impact with the bat, producing scores of 25 and then top scoring with 61 in the second innings which enabled Australia to win a tight game by two wickets.

Australia won the series 4–1 and Carter not only established himself as Australia's leading wicket-keeper, but in addition notched vital runs, scoring half-centuries in the second and fourth Tests both at the MCG with 53 and 66 respectively. Indeed, his innings of 66 was a flamboyant knock scored in only 82 minutes, which included 11 fours, 5 of them coming off two overs from Wilfred Rhodes. By this time Carter had begun working with his father's flourishing undertaking business at Waverley and he often had to rush to District games in the company's hearse.

After a successful tour of England in 1909 in which he was part of a winning team (2–1 in the series), he and his team came down to earth two years later, when a Syd Barnes and Frank Foster inspired England triumphed 4–1 down under. However, during the series Hanson notched his highest Test score (72) in the third Test at Adelaide.

A few weeks later he was one of the 'Big Six' who refused to tour England for the triangular tournament involving England, Australia and South Africa. In Australia at the time the players had the right to choose their own tour manager and they wanted Frank Laver, a former Test player who had been manager to England in 1905 and 1909. However, the Cricket Board wanted more control and refused their choice. There was fisticuffs between the chairman of selectors Peter McAllister, himself a former Test player, and Clem Hill the Australian captain. The incident left McAllister with a bruised face and nose and Hill resigned as a selector and captain. Hill, Carter, Victor Trumper, Warwick Armstrong, Albert Cotter and Vernon Ransford declined the invitation to tour. Hill retired from Test cricket and only Carter and Armstrong played Test cricket again.

Immediately after the World War One, Hanson's position came under threat from the emerging talents of Bert Oldfield, but he was still able to claim his share of Tests, even when he was over 40 years of age.

On the Australian tour of England in 1921 in the third Test at Headingley he was the only Yorkshireman on the field, England did not select one. In the following Test at Old Trafford with England 341 for 4, Lord Tennyson, the England captain, wanted to declare and have 20 minutes at the Australians. However, he had neglected or did not know law 55 (amended in 1914) which stated that in a two-day match (which this had become because of rain) an innings could not be closed later than 100 minutes before the scheduled close of play. Hanson Carter, who was well educated in the laws of the game, reminded the Australian captain Warwick Armstrong of this, and after a 20-minute break for the umpires to sort it out, Armstrong, who had bowled the last over before the interruption, bowled again thus breaking another rule, becoming the only bowler in Test history to bowl successive overs.

Carter went on to play two further Tests against South Africa later that year, his last being at Newlands, Cape Town, where he notched 31 not out in an Australian 10-wicket win, thus being the last wicket-keeper in Test history to wear slatted pads.

He played his last first-class match for N.S.W. versus an Australian XI at Sydney came at the age of 46, and he showed he could still bat by scoring 58 in the first innings. For New South Wales he played 44 matches, scored 1,262 runs at 23.37 and took 121 dismissals (81ct and 40st).

On retirement, in addition to his undertaking business (which incidentally is still operating in Bondi Junction Sydney), he opened a sports retail shop with fellow Australian great Victor Trumper. Hanson, a shrewd and successful businessman, died in Sydney at the age of 70 in June 1948.

Denis Brian Close CBE

LHB & RM/OB, 1949–77

Born: 24 February 1931, Rawdon, Leeds.
Played for: Yorkshire and Somerset.
Test Matches: (22) 1949–76 Cap No. 344

Batting Career for England

I	NO	HS	Runs
37	2	70	887
AV	**100**	**50**	**Catches**
25.34	-	4	24

Bowling for England

Balls	Runs	Wkts	Av
1,212	532	18	29.55
Best	**5wl**	**10wl**	**Sr/Rate**
4–35	-	-	67.33

First-Class Career: (786 Matches) 1949–1977

Batting

I	NO	HS	Runs
1,225	173	198	34,994
AV	**100**	**50**	**Catches**
33.26	52	171	813

Bowling

Balls	Runs	Wkts	Av
70,302	30,947	1,171	26.42
Best	**5wl**	**10wl**	**Sr/Rate**
8–41	43	3	60.03

A Yorkshire legend for many reasons, Brian Close was a natural sportsman from an early age, playing both cricket and football for England Schools. He signed as a professional footballer for Leeds United and later played for Arsenal and Bradford City as an inside-forward, but injury ended his promising football career.

It was as a cricketer that he was to make his name and he burst onto the scene in 1949, making his debut at Fenners against Cambridge University and his County Championship debut seven days later against Somerset at the Athletic Ground, Wells. Before the end of May he had taken 5 for 58 against Essex and top scored with an unbeaten 88, sharing a seventh-wicket partnership of 128 with Alex Coxon.

Close was blessed with immense talent and took everything in his stride. Not only did he manage the 'double' in first-class cricket, 1,098 runs at 27.45 and 113 wickets at 27.87, but he was also the youngest player ever to achieve this feat and the only one to do so in his first season.

Close was selected for the Players versus Gentlemen match at Lord's, and then for the third Test against New Zealand at Old Trafford, and at 18 years and 149 days was, and still is, the youngest ever player to have appeared in a Test for England.

In 1950 he began his national service, but he managed to have it suspended when he was selected for the tour to Australia in the winter of 1950–51. He started well, scoring 108 not out in the opening match, but in the second Test at Melbourne, where he became the youngest ever to represent England against Australia (19 years and 301 days), he scored only one run in two innings, suffered a groin injury and disappeared from Test cricket for the next five years.

Back with Yorkshire he completed a second 'double' in 1952 by scoring 1,192 runs at 33.11 and taking 114 wickets at 24.08, which amazingly, considering his ability, was the last occasion he achieved the feat.

The years between 1951 and 1955 were a period of consolidation for Brian and it was not until 1954 that he scored his first century for the county, 123 not out against the Pakistanis. He had to wait a further 12 months before scoring his first Championship century, 143 against Somerset at Taunton. He also took 7 for 62 against Essex at Bradford and played his third Test against South Africa at the Oval.

In the summers of 1959 and 1960 he achieved his best performances in first-class cricket, taking 8 for 41 against Kent at Headingley and scoring 198 against Surrey at the Oval.

In 1961 Close scored 1,985 first-class runs at 35.44, his best return for a season, and was given a benefit which raised £8,154.

Two years later he was appointed captain, replacing Vic Wilson, and in his first season in charge retained the Championship title and showed a tactical awareness and knowledge that benefitted both Yorkshire and Somerset over the coming years.

Close led by example, being a brave and magnificent fielder at short leg, where he was hit many times, but never showed fear. In his eight years as captain, Yorkshire won the title on four occasions, and he received a testimonial in 1970 which raised £6,540. He was also named one of *Wisden's* Five Cricketers of the Year in 1964.

Thorughout this period he had made sporadic appearances for England, taking his best figures of 4 for 38 against India at Headingley in 1959 and scored his highest Test score (70) against the West Indies at Lord's in 1963. Against Australia in the Old Trafford Test of 1961, a reckless shot against Benaud contributed to an unexpected defeat, but he showed courage beyond duty in 1963 against the quick bowlers of the West Indies, Hall and Griffiths, which won him enormous respect. Three years later he was asked to captain England in the last Test at the Oval, against the West Indies, and he steered England to a remarkable innings victory. Retained for the summer Tests of 1967 against India and Pakistan, five of the six Tests were won by England, but he lost the captaincy as a disciplinary measure after he used delaying tactics in a Championship match against Warwickshire.

Close's reign as Yorkshire captain ended in 1970, with the committee announcing he would not be reappointed for the following season. As a consequence he accepted the captain's job at Somerset and left Yorkshire after playing 536 matches, in which he scored 22,650 runs at 31.94, including 33 centuries, and took 967 wickets at 24.29, with 40 five-wicket hauls and a mere 564 catches held.

As a batsman, the left-handed Close always played for the team, but his attacking nature sometimes let him down and his ability deserved a better average. With the ball he could be a fast-medium or off-spin bowler and his bowling was as unpredictable as his batting.

For Somerset he captained the team from 1971 to 1977, playing 142 matches, scoring 7,567 runs at 39.41 (with a best of 153 not out against Middlesex at Lord's in 1973), and he took 74 wickets at 34.98, the best of which was 5 for 70 against Lancashire at Taunton in 1974. He took 140 catches, and his total of 813 puts him fifth highest in first-class cricket.

His final game was at Scarborough in 1986, at the age of 55, when he played for his own XI against New Zealand, and he was an England selector from 1979 to 1981. He then returned to the Broad Acres once more, serving on the Yorkshire committee during the 1980s and 1990s.

Geoffrey Cook

RHB & SLA, 1971–90

Born: 9 October 1951, Middlesbrough.
Played for: Northamptonshire, Eastern
Province and Durham.
Test Matches: (7) 1983–88 Cap No. 493
Batting Career for England

I	NO	HS	Runs
13	0	66	203
AV	**100**	**50**	**Catches**
15.61	-	2	9

Bowling for England

Balls	Runs	Wkts	Av
42	27	0	-
Best	**5wl**	**10wl**	**Sr/Rate**
-	-	-	-

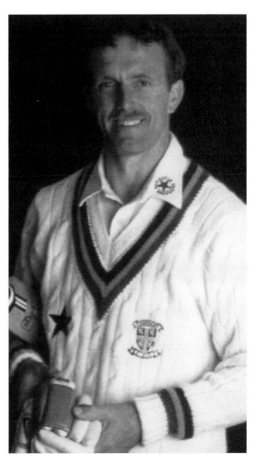

First-Class Career: (460 Matches) 1971–90
Batting

I	NO	HS	Runs
793	65	203	23,277
AV	**100**	**50**	**Ct/St**
31.97	37	112	419/3

Bowling

Balls	Runs	Wkts	Av
1,238	806	15	53.73
Best	**5wl**	**10wl**	**Sr/Rate**
3–47	-	-	82.50

Geoff Cook arrived at Northamptonshire in 1968 on a trial basis, as the young middle-order batsman followed a long line of Durham-born cricketers such as Colin Milburn, Peter Willey, George Sharpe, Alan Hodgson and Alan Tait to the County Ground. The 17-year-old, who hailed from a family steeped in cricket, served his apprenticeship in the second XI before making his first-team debut against Leicestershire in 1971. His sound technique soon saw him promoted to opening the innings, but his progress was steady rather than spectacular, and it was not until 1975 that he first passed 1,000 runs in a season.

The following summer Cook was an integral part of a Northamptonshire side that finished runners-up to Middlesex in the County Championship and reached a Lord's Cup Final (the Gillette Cup) for the first time in their history. Not many gave them much of a chance against the hot favourites Lancashire, but the Midland county emerged the victors by four wickets, with Cook contributing 15 runs and a brilliant catch.

In 1978, Cook, an intelligent, self-assured and popular player with his colleagues and supporters, was appointed vice-captain to Jim Watts. In the same year he began an opening partnership with the attacking and flamboyant Wayne Larkins, which lasted for more than a decade.

In 1981 Northants secured their second final win at Lord's, this time beating Essex by six runs in the Benson and Hedges Cup, and the following summer they made it a hat-trick of appearances at the game headquarters, this time with Cook at the helm. Unfortunately, this time they were beaten on the last ball by Derbyshire, but Cook had the consolation prize of Man of the Match with a well constructed 111 innings from 148 balls. The innings earned him a place on England's winter tour to India and Sri Lanka, and he made his Test debut at Colombo, making 11 and 0. In total he made seven appearances for his country, but 203 runs from 13 innings, with only two half-centuries, meant that he never seized the opportunity to transfer his consistent county form to the Test arena.

However, he did sterling work for his adopted county and acted as skipper from 1981 to 1988, which made him the longest serving captain that the county had during the 20th century. He took Northamptonshire to two more finals in 1987, losing in a tie to Yorkshire in the Benson and Hedges Cup and to Nottinghamshire in the Natwest Final.

His best season was in 1981 when he recorded 1,759 runs at 43.97 and his highest score was 203 against Lancashire in 1986 at Wantage Road, when he and Robin Boyd-Moss put on 344 for the second wicket – which is still a county record. He was highly thought of by his fellow professionals and was elected secretary and chairman of the Cricketers' Association before departing from Northamptonshire in 1991 with nearly 21,000 runs under his belt.

In 1992 Cook was offered the role of director of cricket at his native county, Durham, and he decided it was an offer too good to refuse and set out to prepare for the club's maiden season as a first-class county. With the help of David Graveney he chose the Durham squad and coached the team, but he reverted to director of cricket when Martyn Moxon joined from Yorkshire as county coach in 2001. There is no doubt that Cook, an intense thinker about the game, helped shape Durham's early years and contributed significantly to the development of current England players such as Paul Collingwood, Steve Harmison and Liam Plunkett.

In 2007, when Moxon returned to Yorkshire, Cook again took up the role of coach and guided the county to their first silverware, the Friends Provident Trophy, and to runners-up position in the LV County Championship behind winners Sussex.

However, the ultimate goal was not far away and in September 2008, when Durham beat Kent at Canterbury, the County Championship was theirs at last, and a modest Geoff Cook announced that it was his proudest achievement in the game.

Geoffrey Alan Cope

RHB & OB, 1966–80

Born: 23 February 1947, Burmantofts, Leeds.
Played for: Yorkshire.
Test Matches: (3) 1977–78 Cap No. 475
Batting Career for England

I	NO	HS	Runs
3	0	22	40
AV	**100**	**50**	**Catches**
13.33	-	-	1

Bowling for England

Balls	Runs	Wkts	Av
864	277	8	34.62
Best	**5wl**	**10wl**	**Sr/Rate**
3–102	-	-	108.00

First-Class Career: (246 Matches) 1966–80
Batting

I	NO	HS	Runs
261	93	78	2,383
AV	**100**	**50**	**Catches**
14.18	-	5	71

Bowling

Balls	Runs	Wkts	Av
43,448	16,948	686	24.70
Best	**5wl**	**10wl**	**Sr/Rate**
8–73	35	6	63.33

A talented schoolboy, Geoff Cope played for England Schools, followed by club cricket with Leeds Zingari and then for Leeds Cricket Club in the Yorkshire League. He began his Yorkshire career playing four matches for the second XI in 1965, before making his first-class debut a year later against Hampshire at Bradford, deputising for Ray Illingworth who was on Test duty.

It was hard for Cope in his early career, with Illingworth the main finger spinner in the side, but in the following summer he managed to play in 11 first-class games, taking 40 wickets at 13.82, and in the process he topped the county averages.

He did not win a regular place until 1969, when Illingworth had departed to captain Leicestershire, and he was seen as the natural successor. An off-spinner with a high action, he was never a huge turner of the ball, instead relying on accuracy to deny the batsman runs and exert pressure, while he was also a useful late order batsman.

There were rumours regarding Cope's throwing action in 1968, but two years later he had a fine season taking 83 first-class wickets at 25.43 and was awarded his county cap. Against Essex at Colchester he took 10 for 80 in the match (7 for 36 and 3 for 44), which included a hat-trick. Other notable returns were 6 for 55 against Surrey at Bradford and 6 for 81 against Somerset at Taunton.

In 1972 the 'throwing' issue reared its head once again and he was suspended by the TCCB for having a suspect bowling action. He decided he had to fight to save his career and worked on his action with former Yorkshire great Johnny Wardle, who was forever encouraging him and the two developed a great friendship.

In 1974 and 1975 he had two very good seasons, taking 77 wickets at 21.83 and 69 at 21.86 respectively, and in the latter he recorded his best first-class figures, 8 for 73 against Gloucestershire at the County Ground, Bristol.

In May 1976 he was selected for an England trial at Bristol, and with Derek Underwood as his bowling partner they bowled out the Rest of England for a paltry 48 in their second innings. Cope took 5 for 27, and with his confidence sky high he had his best season for Yorkshire, taking 87 wickets at 24.58, which included 11 for 167 (6 for 60 and 5 for 107) against Middlesex at Bradford.

In the winter of 1976–77 he was selected for the MCC tour to India, but he had to fly home early when his father died. The following winter he went on tour to Pakistan and played in all three Tests, making his debut at Lahore, where he took 3 for 102 and came tantalisingly close to a hat-trick. He had dismissed Abdul Qadir lbw and had bowled Sarfraz Nawaz, and then he had Iqbal Qasim caught at slip by captain Mike Brearley, or so he thought, for the umpire had given him out. However, Brearley, uncertain that he had caught it, recalled Qasim to the crease, but it did not give England any brownie points for they had six lbws given against them in their first innings.

Unfortunately for Cope, the throwing issue still would not go away and the TCCB suspended him again in 1978, which effectively meant that his Test career was over. However, he re-modelled his action once more and battled on for a further three years at Yorkshire and took 42 wickets at 37.09 in 1980, his last season with the county. His last first-class match was against Derbyshire at Scarborough. In 230 first-class matches he took 630 wickets at 24.80 with 33 five-wicket hauls and he held 64 catches. He was also a determined late-order batsman who notched up five first-class fifties, with a best of 78 against Essex at Middlesbrough in 1977 and scored 2,241 runs at an average of 14.00.

In 1980 he had a joint benefit with Barrie Leadbeater which raised £33,846 before he departed to play minor county cricket with Lincolnshire. He also played League cricket for Yeadon, before retiring from the game at the age of 40.

He was elected to the Yorkshire committee after Brian Close had retired from his seat and he is still actively involved with the county.

Alexander Coxon

RHB & RMF, 1945–50

Born: 18 January 1916, Huddersfield.
Died: 21 January 2006.
Played for: Yorkshire, Roker, Sunderland.
Test Matches: (1) 1948 Cap No. 334

Batting Career for England

I	NO	HS	Runs
2	0	19	19
AV	**100**	**50**	**Catches**
9.50 -	-	-	-

Bowling for England

Balls	Runs	Wkts	Av
378	172	3	57.33
Best	**5wl**	**10wl**	**Sr/Rate**
2–90	-	-	126.00

First-Class Career: (146 Matches) 1945–50

Batting

I	NO	HS	Runs
188	33	83	2,817
AV	**100**	**50**	**Catches**
18.17	-	13	127

Bowling

Balls	Runs	Wkts	Av
26,513	9,893	473	20.91
Best	**5wl**	**10wl**	**Sr/Rate**
8–31	24	2	56.05

Alexander Coxon was born in Huddersfield, one of 11 children, and played first for Dalton Cricket Club and then as a professional in the Bradford League with Brighouse and Saltaire. He also played wartime Association Football as a centre-forward for Bradford, before joining Yorkshire in 1945 at the age of 29. Unfortunately, World War Two caused him to miss an important early part of his career.

He made his Yorkshire debut against Lancashire in the Roses match at Bradford in August 1945, taking 4 for 65 in the match, and the following season he played 28 matches, making quite an impact with his aggressive fast-medium bowling. Coxon took 69 wickets at 19.19 with a best of 8 for 31 against Worcestershire at Headingley, his best first-class figures, which included a hat-trick when he took the last three Worcestershire wickets in their second innings. It was a match Yorkshire nervously won by just one wicket. Apart from his bowling he was also a determined late-order batsman, notching up his first half-century with a score of 53 against Oxford University in the Parks.

In 1947 he opened the attack with Bill Bowes and continued his good form by taking 80 first-class wickets at 23.35, with a best of 6 for 42 against Gloucestershire at Bristol. He also worked his way up the batting order, scoring 573 runs at 16.73 and was awarded his county cap in the match against Sussex at Bradford. While batting, skipper Brain Sellers took off his cap and placed it on Coxon's head saying, 'Does it fit? You have earned it.'

The following season Coxon established a regular place in the top seven of the batting order and produced his best score for the county when he scored 83 against Nottinghamshire at Headingley out of a total innings score of 177. In addition he took 79 first-class wickets.

However, his best days were still ahead of him, even though he was now 32 years of age. During the summer he was selected for England, playing against the Australia 'Invincible' team at Lord's for his one and only Test match. He took 3 for 172 off 63 overs, dismissing Brown for a duck and removing Morris as well. He also believed that he trapped Don Bradman lbw, and it is said that he called the Australian legend 'a lucky bugger' after he had excaped the appeal. He also had an exchange of words with Denis Compton, and according to many was unlucky not to win more caps.

Indeed, in 1949 he proved what a fine aggressive bowler he was by taking 101 wickets at 20.79 and in 1950 went even better with 129 at 18.59, which included 10 for 80 against Hampshire at Portsmouth (4 for 32 and 6 for 48), in the last match of the season. His best return of the summer came in his last first-class match for Yorkshire with 7 for 51 against the MCC at Scarborough.

The following winter he coached in South Africa and then left the White Rose County after accepting an offer from Sunderland to play in the Durham Senior League, thereby becoming the highest paid professional in the League. Alex always denied he was sacked by Yorkshire, but his fiery temperament did not go down well with some of the committee.

For Yorkshire he played 142 matches, took 464 wickets at 20.53 with 24 five wicket hauls, scored 2,747 runs at 18.43 and held 124 catches.

As well as playing for Sunderland, Durham also secured his services, and in three years with the minor county team he took 127 wickets at 14.84 in only 29 matches, with a best of 9 for 28 against Staffordshire and 122 not out against Yorkshire Seconds, both in 1952. His last game for Durham was in 1954 against Lancashire Seconds at Old Trafford. After a shower of rain had sent the players off the field, Coxon asked for some sawdust. When the inexperienced ground staff boy asked where to put it, Alex said, 'Right there', in front of the stumps on a good length. The players and umpires fell about laughing, but unfortunately the Durham captain, a certain Roland Barton Proud (a big man, known as the 'Durham Ox'), was not amused and Coxon never played for the county again.

Coxon then played League cricket for South Shields and Wearmouth, for whom he took 71 wickets in 1971 at the age of 50.

He became junior coach at South Shields at the age of 76 in 1992, and died three days after his 90th birthday.

Willis Robert Cuttell

RHB & LB, 1896–1906

Born: 13 September 1864, Sheffield.
Died: 9 December 1929, Nelson, Lancashire.
Played for: Lancashire.
Test Matches: (2) 1899–99 Cap No. 112

Batting Career for England

I	NO	HS	Runs
4	0	21	65
AV	**100**	**50**	**Catches**
16.25	-	-	2

Bowling for England

Balls	Runs	Wkts	Av
285	73	6	12.16
Best	**5wl**	**10wl**	**Sr/Rate**
3–17	-	-	47.50

First-Class Career: (227 Matches) 1896–1906

Batting

I	NO	HS	Runs
315	31	137	5,938
AV	**100**	**50**	**Catches**
20.90	5	21	140

Bowling

Balls	Runs	Wkts	Av
44,411	15,519	792	19.59
Best	**5wl**	**10wl**	**Sr/Rate**
8–105	50	8	56.07

Willis Cuttell was the son of William Cuttell, a useful all-rounder who played 15 matches for Yorkshire from 1862 to 1871 and also played with several Lancashire League Clubs, Eccles and Bolton in particular. Like his father, Willis was born in Sheffield and played his early cricket as a professional for Bankers Cricket Club in Sheffield and also for Worksop. He also had a spell with Accrington, before trying to gain a place on the Yorkshire staff. He played a couple of matches against opposition that was not considered first-class, but did not do enough for Yorkshire to further their interest.

Willis therefore returned to Lancashire League cricket and in 1892 moved to Nelson. A year later he took 118 wickets, and in 1895 he proved himself the best bowler in the League with 106 wickets at only 8.5 runs per wicket.

By now Cuttell had served his residential qualifications for Lancashire and at the age of 31 was finally engaged by the Red Rose County for the 1896 season, but he played only two games.

As a cricketer, like his father, he was an all-rounder, whose bowling was medium pace with a beautiful high action, and he possessed the ability to turn the ball both ways, bowling both the leg-break and off-break. His first captain, Albert Neilson Hornby, said that his best ball was the one that went straight on with the arm. Willis could deliver all three with exceptional accuracy, with no apparent change of action, and his bowling surprised some of the best batsmen in the country. In addition he was an outstanding fielder and a hard-hitting batsman.

In 1897 he played a major part in Lancashire winning the County Championship for the first time since 1881. He took 102 wickets at 17.70, finishing second to the great Johnny Briggs in the Lancashire averages, and only Tom Richardson and Briggs took more wickets in the country.

The following summer he had his best season in first-class cricket when he achieved the 'double', 1,003 runs at 25.71 and 114 wickets at 21.21, becoming in the process the first Lancashire player to do so. On a good pitch at Old Trafford he took a career best of 8 for 105 against Gloucestershire, dismissing W.G. Grace in both innings. He also took 7 for 19 against Derbyshire, and when playing for the North against the South he took 8 wickets for 41 runs in the match. Once again he got the upper hand against the great doctor, clean bowling Grace in both innings. His performances not only earned him an England call-up for the winter tour to South Africa under Lord Hawke's leadership, but also got him named as one of *Wisden's* Five Cricketers of the Year.

In the Test match series he scored 65 runs at 16.25 and took 6 wickets at 12.16. His best score was 21 at Johannesburg and he took 3 for 17 in the same match.

In 1899 he made his highest first-class score of 137 against Nottinghamshire at Old Trafford, but could not force his way back into the England team, mainly because of the bowling on sticky wickets of the Yorkshire pair, Wilfred Rhodes and Schofield Haigh.

In the summer of 1903 he took a joint benefit with Charles Smith, also a Yorkshireman, which raised £657. A year later he took 100 championship wickets at 19.92.

In 1906 he was third in the national bowling averages with 67 wickets at 13.56, but at the end of the season he decided to end his playing career and took up a coaching position at Rugby School, which he held for the next 20 years. For Lancashire he scored 5,938 runs at 20.9, with five centuries, took 792 wickets at 19.59 and held 140 catches. He also scored 1,000 runs twice in a season and took 100 wickets in a season on four occasions.

At the age of 63 he became a first-class umpire, but he could only carry out the role for two years, due to a deterioration in his health.

On retiring he purchased a tobacconist shop in Nelson, where he lived for the remainder of his life.

Richard Kevin James Dawson

RHB & OB, 2000–to date

Born: 4 August 1980, Doncaster.
Played for: Yorkshire, Northamptonshire and
Gloucestershire.
Test Matches: (7) 2001–03 Cap No. 608

Batting Career for England

I	NO	HS	Runs
13	3	19*	114
AV	**100**	**50**	**Catches**
11.40	-	-	3

Bowling for England

Balls	Runs	Wkts	Av
1,116	677	11	61.54
Best	**5wl**	**10wl**	**Sr/Rate**
4–134	-	-	101.45

First-Class Career: (96 Matches) 2000–to date

Batting

I	NO	HS	Runs
143	17	87	2,673
AV	**100**	**50**	**Catches**
21.21	-	11	51

Bowling

Balls	Runs	Wkts	Av
14515	8160	187	43.63
Best	**5wl**	**10wl**	**Sr/Rate**
6–82	5	-	77.60

Born in the South Yorkshire town of Doncaster, Richard Dawson was a promising schoolboy cricketer and was captain of the England Under-15 team. In 1997 he toured Bermuda with the England Under-18s and in the winter of 1998–99 he went to New Zealand with the Under-19 team.

An off-spin bowler who was a more than useful late-order batsman, he first played for the Yorkshire Second XI as a 17-year-old in 1998, making his debut against Worcestershire at

Harrogate. He played five games that season with a top score of 52 not out against Northamptonshire at York and 4 for 40 against Hampshire at Todmorden.

A pupil at Batley Grammer School, he went on to Exeter University and made his first-class debut for the British Universities against the touring Zimbabweans in the summer of 2000.

The following season he burst onto the first-class scene in a big way, playing nine games for Yorkshire and taking 30 wickets at 33.80. He made his debut at Headingley against Leicestershire, scoring a fine 37, and a month later he took 6 for 98 against Surrey, also at Leeds. Along with Steve Kirby he was instrumental in assisting Yorkshire to their first Championship title since 1968, and it was fitting that his best bowling performance for the county, 6 for 82, was in the Championship clincher against Glamorgan at Scarborough. He also won the NBC Denis Compton award for the Most Promising Young Yorkshire Cricketer.

It seemed that Yorkshire had unearthed another in a long line of good slow bowlers, and the England selectors plunged him straight into international cricket, selecting Dawson for the tour to India in the winter of 2000–01. He made his debut at Mohali in the first Test, taking 4 for 134 off 34 overs, with nightwatchman Anil Kumble as his first victim in Test cricket.

In the 2002 domestic season with Yorkshire he scored a useful 496 runs, with a first-class best of 87 against Kent at Canterbury, when he and Richard Blakey (90) shared a seventh-wicket partnership of 162. He also took 39 wickets at 39.38, with a best of 5 for 42 against Lancashire in the Roses match at Old Trafford, and in the following game at the Rose Bowl against Hampshire he took 5 for 69.

Selected as second spinner for the tour to Australia in 2002–03, an injury to Ashley Giles meant that he was now the main spin bowler, but 5 wickets at 79.60 in four Tests showed he was somewhat out of his depth. However, he did bat bravely on several occasions, particularly at Perth, where he made his best Test score of 19 not out, facing Brett Lee and company on a bouncy wicket.

He had an average season in 2003, taking only 17 wickets, although he did score 564 runs, his highest aggregate in a season. It seemed that his bowling was somewhat static, but even so he was named in England's 30 player pool for the Champions Trophy, after which he disappeared from the international scene as quickly as he had appeared.

With Yorkshire his form slumped to such a degree that in 2006 he was asked to captain the second XI, and at the end of the season he was released from his contract. It was a sad end to his Yorkshire career, which had seen him take 181 first-class wickets at 42.42 and score 2,496 runs at 21.33.

Dawson joined Northamptonshire for the 2007 season but played only two games before being released yet again. He began training as a journalist, using his university experience to the full, and he did some coaching at Gordonstoun School in Scotland until Gloucestershire offered him a short-term stint towards the end of the season.

Fortunately for Dawson, in August 2008, he was given a two-year deal with Gloucestershire, and as at the time of writing he is still only 28 years of age, he has plenty of time to fulfil the potential of his early career.

David Denton

RHB & RM, 1894–1920

Born: 4 July 1874, Thornes, Wakefield.
Died: 16 February 1950, Thornes, Wakefield.
Played for: Yorkshire.
Test Matches: (11) 1905–1910 Cap No. 142

Batting Career for England

I	NO	HS	Runs
22	1	104	424
AV	**100**	**50**	**Catches**
20.19	1	1	8

D. DENTON.

First-Class Career: (742 Matches) 1894–1920

Batting

I	NO	HS	Runs
1,163	70	221	36,479
AV	**100**	**50**	**Ct/St**
33.37	69	187	396/1

Bowling

Balls	Runs	Wkts	Av
1,681	983	34	28.91
Best	**5wl**	**10wl**	**Sr/Rate**
5–42	1	-	49.44

David Denton was one of the best batsmen that the county produced during the 'Golden Age of English Cricket'. Only Herbert Sutcliffe scored more runs for Yorkshire, Sutcliffe, Boycott, Hutton and Leyland had more centuries and only Rhodes and Hirst played more matches.

A native of Thornes, Wakefield, Denton was the younger brother of Joseph Denton who played 15 matches for Yorkshire in 1887 and 1888. David played his early cricket with Hodgson's and Simpson's at his home club in Thornes, scoring his first century in 1892 against Pudsey Britannia before he moved to Castleford in 1894.

He made his first appearance for Yorkshire in 1894 against Warwickshire at Bramall Lane, but it was another 12 months before he secured a regular place in the Yorkshire team. In 1896 he scored his first century for the county, 113 against Derbyshire at Derby, and in addition notched up 1,028 runs. He had originally been recommended to Yorkshire as a right-arm medium-fast bowler, and in the same year he took his best bowling figures, 5 for 42 against the South of England XI at Scarborough.

However, it was as a batsman that he became a Yorkshire icon. A slightly built figure, Denton was superbly quick on his feet and attacked the bowling whenever possible. Indeed, he was nicknamed 'Lucky Denton' because of the amount of chances he gave while batting that were not taken, but his strong, flexible wrists and superb timing enabled him to score freely all around the wicket. He was particularly strong on the off-side and he was always eager to cut, pull or hook the ball at every opportunity. He did not take kindly to his nickname, saying that a man who has the ability to score in excess of 30,000 first-class runs must have something more than luck at the back of him. In addition, he was a brilliant out-fielder, fast on his feet with a fine throw, and had the reputation of hardly ever dropping a catch.

Between 1899 and 1904 he scored well over 1,000 runs a season, and in 1905 he notched up over 2,000 for the first time (2,258 at an average of 45.16), which was in fact his best aggregate for a season. Included in the total was a highest score of 172 against Gloucestershire at Bradford Park Avenue, which was one of eight centuries that he scored that season. He was not only rewarded with the honour of being named one of *Wisden's* Five Cricketers of the Year, but was also selected for his Test debut against the visiting South Africans at Headingley, which, incredibly, was the only Test match that he played in his home country.

In the winter of 1906 he was selected for the MCC tour to South Africa under the leadership of 'Plum Warner', but he had a disappointing trip and scored only 172 runs at an average of 17.2 in the five Tests, although he did score 61 in the second innings of the third Test in Johannesburg. He was dropped from the Test scene for another four years, before he reappeared once more against South Africa in 1910. Once again for a batsman of his ability, his performances were somewhat disappointing and, despite his maiden century (104 at Johannesburg), an average of only 20.19 from 22 innings spelled the end to his Test career.

However, he continued to plunder runs for Yorkshire and in 1906 he scored a century in each innings against Nottinghamshire at Trent Bridge (107 and 109 not out). He repeated the performance two years later at Scarborough with 133 and 121 against the MCC In the meantime he received a well-earned benefit which realised £1,915.

In the summers of 1911 and 1912 he hit over 2,000 runs each season (2,161 at 42.37 in the former and 2,088 at 44.23 in the latter), and included his highest first-class score, 221 against Kent at Tunbridge Wells.

In 1920, his last season in first-class cricket, he scored 1,324 runs, which included the last of his 61 centuries for Yorkshire, with a score of 145 against Kent. In 21 years with the county he scored 1,000 runs a season every year, with the exception of 1898.

Denton was a member of nine Championship-winning teams, and in 676 matches for Yorkshire he scored 33,282 runs at an average of 33.38, took 34 wickets at 28.14, held 360 catches and made 1 stumping.

On retirement his health precluded him from a coaching role and he became the Yorkshire scorer for a period. However, his health improved for a while and he became a first-class umpire from 1925 to 1937. A keen Methodist, he collected a large volume of cricket memorabilia from his playing days, and on his death, at the age of 75 in February 1950 he showed what a shrewd and careful man he had been by leaving in excess of £10,000.

Arthur Dolphin

RHB & WK, 1905–27

Born: 24 December 1885, Wilsden, Bradford.

Died: 23 October 1942, Lilycroft, Heaton, Bradford.

Played for: Yorkshire and Patiala.

Test Matches: (1) 1920–21 Cap No. 188

Batting Career for England

I	NO	HS	Runs
2	0	1	1
AV	100	50	Ct/St
0.50	-	-	1

First-Class Career: (449 Matches) 1905–27

Batting

I	NO	HS	Runs
465	164	66	3,402
AV	100	50	Ct/St
11.30	-	7	609/273

Bowling

Balls	Runs	Wkts	Av
66	28	1	28.00
Best	5wl	10wl	Sr/Rate
1–18	-	-	66.00

Arthur Dolphin was a native of Wilsden, near Bradford, and lived there for most of his life. He first played for Wilsden Britannia when he was only 14 years of age and made his first-class debut for Yorkshire against Cambridge University at Fenners in 1905 at the age of 19, deputising for David Hunter. In doing so, he became the first Bradford League player to represent the county.

When Hunter retired at the end of the 1909 season, Dolphin took over the wicket-keeping gloves after serving his apprenticeship with the second XI. He retained the position for the following 17 seasons, following an illustrious list of Yorkshire wicket-keepers, including Ned Stephenson, George Pinder and the two Hunters, Joseph and David, and he gave 22 years of loyal service to Yorkshire.

A small but lively cricketer, he kept wicket to some of the greatest bowlers of all time, including Wilfred Rhodes and George Hirst. In addition, he had to contend with the varied pace, swing and spin of Alonzo Drake, Roy Kilner and Abe Waddington, all left-arm bowlers, as well as the medium-pace variations of Schofield Haigh and George Macauley.

If the deliveries were often too good for the batsman, few eluded Dolphin's grasp, and he performed his duties with the minimum of fuss, a characteristic which defines all the very best wicket-keepers. He played in an era when the skills of pure wicket-keepers, often standing up to the medium-fast bowlers on uncovered, rain affected wickets, were sometimes prized above batting skills. However, it was his lack of runs when at the crease which probably hampered his chances of Test match cricket, though he did, of course, have to contend with the great Surrey 'keeper Herbert Strudwick for most of his career.

Dolphin did play one Test match at Melbourne on the disastrous 1920–21 tour of Australia, as a member of Johnny Douglas's party, but like all his colleagues he suffered at the hands of an unrestrained home team.

As a batsman he could defend doggedly with a straight bat when the situation demanded it, and in 1914, going in as nightwatchman against Essex, he made his highest first-class score (66), sharing a second-wicket partnership of 124 with Benjamin Wilson.

During the war he served alongside his county colleagues Roy Kilner and Major Booth with the 'Leeds Pals', and he returned to the Yorkshire ranks in 1919. It was then thast he enjoyed his most successful season with the gloves, claiming 82 dismissals (52 catches and 30 stumpings), which included nine dismissals against Derbyshire at Bradford (eight caught and one stumping). He also scored a gritty 62 not out in a partnership with Ernest Smith (49), of 103 for the last wicket against Essex at Leyton, thereby saving Yorkshire from the follow-on.

In 1921, when Hampshire made 456 for 2 in a day, Dolphin retained his concentration to such an extent that he only conceded two byes in the innings. The following summer he was given a benefit match against Kent at Headingley, which raised a hefty sum of £1,891, and he hit the winning runs after scoring 20 of the 24 required needed to secure victory by 10 wickets.

At various times in his career he suffered from sciatica, and he played his last match for Yorkshire in the summer of 1927 at the age of 41 and was not re-engaged for the following season. For Yorkshire he played 427 matches, scored 3,325 runs at 11.50 and took 829 dismissals (569 catches and 260 stumpings).

He then became a popular and well-respected first-class umpire for a decade and officiated in six Test matches. He was well-known during his umpiring days for never wearing a hat, even on the hottest of summer days.

Thomas Emmett

LHB & LF, 1866–88

Born: 3 September 1841, Halifax.
Died: 30 June 1904, Leicester.
Played for: Yorkshire.
Test Matches: (7) 1876–82 Cap No. 3

Batting Career for England

I	NO	HS	Runs
13	1	48	160
AV	100	50	Catches
13.33	-	-	9

Bowling for England

Balls	Runs	Wkts	Av
728	284	9	31.55
Best	5wl	10wl	Sr/Rate
7–68	1	-	80.88

First-Class Career: (426 Matches) 1866–88

Batting

I	NO	HS	Runs
700	90	104	9,053
AV	100	50	Catches
14.84	1	24	276

Bowling

Balls	Runs	Wkts	Av
60,333	21,314	1,571	13.56
Best	5wl	10wl	Sr/Rate
9–23	121	29	38.40

Tom Emmett was one of the great characters of Yorkshire and English cricket in the second half of the 19th century second only to W.G. Grace in being the most popular cricketer of his day. Born in Halifax, he played his early cricket with the Illingworth club before taking his first professional engagement at Halifax, followed by three years at Keighley.

He made his first-class debut for Yorkshire at the age of 24 in 1866 against Nottinghamshire at Trent Bridge, (his fee was £5, which included travelling expenses and accommodation) and he took 5 for 33.

During his first few years with the county he showcased several outstanding bowling performances, such as when he took 6 for 7 in 12 overs against Surrey at Sheffield in 1867. Two years later he achieved his best individual performance and best aggregate of wickets for a match when he took 16 for 39 against Cambridgeshire at Hunslet, which included 7 for 15 and his best-ever, 9 for 23.

When he first joined the county he was a fast left-arm bowler with a near round-arm action who intelligently used the crease to its maximum to vary his angle and would occasionally bowl from behind it. Known to be wayward at times, he nevertheless had the best batsmen in England in trouble, including W.G. Grace, with his ability to pitch the ball middle and leg and hit the off-stump. As his pace diminished in later years he pushed the ball wider, inviting the batsman to edge the ball to the slip cordon, and he developed a slower break-back which he called his 'sosteneuter'. He was also an attacking batsman, who opened the innings at various times during his career.

From 1867 his partnership with fellow opening bowler George Freeman was one of the most feared in county cricket, and in 1868 they bowled out Lancashire for 30 and 34 at Holbeck, Leeds, with Emmett taking 8 for 24 and Freeman 12 for 23. In the same season they repeated the act, this time against Middlesex at Sheffield, with Emmett taking 6 for 57 and Freeman 12 for 62. Indeed, during his Yorkshire career he bowled unchanged throughout a match in which the opposition were dismissed twice on no less than 12 occasions, six with George Freeman, five with Allen Hill and once with Billy Bates, a magnificent achievement and unmatched by any other Yorkshire bowler.

In 1873 he scored his one and only century, 104 against Gloucestershire at Clifton College, Bristol, and took 12 for 84 (6 for 38 and 6 for 46) against Surrey at Sheffield.

Four years later he went on the first of three trips to Australia and played in the inaugural Test match at the MCG In the second Test, also at Melbourne, he hit his highest Test score of 48 and shared a sixth-wicket stand of 74 with fellow Yorkshireman George Ulyett. Two years later, again at the MCG, he achieved his best bowling figures in Test cricket, 7 for 68 off 59 overs, thus becoming the first English bowler to take seven wickets in a Test innings. He toured Australia once more in 1881–82 and he also visited North America, playing a total of seven Test matches for his country.

In 1878 he was elected the first professional captain of Yorkshire, a position he held until 1982, and he was the last professional captain until Vic Wilson was appointed in 1960.

The charm of Emmett was his keen and obvious enjoyment of the game, and to the end of his playing days he played with the enthusiasm of a schoolboy. In addition he had a wonderful wit, and on one occasion when Yorkshire were being slipshod in the field he quipped, 'There's an epidemic here, and it ain't catching.' On another occasion when Yorkshire were suffering at the hands of W.G. Grace (he scored 318 against them), Emmett's response was, 'Grace before meat, Grace after meat, and Grace all bloody day.'

He played his last match for Yorkshire in 1888, the last of 298 matches for the county, in which he scored 6,315 runs at 15.10, took 1,208 wickets at 12.78 with 92 five wicket hauls and held 177 catches. He was the first bowler to take 1,000 wickets for Yorkshire, and no other has done so at a lower average.

Emmett was 47 when he retired and deservedly had a benefit match that raised £620. He later played for a short period as a professional at the Bradford and Leicester clubs and coached at Stonyhurst College. He then became groundsman and coach at Rugby School, where one of his pupils was Pelham (Plum) Warner, who went on to captain England. He later coached at Leicestershire, for whom his eldest son Arthur appeared in 1902.

A renowned family man (he had four daughters and two sons), he died at the age of 62 in Leicester from an attack of apoplexy.

Paul Anthony Gibb

RHB & WK, 1934–1956

Born: 11 July 1913, Acomb, York.
Died: 7 December 1977, Guildford, Surrey.
Played for: Scotland, Cambridge University,
Yorkshire and Essex.
Test Matches: (8) 1938–47 Cap No. 305
Batting Career for England

I	NO	HS	Runs
13	0	120	581
AV	**100**	**50**	**Ct/St**
44.69	2	3	3/1

First-Class Career: (287 Matches) 1934–56
Batting

I	NO	HS	Runs
479	33	204	12,520
AV	**100**	**50**	**Ct/St**
28.07	19	51	425/123

Bowling

Balls	Runs	Wkts	Av
269	161	5	32.20
Best	**5wl**	**10wl**	**Sr/Rate**
2–40	-	-	53.80

The eldest son of a railway executive, Paul Gibb attended St Edwards School, Oxford, and made his first-class debut for Scotland against the Australians at Raeburn Place in 1934, although he did tour North America and Bermuda in 1933 with Sir Julian Cahn's team. A year later he went up to Cambridge and made his debut for Yorkshire against Nottinghamshire at Bramall Lane, scoring 157 not out and sharing a sixth-wicket partnership of 178 with Herbert Sutcliffe. In the process he became the first and only amateur to make a century on their debut for the county.

Although a wicket-keeper, it was as an opening batsman that he first played for the county, and in the winter of 1935–36, as the only available amateur, he captained the county on their first-ever overseas tour to Jamaica. On tour he took his turn at bowling and took a career best of 2 for 40 with the ball.

During his four years at Cambridge he established himself as the regular wicket-keeper, controversially taking over the role from Billy Griffiths in his third year. He notched up five centuries for the university, with a highest first-class score of 204 against the Free Foresters in 1938. It was his best season for Cambridge, a season which saw him score 1,658 runs. In addition to scoring 122 in the varsity game against Oxford at Lord's, he carried his bat through the university's innings of 163 against Bradman's touring Australian team with 80 not out.

Known as a somewhat dour opening batsman, he was immensely strong on the back foot and although he had a tendency to overdo the hook shot, when set he could score all around the wicket. He was also a very brave and competent wicket-keeper, with an excellent reputation for standing up to the wicket.

In July 1938 he was chosen to play in the third Test against Australia in place of the injured Les Ames, controversially ahead of his Yorkshire colleague Arthur Wood, but in the event the match was abandoned without a ball being bowled.

For the winter tour of South Africa in 1938–39 he was chosen as Ames's deputy and played all five Tests purely as a batsman, opening the innings with Len Hutton. In the first Test at Johannesburg he scored 93 and 106, thus becoming the first Yorkshire player to score a century in his first Test match. At Durban in the fifth and final Test he scored 120 in the second innings, a match which was abandoned as a draw after 10 days of play (England having reached 654 for 5 chasing 696 to win) as England's boat was due to leave for home. The match was famous for being known as the 'Timeless Test'.

The war disrupted his career somewhat, just when, as a batsman in particular, he was reaching his prime. Immediately after the war he played for Yorkshire in the 1946 season as senior 'keeper and scored his second century for the county, with a score of 104 against Warwickshire at Edgbaston.

Gibb appeared in the first two Tests against India, and at Lord's he scored 60 in a fifth-wicket partnership of 182 with Joe Hardstaff Jnr (205 not out), but he lost his place to Godfrey Evans for the remainder of the series. In the winter he went to Australia and played in the Brisbane Test, but again he lost his place to Evans and did not play for England again, despite having a batting average of 44.68 from eight matches. On his return to England he decided to quit Yorkshire cricket and was lost to the game until the summer of 1951, when he joined Essex as a professional. For Yorkshire he played 36 matches, scored 1,545 runs at 32.87, took 3 wickets at 27.33 and made 33 dismissals (25 caught and eight stumped).

With Essex he became the first Blue to turn professional, and in his first season he scored four centuries, including his highest for the county, 141 against Kent at Blackheath. In the process he shared what was then a record partnership of 343 with fellow Yorkshireman Richard Horsfall (206) for the third wicket. He also made over 1,000 runs for the season (1,330), as he did on three other occasions for the county.

In 1952 he was second only to Jack Firth of Leicestershire as the leading wicket-keeper, with 77 dismissals, and the following year he went one better, topping the list with 71 (58 caught and 13 stumped).

In the winter of 1953–54 he made his last tour, as a member of the Commonwealth team to India, and scored 154 against Assam Governor's XI at Jorkat.

He played 145 matches for Essex, scoring 6,328 runs at 26.58, including eight centuries, and took 336 dismissals (273 caught and 63 stumped), before retiring to become a first-class umpire from 1957 to 1966. He was a popular figure on the county circuit with his dry humour. He later did some coaching in South Africa before becoming a bus driver in Guildford, where he died suddenly in the station in 1977 at the age of 64. Inexplicably, he was left out of *Wisden's* obituary section the following year.

George Keyworth Glover

RHB & OB, 1889–90 to 1897–98

Born: 13 May 1870, Wakefield, Yorkshire.

Died: 15 November 1938, Kimberley, Cape Province, South Africa.

Played for: Kimberley and Griqualand West.

Test Matches: (1) 1895–96 Cap No. 36

Batting Career For South Africa

I	NO	HS	Runs
2	1	18*	21
AV	**100**	**50**	**Catches**
21.00	0	0	0

Bowling for South Africa

Balls	Runs	Wkts	Av
65	28	1	28.00
Best	**5wl**	**10wl**	**Sr/Rate**
1–28	0	0	65.00

First Class Career: (16 Matches)
1889–90 – 1897–98

Batting

I	NO	HS	Runs
29	3	78	621
AV	**100**	**50**	**Catches**
23.88	0	4	10

Bowling

Balls	Runs	Wkts	Av
2,760	1,317	72	18.29
Best	**5wl**	**10wl**	**Sr/Rate**
8–35	5	2	38.33

George Keyworth Glover, who was born in Wakefield, was taken to South Africa as youngster and emerged as one of South Africa's leading all-round cricketers in the 1890s. A right-handed attacking stroke-player, he was in addition a fine off-spin bowler with a high action.

Glover made his debut for Kimberley (later to become Griqualand West) in their initial first-class match against Natal in December 1889 and was their most successful bowler with 3 for 29 and 2 for 24 in his team's win by 52 runs. In the return match, again at the Electic's ground in Kimberley, he registered his maiden first-class fifty to help his side win by an innings.

Three months later, in April 1890, George appeared for Kimberley in the first-ever Currie Cup match against Transvaal, and although he failed with the bat, captured 6 for 50 in his opponents' first innings and was consequently the first bowler to take five or more wickets in an innings in the competition.

By now playing as Griqualand West, the Kimberley side took part in the last of the Champion Bat Tournaments in 1890–91 and once again Glover was the leading bowler with figures of 3 for 48 and 4 for 37 against Eastern Province and 4 for 60 versus Western Province. At the end of the season in April 1891 the Kimberley side beat Transvaal to win the Currie Cup for the only time, George taking 4 for 168 in a match that lasted seven days.

In the following tournament in 1892–93 he was the outstanding player with 131 runs at 43.66 with a top score of 78 against Western Province, which was indeed his highest first-class score. In addition he took 8 wickets in the match at 22.00 with a best of 5 for 94, but despite his great all-round performance it failed to bring victory and Western Province won the match and the trophy.

Although Griqualand West played only two matches in the 1893–94 Currie Cup, Glover claimed 18 wickets at 7.11. Against Natal he took 3 for 60 in the match and then followed this with the outstanding bowling performance of his career, 15 for 68 versus Eastern Province (8 for 35 and 7 for 33) at Newlands, which at the time was the best figures in a Currie Cup match. Indeed, only Johnny Briggs, for England versus South Africa with 15 for 28, also at Cape Town in 1888–89, had taken 15 wickets in a match in South Africa, and no other bowler had managed eight or more wickets in a Currie Cup innings.

In the summer of 1894 he was chosen to tour the United Kingdom with the first-ever South African team to venture overseas. None of the matches were deemed first-class, but George finished third in the bowling averages with 56 wickets at 17.44, which included 6 for 39 against Scotland, 5 for 36 and 4 for 43 against Lord Cantelupe's XI and 4 for 65 versus Derbyshire. However, he failed to do himself justice with the bat, scoring 377 runs at 13.96 with a best of 41 against Surrey at the Oval.

In the South African season of 1895–96 he bowled unchanged throughout the second innings of the game against Lord Hawke's English touring team to take 6 for 75 for the Griqualand West 15 and this effort earned him selection for the third and final Test of the series at Newlands. In his one and only Test he batted soundly to make 18 not out at number eight in a first-innings total of 115, but he was out for three in the second knock of 117, and took 1 for 28 in England's only innings of 265.

Glover's consistent performances continued in the following Currie Cup season of 1896–97, scoring 46 not out in a total of 131 and 76 out of 180 against Natal and in addition taking 5 for 102 in the match.

His first-class career ended at the close of the following season when he topped the batting averages with 147 runs at 29.40, with a best of 62 against Natal, and took the most wickets, 13 at 21.15 with 10 for 99 (4 for 50 and 6 for 49) when he helped his team beat Border by three wickets.

Two of George's brothers, Fred and Charles, also played for Griqualand West, all three appearing in the same team in the Currie Cup competitions of 1893–94 and 1896–97. His son George Ernest Glover (1925 to 1932) and his grandson Michael Keyworth Glover (1958 to 1964) also represented Griqualand West.

A farmer by occupation, George Keyworth died at the age of 68 in Kimberley, Cape Province, in November 1938.

Darren Gough

RHB & RFM, 1989–2008

Born: 18 September 1970, Barnsley.
Played for: Yorkshire and Essex.
Test Matches: (58) 1994–2003 Cap No. 568

Batting Career for England

I	NO	HS	Runs
86	18	65	855
AV	**100**	**50**	**Catches**
12.57	-	2	13

Bowling for England

Balls	Runs	Wkt	Av
11,819	6,503	229	28.39
Best	**5wl**	**10wl**	**Sr/Rate**
6–42	9	-	51.61

First-Class Career: (248 Matches) 1989–2008

Batting

I	NO	HS	Runs
326	60	121	4,607
AV	**100**	**50**	**Catches**
17.31	1	20	51

Bowling

Balls	Runs	Wkts	Av
44,023	2,317	855	27.15
Best	**5wl**	**10wl**	**Sr/Rate**
7–28	33	3	51.4

Barnsley-born Darren 'Dazzler' Gough started his Yorkshire career with the Barnsley and Yorkshire Boys and the Yorkshire Cricket School. He made his White Rose debut at the age of 18 in 1989 against Middlesex at Lord's, claiming Mike Gatting as his first wicket in first-class cricket and taking five wickets in the match.

A fast-medium bowler at the time, he unfortunately suffered a stress-fracture soon after his breakthrough, but he soon lost weight and became fitter and stronger. In 1993, Yorkshire's foreign player Ritchie Richardson encouraged him to bowl as a fast bowler and he finished the season with 57 wickets at 26.61, which included his best first-class bowling figures of 7 for 42 against Somerset at Taunton. He was awarded his county cap and selected for England's A tour to South Africa.

The following summer, after making his one-day debut against New Zealand, he won his first Test cap in the third Test, scoring 65 (his highest Test score) in his first innings. In addition he took a wicket in his first over.

In the winter, brimming with confidence, Gough went on his first tour to Australia and scored a thrilling 51 in the third Test at Sydney, followed by 6 for 49 in Australia's first innings total of 116. His first tour 'down under' saw him take 20 wickets in the three Tests at 21.25, but he returned home with a broken bone in his left foot. However, he was boosted by the knowledge that he had been England's best bowler. He had not only bowled quickly but had also begun to reverse-swing the ball and had learned a change of pace, a technique which was to benefit him in later years.

In 1995 he took his first hat-trick, which included four wickets in five balls against Kent, and his best bowling figures of 7 for 28 against Lancashire, both at Leeds. The following summer he hit his highest first-class score (121) against Warwickshire and took 67 first-class wickets. As a batsman he always wanted to attack the bowling, when, arguably, if he had reigned himself in he would have scored many more runs. He could defend and bat properly when he wanted to, the innings against Warwickshire proved that, but he was always looking for the big shots. Indeed, as a youngster both at schoolboy and club level he was equally as good a batsman as he was a bowler.

Gough's best figures for England came in 1998, when he took 6 for 42 against South Africa. While on his second tour to Australia, he took a Test hat-trick at Sydney, the first by an England bowler since J.T. Hearne at Leeds in 1899. He was also named one of *Wisden's* Five Cricketers of the Year in 1999.

Together with Andrew Caddick, he formed a fine opening attack, while nobody contributed more to England's four series wins in a row in 2000 and 2000–01 than Gough, who was Man of the Match in the series against the West Indies and Sri Lanka and was later voted the Vodaphone England Cricketer of the Year.

Against Pakistan at Lord's in 2001, he took his 200th Test wicket (Rashid Latif) in his 50th Test and in the same match he passed John Snow's record of 202 wickets to move into seventh place on the list of England's Test match bowlers. He also took 5 for 61 in Pakistan's first innings, his first Test five-wicket return at Lord's.

In 2001–02, against India at Cuttack, he became the first England bowler to take 150 one-day international wickets, but on the England tour of Australia in 2002–03 he had to return early due to an injury to his right knee. Fortunately he recovered, but after the second Test against South Africa at Lord's in 2003 he decided to call time on his Test career, after taking 229 wickets at 28.39 and scoring 855 runs at 12.57, to concentrate on his one-day cricket.

However, he was overlooked for the one-day series in Bangladesh and Sri Lanka the following winter, and in January 2004, after 15 years' service, he decided to call time on his Yorkshire career and joined Essex, citing family reasons.

Gough returned to the international stage in 2004, and in September of that year he became the first Englishman to take 200 wickets in one-day cricket. In January 2005 he played for the World XI, who were facing the Asian XI in the World Cricket Tsunami Appeal.

He asked not to be considered for the England tour of Pakistan in October 2005 so that he could spend more time with his family, but it was discovered that he had signed up with the BBC to take part in the *Strictly Come Dancing* TV show, a competition he won, along with his partner Lilia Kopylova.

He was again omitted from the one-day party to India in February and March 2006, but he did play again, his final game being against Pakistan at Lord's in September of that year. In one-day international cricket he took 234 wickets at 26.29, which is still the most wickets by an English bowler to date.

In 2007 he returned to his native county as captain, playing 14 games in his first season and taking 37 wickets at 23.67. However, he could only manage eight games in 2008 and decided to call it a day at the end of the season, bowing out after Yorkshire's last home Championship match against Somerset at Scarborough. For Yorkshire he played 146 matches, scored 2,922 runs at 16.70, took 453 wickets at 27.56 and held 31 catches.

Andrew Greenwood

RHB, 1869–80

Born: 28 August 1847, Cowes Lepton,
        Huddersfield.
Died: 12 February 1889, Huddersfield.
Played for: Yorkshire.
Test Matches: (2) 1876–77 Cap No. 4
Batting Career for England

I	NO	HS	Runs
4	0	49	77
AV	**100**	**50**	**Ct/St**
19.25	-	-	2

First-Class Career: (141 Matches) 1869–80
Batting

I	NO	HS	Runs
249	14	111	4,307
AV	**100**	**50**	**Ct/St**
18.32	1	18	70

Bowling

Balls	Runs	Wkts	Av
16	9	-	-
Best	**5wl**	**10wl**	**Sr/Rate**
-	-	-	-

A nephew of Luke Greenwood, who played
50 matches for Yorkshire from 1861 to 1874,
Andrew Greenwood was part of a family who
had connections with Huddersfield League
club Lascelles Hall, which was something of a
nursery for Yorkshire players in the mid to late
1800s.

Greenwood was a diminutive figure, who
made his debut for Yorkshire in 1869 against
Nottinghamshire at Trent Bridge. He was a
sound and fearless right-hand opening or
middle-order batsman, who was also brilliant
in the outfield. Two years later, after scoring
50 for Yorkshire against Lancashire in the
Roses match, he was selected for the North

of England XI against an Eleven Colts of England. Also in the team was his uncle Luke, and Andrew carried his bat for 40 not out in a score of only 78.

In 1872 he was selected again for the North of England, this time against the South at Canterbury, a game in which he made a fine 52 and once again excelled in the field.

Eighteen months later he made the first of two trips to Australia, returning to England to record his highest aggregate of runs, 456, which included a best of 78 not out against Lancashire at Bradford Park Avenue.

In 1876 Greenwood notched up his one and only first-class century, 111 for the North against the South of England, and was selected for James Lillywhite's 1876–77 team to tour Australia in the winter of that year. It was the tour that included the first official Test match against a combined Australian team, which was made up of players from New South Wales and Victoria, the match taking place at the Melbourne Cricket Ground. Greenwood was one of five Yorkshiremen making their Test debut, alongside Tom Armitage, Allen Hill, Tom Emmett and George Ulyett. He only made scores of 1 and 5, but in the second Test, also at the MCG, he scored 49, which was his highest Test score as these proved to be the only Test matches that he played in.

On his return to domestic cricket in 1877 he scored 373 runs for Yorkshire at 26.90, which was his best average for a season. He not only opened the batting, but also produced his highest score for Yorkshire (91) against Gloucestershire at Bramall Lane.

During the latter part of his career he was regarded as one of the best professional batsmen in England, and although his first-class career average of only 18.32 suggested otherwise, his runs were nearly always made on difficult wickets.

For Yorkshire, Greenwood played 95 matches, scoring 2,762 runs at 17.93 and held 33 catches.

When his cricketing career ended in 1880, he became the landlord of the Peacock Hotel in Elland Road, Leeds. He died at the age of 41 in his native Huddersfield.

Schofield Haigh

RHB & RFM, 1895–1913

Born: 19 March 1871, Berry Brow,
        Huddersfield.
Died: 27 February 1921, Taylor Hill,
        Huddersfield.
Played for: Yorkshire.
Test Matches: (11) 1898–1912 Cap No. 113
Batting Career for England

I	NO	HS	Runs
18	3	25	113
AV	**100**	**50**	**Catches**
7.53	-	-	8

Bowling for England

Balls	Runs	Wkts	Av
1,294	622	24	25.91
Best	**5wl**	**10wl**	**Sr/Rate**
6–11	1	-	53.91

First-Class Career: (561 Matches) 1895–1913
Batting

I	NO	HS	Runs
747	119	159	11,713
AV	**100**	**50**	**Catches**
18.65	4	47	299

Bowling

Balls	Runs	Wkts	Av
78,819	32,091	2,012	15.94
Best	**5wl**	**10wl**	**Sr/Rate**
9–25	135	30	39.17

Born in Berry Brow, Huddersfield, Schofield Haigh joined the Berry Brow Solem Cricket Club at the age of 14, but moved to Armitage Bridge in 1877, where he was coached by Yorkshire opening-batsman Louis Hall. On the advice of Hall he moved to Aberdeen as a professional, and later played at Perth in 1894 and 1895.

In his second season he played for Scotland and took 7 for 84 against Lancashire. The following week he took 7 for 12 against his native county and was soon persuaded to return to England to play for Yorkshire.

He made his Yorkshire debut later that season against Derbyshire at Derby, scoring 25 in a ninth-wicket partnership of 50 with Frank Milligan (38), and in the following season he took 8 for 78

against the Australians at Bradford, five of them bowled, and 12 for 115 against Derbyshire at Bramall Lane.

In 1897 Haigh took the first of three hat-tricks for the county against Derbyshire at Bradford, and 7 for 17 against Surrey at Headingley, all of them bowled in 12 overs.

Originally a right-arm, fast-medium bowler, who always had a peculiar run up and final stride, he experimented with his bowling in his early years, first shortening his run-up and slowing his pace and then developing spin as his career progressed. Eventually, he could bowl nearly every type of delivery, but his main weapon was a quick off-break and fast yorker, and he believed in bowling at the stumps. His favourite observation after inspecting a sticky pitch was, 'Methinks they'll deviate today', and Plum Warner rated him virtually unplayable on wet wickets. He was also a sound and capable batsman, who could defend or attack when the situation demanded.

In 1898, against Hampshire at Southampton, he took 14 wickets in the match for only 43 runs (8 for 21 and 6 for 22) and within a few months he had made his Test debut against South Africa at Johannesburg as a member of Lord Hawke's team. In the second Test at Cape Town he notched up his highest Test score (25) and proceeded to take 6 for 11 off 11.4 overs to bowl South Africa out for only 35, his best bowling performance in Test cricket. He proceeded to play a further nine Tests, visiting South Africa again on the next tour in 1906 and played four Tests against the Australians In Britain. He was never selected to tour the southern hemisphere as the selectors probably felt that his type of bowling would not have been suitable to the hard and dry wickets in Australia.

On drying wickets he continued to torment the best batsmen in the country, and in 1901 took 145 Championship wickets at 14.16. The following year he hit his highest first-class score, 159 against Nottinghamshire at Bramall Lane, and was named as one of *Wisden's* Five Cricketers of the Year along with three of his Yorkshire colleagues, George Hirst, John Tunnicliffe and the Cambridge amateur batsman, Tom Launcelot Taylor.

The following year he took another hat-trick against Somerset at Sheffield and finished top of the County Championship bowling tables with 123 wickets at 11.99 and 154 wickets in total.

In 1904 he did the double, scoring 1,055 runs at 26.37, which included two first-class centuries (104 and 138 against Derbyshire and Warwickshire respectively), and took 121 wickets at 19.86. This included bowling unchanged against Hampshire at Headingley, when he took 10 for 49 in tandem with Wilfred Rhodes's 10 for 39. Two years later he snared 174 wickets at 14.59, his highest for any season, and from 1907 to 1909 he topped the County Championship bowling averages with 260 wickets at only 12.10. In the latter year he took 7 for 25 against Lancashire at Old Trafford, which included the hat-trick, and he also received a benefit that realised the sum of £2,071.

After a poor season by his standards in 1910, he returned to form in 1911, and he was as irresistible as ever the following summer, his 96 wickets at 11.41 being decisive in Yorkshire's Championship win. He also took 9 for 25 against Gloucestershire, his best performance in first-class cricket.

Along with Rhodes and Hirst, he was an integral part of a trio of bowlers who were largely responsible for Yorkshire's eight Championship titles between 1896 and 1912, in what was known as the 'Golden Age of English Cricket'.

A popular and well liked cricketer (he was dubbed 'The Sunshine of Yorkshire'), Haigh played 513 matches for Yorkshire, taking 1,876 wickets at 15.61, which included 127 five-wicket hauls, scoring 10.993 runs at 19.05 and holding 276 catches. In addition he took 100 wickets in a season 11 times and he is one of only four players to score in excess of 10,000 runs and take 1,000 wickets for the county. Rhodes, Hirst and Illingworth are the other three, and none of them took their wickets at a lower cost.

After he retired in 1913 he played for Keighley Cricket Club, and in World War One he worked on munitions before taking up a coaching position at Winchester School, where one of his pupils was Douglas Jardine. He umpired several first-class matches at the Scarborough festival, and died prematurely at the age of 50 in February 1921.

John Harry Hampshire

RHB & LB, 1961–84

Born: 10 February 1941, Thurnscoe.

Played for: Yorkshire, Tasmania and Derbyshire.

Test Matches: (8) 1969–75 Cap No. 442

Batting Career for England

I	NO	HS	Runs
16	1	107	403
AV	**100**	**50**	**Ct/St**
26.86	1	2	9

First-Class Career: (577 Matches) 1961–84

Batting

I	NO	HS	Runs
924	112	183*	28,059
AV	**100**	**50**	**Ct/St**
34.55	43	156	446

Bowling

Balls	Runs	Wkts	Av
2,539	1,637	30	54.56
Best	**5wl**	**10wl**	**Sr/Rate**
7–52	2	-	84.63

Born in the South Yorkshire town of Thurnscoe, John Harry Hampshire was the son of John Hampshire Snr, a fast bowler who played three games for the county in 1937, and the elder brother of Alan Hampshire, who played a single first-class game for Yorkshire in 1975.

John Jnr played his early cricket for Rotherham and Yorkshire Boys and later for Rotherham Town in the Yorkshire League, winning the junior batting prize in the Yorkshire Council at the age of 18.

After playing for the Yorkshire Second XI in 1960 as an opening batsman, he made his debut for the county the following year against Leicestershire at Grace Road, where he scored 61 in the second innings, adding 96 for the fifth wicket with Doug Padgett.

His first century for Yorkshire was against Surrey (120) at Bramall Lane, Sheffield, in 1963, and he notched up 1,236 runs at 26.86. He took a career best of 7 for 52 against Glamorgan at Cardiff, his wickets coming in only 13 overs in a Yorkshire victory by an innings and 66 runs.

During the rest of the decade he established himself as a regular in the middle-order, where his attacking style was better suited. A strongly-built man, he was adept at cutting and pulling the ball, and he could drive powerfully when in he was in form. Indeed, as a batsman one felt that he never scored the runs that he should have, as shot selection and concentration let him down on numerous occasions. As a bowler he was used sparingly as a leg-spinner, having to compete with Illingworth and Wilson for slow bowling overs in his early career.

In 1969 he was a surprise selection for the second Test against the West Indies at Lord's, but he justified his place by scoring 107 and becoming the first Englishman to score a Test century on his debut at Lord's. Surprisingly, he was dropped after the next match at Headingley, and although he made the tour to Australia and New Zealand in 1970–71 and scored 192 runs at only 24.00, it was not sufficient to keep him in the team. He did have a further two Tests against Australia in 1972 and 1975, again without success, and soon faded away from the Test arena.

In 1971 he hit his highest score for Yorkshire, 183 not out against Sussex at Hove, and continued to score two or three centuries per season on a regular basis. In 1976 he had a benefit which raised £28,425.

His best season in terms of aggregate runs was 1978, with 1,596 at an average 53.20, and a best of 132 against Warwickshire at Bradford. However, this was a season which was more notable for the infamous match at Northampton. It was a game that a great many Yorkshire supporters and members felt ashamed by, and although there were differing opinions, the fact is that two Yorkshire players refused to score runs for their county on purpose. Geoff Boycott had admittedly scored a painstaking 113 when he opened the batting, but Hampshire and Colin Johnson, a junior batsman, in protest at his slow scoring, had batted so slowly that Yorkshire missed a bonus point. Johnson was dropped for the next match but Hampshire was not, he was merely criticised by the committee. There were many Yorkshire followers who felt that Hampshire, as senior batsman and instigator of the tactics, had escaped lightly and was lucky to still be a Yorkshire player. The irony of it was that when Boycott was sacked at the end of the season, Hampshire was given the captaincy, but he did not have the personality for the job. The decision to hand him the role was, like many of the committee decisions in those days, baffling to say the least.

He left Yorkshire in 1982, after scoring 21,979 runs at 34.61, with 34 centuries, holding 368 catches and taking 24 wickets at 46.16 with two five-wicket hauls.

He played 57 matches for Derbyshire between 1982 and 1984, scoring 1,256 runs at 41.86 in his first season.

On his retirement he also spent some time in Tasmania, where he played and coached from 1967 to 1979. After leaving Yorkshire he joined the first-class umpires list and was promoted to the international panel in 2000. He is currently an assessor of umpires for the ECB.

Allen Hill

RHB & RMF, 1871–82

Born: 14 November 1843, Newton,
     Kirkheaton, Huddersfield.
Died: 28 August 1910, Leyland, Lancashire.
Played for: Yorkshire.
Test Matches: (2) 1876–77 Cap No. 5
Batting Career for England

I	NO	HS	Runs
4	2	49	101
AV	**100**	**50**	**Catches**
50.50	-	-	1

Bowling for England

Balls	Runs	Wkts	Av
340	130	7	18.57
Best	**5wl**	**10wl**	**Sr/Rate**
4–27	-	-	48.57

First-Class Career: (193 Matches) 1871–82
Batting

I	NO	HS	Runs
312	35	49	2,478
AV	**100**	**50**	**Catches**
8.94	-	-	142

Bowling

Balls	Runs	Wkts	Av
30,024	10,686	750	14.34
Best	**5wl**	**10wl**	**Sr/Rate**
8–48	57	10	40.30

Allen Hill was born in Kirkheaton and learnt his cricket with his home village and Lascelles Hall, before he joined Dewsbury Savile and then Mirfield for five shillings a match plus expenses.

The young Hill soon gained a reputation as a fast bowler of some merit and in 1867 he was engaged as coach and groundsman at Stonyhurst College on the recommendation of Yorkshire cricketer Luke Greenwood. He then joined the Lancashire groundstaff and became a professional at Burnley in 1871. In the same year he made his debut for Yorkshire against the MCC at Lord's in the opening match of the summer, deputising for George Freeman.

During that first season Hill's appearances were restricted due to Burnley being reluctant to release him, but on one occasion that they did he destroyed Surrey at the Oval by taking 12 for 59 in the match (6 for 35 and 6 for 24), his best match analysis for Yorkshire. He also top scored with 28 in Yorkshire's first innings and was presented with a silver cup by a London-based Yorkshire follower.

From 1872 he was a regular in the Yorkshire team and was seen as one of the quickest bowlers in the country. Although it had been legal to bowl over-arm, he continued to bowl round-arm, generally from a short run-up, and generated a fearsome pace. Wisden said of him, 'his action was one of the best of its kind' and although he bowled a sharp beak-back from the off, it was his pace and accuracy that enabled him to take so many wickets.

In 1873 he took his most wickets for a season (82 at 12.10), and in the following summer against the United South of England at Bradford he had the outstanding figures of 15 overs, 7 maidens and 6 wickets for 9 runs, which included a hat-trick. It was a match in which the South needed only 66 runs to win in their second innings, but fell for 39 all out, with W.G. Grace the only one to reach double-figures with 15. In the same season he took his best first-class bowling figures of 8 for 48 for the North against the South at Prince's and took his second hat-trick, this time for the Players against the Gentlemen. He also bowled unchanged throughout the innings against Lancashire at Old Trafford, taking 10 for 38, with Tom Emmett (8 for 74), which was one of five occasions that he did so for Yorkshire.

Two years later, in 1876, he scored his highest first-class score for Yorkshire, 49 against Middlesex at Bramall Lane, and continued to take wickets on a regular basis, including 7 for 39 against the MCC at Scarborough and 7 for 62 against Surrey at Sheffield. Indeed, it was at Bramall Lane that year that he pulled of a remarkable win for Yorkshire against Lancashire in the Roses match. With Lancashire needing only 89 to win in their second innings, he made an astonishing catch to dismiss Albert Hornby off Tom Emmett and then proceeded to take five wickets for three runs to bowl out their arch rivals for 70.

In the winter of 1876–77 he toured Australia with James Lillywhite's team, playing in both of the inaugural Test matches at the MCG. He had the honour of taking the first wicket in Test cricket when he bowled Nathaniel Thomson, and he also took the first catch, Thomas Horan, off the bowling of Alfred Shaw. In the second Test he took 4 for 27 and scored 49 – his best performances with both bat and ball in Test cricket. He also had the privilege of taking all 10 wickets for nine runs against the 16 of Adelaide in a country game.

Two years later, in 1879, he took his best bowling figures for Yorkshire, 7 for 14 against Surrey at Argyle Street, Hull, and in the following summer he took 6 for 26, once again against Surrey, this time at the Oval, which included a hat-trick with the last three balls of the innings.

He retired from Yorkshire in 1882 after playing 140 matches, in which he scored 1,705 runs at 8.61, took 542 wickets at 12.91, including 39 five-wicket hauls, and held 91 catches.

A benefit game was held for him two years later against Lancashire at Bramall Lane, with 6,000 attending on the first day's play. The match realised the sum of £376 on his behalf.

His career ended in 1884 when he broke his collarbone in a match in Birmingham, and then this cheerful and popular cricketer turned to umpiring, officiating in the first Test at Lord's in 1890 between England and Australia.

George Herbert Hirst

RHB & LMF, 1891–1929

Born: 7 September 1871, Kirkheaton,
Huddersfield.
Died: 10 May 1954, Egerton, Huddersfield.
Played for: Yorkshire.
Test Matches: (24) 1897–1909 Cap No. 108
Batting Career for England

I	NO	HS	Runs
38	3	85	790
AV	**100**	**50**	**Catches**
22.57	-	5	18

Bowling for England

Balls	Runs	Wkts	Av
4,010	1,770	59	30.00
Best	**5wl**	**10wl**	**Sr/Rate**
5–48	3	-	67.97

First-Class Career: (825 Matches) 1891–1929
Batting

I	NO	HS	Runs
1,215	151	341	36,356
AV	**100**	**50**	**Catches**
34.13	60	201	604

Bowling

Balls	Runs	Wkts	Av
123,192	51,282	2,742	18.72
Best	**5wl**	**10wl**	**Sr/Rate**
9–23	184	40	44.97

That a village the size of Kirkheaton should produce two of the best cricketers ever, George Hirst and Wilfred Rhodes, is truly remarkable. Even more so was the fact that they that they both batted right-handed and bowled left-arm.

Hirst left school at the age of 10 and first appeared on a cricket field for Kirkheaton, playing in the first team at 15 years of age. In 1990 he moved to Elland as a professional and later played for Mirfield and Huddersfield.

Essentially a self-taught batsman, Hirst was an aggressive quick-footed middle-order stroke-maker, who, from a two-eyed stance, saw the ball very early and was a master of the pull and hook shots. He could dominate an attack when required or defend doggedly if his team was in trouble, but as Yorkshire dominated the County Championship through most of his career, that was not very often.

G.H.HIRST Y

In his early days Hirst was a left-arm fast bowler, who had a long bounding run, and he delivered the ball with a free, easy action, often making the ball swerve. As he got older he slowed his pace, and from the turn of the century not only could he bowl a vicious yorker, but he had also completely mastered the art of swing bowling. One helpless victim, Sammy Woods, the Australian import who played for Somerset, described his bowling as being like a very good throw from cover point.

He made his first-class debut for Yorkshire in 1891, against Somerset at Taunton, but in his first three years with the county he played only a single game each season.

It was his bowling which gave him his first real impact, when in 1893 his 99 first-class wickets saw him finish behind Peel and Wainwright in the county averages. Against the MCC at Lord's he returned 12 for 48 (6 for 25 and 6 for 23) and then he took 7 for 38 against the MCC at Scarborough. His first hundred for Yorkshire came in 1894, an unbeaten 115 against Gloucestershire at Bristol, and he finished the season with 95 wickets at 15 runs per wicket. The first of his two hat-tricks came the following season at Leicester, and the wickets taken that day were among 150 first-class wickets that year.

The season of 1896 saw Hirst register his first double (1,222 runs at 28.20 and 104 wickets at 21.64), and in the winter he toured

Australia in the first of two trips, making his Test debut against Australia at Sydney in December 1897, scoring 62, while at Adelaide, in the third Test, he hit his highest Test score of 85.

In 1902, in the first Test at Edgbaston, he and Wilfred Rhodes ripped Australia out for only 36, Hirst taking 3 for 15 and Rhodes 7 for 17, but the weather denied England victory. However, in the following game against Yorkshire, the Australians were embarrassed further when they were routed for only 23, their lowest-ever score in England, Hirst taking 5 for 9 and Stanley Jackson 5 for 12 in an emphatic White Rose victory. In the last Test at the Oval, with England needing only 15 runs to win, Wilfred Rhodes as the last man joined Hirst at the wicket. The story goes that George said to Wilfred, 'We'll get them in ones.' Get them they did, but not in ones. George made a match-winning 58 not out following his 43 in the first innings, and he also took 5 for 77 with the ball. On the Ashes tour of 1903–04 he took 15 wickets in the Tests and recorded 5 for 48, his best bowling figures in Test cricket.

In the years of Yorkshire's Championship hat-trick, 1900 to 1902, he made 5,323 runs and took 328 wickets. In 1904 he registered 2,501 runs at 54.36, his highest season aggregate. His benefit of that year raised £3,703, a county record that stood until 1925.

In the County Championship he continued with his colossal performances and in 1905 he recorded the highest-ever score for Yorkshire, 341 against Leicestershire at Leicester, which included 54 boundaries.

The following year he gave the most outstanding county season performance of all time, with 2,385 runs at 45.86 and 208 wickets at 16.50. No player before or since has achieved the 2,000 double and it is unlikely they ever will. In the game against Somerset at Bath he scored 111 and 117 not out and took 6 for 70 and 5 for 45. He is still the only man to achieve two centuries and 10 wickets in the same match.

Hirst's best county bowling figures were in 1910, when, in the Roses match at Headingley against Lancashire, he took 9 for 23.

All told he exceeded 1,000 runs in a season 19 times, including 2,000 on three occasions, and took 100 wickets 15 times. He achieved the double 14 times (only Wilfred Rhodes with 16 beats him), which included 11 seasons in succession: a record. He did the match double, 100 runs and 10 wickets, three times, and scored 100 before lunch on five occasions.

In 718 matches for Yorkshire he scored 32,057 runs at 34.73 (with 56 centuries), took 2,484 wickets at 18.03 (with five wickets or more on 174 occasions) and held 520 catches.

In 1921 he effectively finished his career with Yorkshire and began an 18-year coaching association with Eton College, but he returned to the Broad Acres in 1929 to play his last first-class match for the county. He followed this with coaching young players at Yorkshire, and although in his playing days he was renowned for his blunt and tenacious cricket, as a coach he was loved by the colts that came under his wing.

Matthew James Hoggard

RHB & RFM, 1996–2008

Born: 31 December 1976, Leeds.
Played for: Yorkshire.
Test Matches: (67) 2000–08 Cap No. 602

Batting Career for England

I	NO	HS	Runs
92	27	38	473
AV	**100**	**50**	**Catches**
7.27	-	-	24

Bowling for England

Balls	Runs	Wkts	Av
13,909	7,564	248	30.50
Best	**5wl**	**10wl**	**Sr/Rate**
7–61	7	1	56.00

First-Class Career: (179 Matches) 1996–2008

Batting

I	NO	HS	Runs
229	67	89*	1,458
AV	**100**	**50**	**Catches**
9.00	-	3	50

Bowling

Balls	Runs	Wkts	Av
32,686	16,802	622	27.01
Best	**5wl**	**10wl**	**Sr/Rate**
7–49	20	1	52.5

For the past few years Matthew Hoggard has been one of the world's top swing bowlers, and when he made his England debut in the 100th Test at Lord's in June 2000 he was uncapped by Yorkshire.

Born in Leeds, he played his early cricket with Pudsey Congs and the Yorkshire Academy before making his Yorkshire debut against South Africa A at Headingley in 1996, a match in which he took his first wicket in first-class cricket, that of Jack Kallis, lbw. His breakthrough season for Yorkshire came in 1998, when he took 41 wickets in first-class matches, with a best of 5 for 57 against Essex at Marine Road, Scarborough. To further his experience he spent the winter of 1998–99 and 1999–2000 playing for Free State in South Africa under the watchful eye of Allan Donald.

In 1999 he played in only eight first-class games for the county due to a knee injury, but the following summer he snared 50 wickets at 25.48, with a best of 5 for 50 against Somerset at Scarborough and 5 for 67 against Durham at Chester-Le-Street. He also bowled well in one-day cricket, taking a record 37 wickets in the National League at an average of 12.37, with a best of 5 for 28 against Leicestershire at Grace Road, surpassing Howard Cooper's record of 29 wickets set in 1975.

Still uncapped by the county, he was surprisingly called-up by England for his first Test cap against the West Indies in the 100th Test match to be staged at Lord's. Although he remained wicketless in the match, he impressed with the amount of movement he gained both on and off the pitch and he was given his White Rose County cap in July of that year.

His development of swinging the ball gained him his England place and after just two Test matches he was selected for the arduous tour to Pakistan and Sri Lanka in 2000–01. He returned match figures of 8 for 30 (4 for 13 and 4 for 17) from 22.3 overs against Pakistan Board XI at Lahore and took 17 wickets in two matches. In the one-day series in Zimbabwe he took 5 for 49 at Harare, which won him the Man of the Match award. It thrust him into the international spotlight and gained him a place on the tour to India and New Zealand. He bowled superbly at Christchurch in the first Test and took 7 for 63 against New Zealand, the best innings return by an opening bowler in Tests played against New Zealand at that time, but this record was later beaten by Ryan Sidebottom at Napier in 2008.

In 2002 he won the Man of the Match award at Edgbaston in the second Test against Sri Lanka after taking match figures of 7 for 147 (2 for 55 and 5 for 92), and he also scored 17 not out in England's second innings, sharing a record tenth-wicket stand of 91 with Graham Thorpe.

Over the following two years Hoggard became one of England's senior bowlers and spearheaded Yorkshires attack. For the White Rose County he took a career best of 7 for 49 against Somerset at Headingley in 2003, in his first Championship match after undergoing knee surgery. On the winter tour of the West Indies he took a brilliant hat-trick at Barbados, becoming the third Englishman after Peter Loader (1957) and Dominic Cork (1995) to do so against the Caribbean country.

In the summer of 2004 he hit his highest Test score to date (38) at the Oval against the West Indies, and he proceeded to make his highest Yorkshire score of 89 not out against Glamorgan at Leeds.

On the winter tour to South Africa of 2004–05 he took his best Test figures of 7 for 61 at Johannesburg (12 for 205 in the match) where his sustained spell of swing bowling bowled England into a series by clinching 2–1 victory.

After a quiet start to the summer, he contributed nine wickets in the last two Tests against Australia at Trent Bridge and the Oval (16 wickets in the series at 29.56) as England sealed their first Ashes victory for 18 years.

In the 2006 New Year's Honours List Matthew was awarded the MBE along with his England teammates for his role in the successful Ashes tournament and was named as one of *Wisden's* five Cricketers of the Year in April 2006. He was also ranked as the fourth best Test bowler in world cricket after a magnificent spell of bowling against India in the first Test at Nagpur in March 2006 when he took 6 for 57 in 30.5 overs. He was also England's highest wicket-taker in the series with 13 wickets at 17.84.

Unfortunately, injuries kept him out of most of the home Test matches in 2007, and on the tour to New Zealand in 2008 a disappointing performance in the first Test at Hamilton meant that he was left out of the second Test at Wellington, along with Steve Harmison. At the time of writing Hoggard has not appeared in a Test match since, and it is said that he does not believe he will be picked again. If so it will be good news for Yorkshire, but a sad end to a Test career that has seen him take 248 wickets at 30.50, which places him sixth on the all-time list of wicket-takers for England.

Percy Holmes

RHB & RM, 1913–33

Born: 25 November 1886, Oakes, Huddersfield.
Died: 3 September 1971, Marsh, Huddersfield.
Played for: Yorkshire.
Test Matches: (7) 1921–32 Cap No. 190
Batting Career for England

I	NO	HS	Runs
14	1	88	357
AV	**100**	**50**	**Ct/St**
27.46	-	4	3

First-Class Career: (555 Matches) 1913–33
Batting

I	NO	HS	Runs
810	84	315*	30,573
AV	**100**	**50**	**Ct/St**
42.11	67	141	342

Bowling

Balls	Runs	Wkts	Av
252	185	2	92.50
Best	**5wl**	**10wl**	**Sr/Rate**
1–5	-	-	126.00

Between the two world wars, Percy Holmes, a right-hand opening batsman, was arguably one of the best batsmen to ever play for Yorkshire.

He attended Oakes School in Huddersfield and first played with Paddock, before moving to Golcar, all the while playing for the Yorkshire Second XI. He then moved to Spen Victoria before making his first-class debut for the county against Middlesex in 1913 at the age of 26. However, he soon made rapid progress and in 1919 he became Herbert Sutcliffe's opening partner and forged not only Yorkshire's best ever opening partnership, but also one of the best in English first-class cricket.

In 1919 Holmes notched up his first century for the county, 100 against Nottinghamshire, and together with Sutcliffe he shared a stand of 253 against Lancashire, Holmes making 123 and Sutcliffe 132.

The following year he had a superb season and scored over 2,000 runs for the first time (he did it three times for Yorkshire). The season included a score of 145 not out against Northamptonshire at Northampton, carrying his bat out of a total of 270. In addition he

scored a century in each innings, 126 and 111 not out against Lancashire at Old Trafford. He then notched up over 300 for the first time, with 302 against Hampshire at Portsmouth and sharing an opening stand of 347 with Sutcliffe (131), his innings lasting over seven hours. Not surprisingly, he was the outstanding batsman of the season with 2,144 runs at 54.97.

By reputation, Holmes was the equal to Sutcliffe on technical ability, but he believed in attacking the bowlers more than his partner, and his quick footwork enabled him to hook and cut successfully, and he was forever on the look-out for runs. He was also a very good fielder.

In 1921 he made his Test debut against Australia at Trent Bridge, scoring 30 and 8, but was dropped and did not reappear at Test level until 1927.

The following year he scored two double hundreds against Warwickshire, 209 at Edgbaston and then 220 not out in the return match at Huddersfield. However, it was three years later, in 1925, that he had his best season for the county. Not only did he score his most runs for a season, 2,453 at an average of 58, but he was also the leading batsman in the country. In the month of June he scored 1,021 runs at an average of 102.10 and notched up his second score of over 300, with 315 not out against Middlesex at Lord's. At the time it was the highest individual score ever made at the games headquarters and in doing so he equalled John Brown's record of scoring over 300 runs twice in an innings for Yorkshire.

In the summer of 1927 he carried his bat yet again, scoring 175 not out in a total of 377 against New Zealand at Bradford, and was selected for the winter tour of South Africa, under the leadership of his Yorkshire colleague Ronald Stanyforth. He topped 50 on four occasions with a best Test score of 88 in the third Test at Cape Town, but after the tour was selected for only one more Test match against India at Lord's in 1932. However, by then he was past his peak, aged 45. Although he did not score the volume of runs that he did at county level, he was unfortunate that he was competing for an opening spot not only with his colleague Herbert Sutcliffe, but also the legendary Jack Hobbs and his Surrey partner Andrew Sandham.

The following season he received a greatly deserved benefit of £2,620 and in 1929 carried his bat for 110 not out in a total of 219 against Northamptonshire at Bradford and notched up 285 against Nottinghamshire at Trent Bridge.

In 1932, along with Herbert Sutcliffe, he created history by scoring 555 runs for the first wicket against Essex at Leyton (beating Tunnicliffe and Brown's record of 554 set in 1898), as Holmes made 224 not out and Sutcliffe 313. It was a world-record partnership that stood for 44 years and is still the highest for any wicket in English domestic cricket.

The following year was his last for Yorkshire, an operation now meant that he was not fully fit, but he still managed to make 929 runs at 19.25, with a top score of 65.

For Yorkshire he played 485 matches, scored 26,220 runs at 41.95, with 60 centuries, took one wicket and held 319 catches. His partnership with Herbert Sutcliffe yielded 74 century first-wicket stands (69 for Yorkshire), and he scored five of Yorkshire's 10 highest innings.

On leaving Yorkshire he had a period in the Welsh League as a professional with Swansea, and he also played for a time with Kings Cross in Halifax. He spent one year as an umpire in 1947, and coached at Scarborough College. He died at the age of 84, only a few miles from where he was born.

Joseph Hunter

RHB & WK, 1878–88

Born: 3 August 1855, Scarborough.
Died: 4 January 1891, Rotherham.
Played for: Yorkshire.
Test Matches: (5) 1884–85 Cap No. 49
Batting Career for England

I	NO	HS	Runs
7	2	39*	93
AV	**100**	**50**	**Ct/St**
18.60	-	-	8/3

First-Class Career: (162 Matches) 1878–88
Batting

I	NO	HS	Runs
240	71	60*	1,330
AV	**100**	**50**	**Ct/St**
7.86	-	2	234/122

A native of Scarborough, Joseph Hunter was the eldest of five brothers, three of them wicket-keepers, and he learned his early cricket with Scarborough Cricket Club.

Originally a stonemason by trade, he made his Yorkshire debut in 1878, replacing the injured George Pinder behind the stumps in the Roses match at Old Trafford. However, it was not an auspicious start, as Yorkshire was defeated by an innings and 26 runs. He played 10 games in his debut season, but it was another three years before he made the position his own.

In 1881 he took five victims against Middlesex at Lord's, and although normally he batted at number 10 or 11, two years later, in the match against Derbyshire at Derby, he shared in a ninth-wicket partnership of 98 with Tom Emmett (49), with Hunter scoring a valuable 51 not out after eight wickets had fallen for 195.

While he was not ranked quite as good as his contemporaries, he was nevertheless selected for the Alfred Shaw/Arthur Shrewsbury team which toured Australia in the winter of 1894–95, although he did have to haggle to obtain better terms for his services on the trip. As it was he played in all eight first-class games on tour, which included five Test matches, and he made his debut at Adelaide. In the

Yorkshire, 1884.

second Test at Melbourne he registered his highest Test score, 39 not out, and not only shared in a tenth-wicket partnership of 98, but also assisted Lancashire's Johnny Briggs (121) in obtaining his one and only century in Test cricket. It was a record last-wicket stand for England at the time and is still the fourth largest. He also took 13 catches and four stumpings while on tour and proved to be a popular and valuable member of a team which retained the Ashes. He is still the only Scarborough-born player to play for England.

On his return to England in the summer of 1885 he hit his highest first-class score, 60 not out, against Gloucestershire at Bradford Park Avenue, first sharing in a stand of 64 with Bobby Peel and then ably taking the Yorkshire score from 211 to 325 when the innings closed.

However, within the next three years, ill health and niggling hand injuries restricted his appearances, and after receiving a bad hand injury in the match against Middlesex at Lord's in 1888 he retired from county cricket, holding a record of nearly a third of his dismissals from stumpings. Only his predecessor George Pinder had a better record among Yorkshire wicket-keepers. He was eventually replaced by his younger brother David, who went on to make 521 appearances for the county between 1888 and 1909.

For Yorkshire, Joseph played 143 matches, scored 1,183 runs at 7.78 and took 207 catches with 102 stumpings.

After retiring he returned to play some matches for Scarborough, before becoming the landlord of the Wellington Inn, while later he kept the Wheat Sheaf pub in Rotherham. He died at the age of 35 and was buried in Scarborough cemetery.

Sir Leonard Hutton

RHB & LBG, 1934–60

Born: 23 June 1916, Fulneck, Pudsey.
Died: 6 September 1990, Norbiton, Surrey.
Played for: Yorkshire.
Test Matches: (79) 1937–55 Cap No. 294

Batting Career for England

I	NO	HS	Runs
138	15	364	6,971
AV	**100**	**50**	**Catches**
56.67	19	33	57

Bowling for England

Balls	Runs	Wkts	Av
260	232	3	77.33
Best	**5wl**	**10wl**	**Sr/Rate**
1–2	-	-	86.67

First-Class Career: (513 Matches) 1934–60

Batting

I	NO	HS	Runs
814	91	364	40,140
AV	**100**	**50**	**Catches**
55.52	129	177	400

Bowling

Balls	Runs	Wkts	Av
9,774	5,106	173	29.51
Best	**5wl**	**10wl**	**Sr/Rate**
6–76	4	1	56.50

Len Hutton was born in Fulneck near Pudsey and was arguably the best technical batsman to play for Yorkshire, and possibly England as well. Even as a young boy he was spoken of as a future England batsman, and he appeared for Pudsey St Lawrence's second team when he was only 12 years old. Indeed, his coach at Yorkshire, George Hirst, admitted that there was little he could teach the young protégé.

In 1934 he made his debut for Yorkshire and in his first Championship game against Warwickshire at Edgbaston he scored 50 in his only innings, and in July he became the youngest Yorkshire player to score a century, with 196 against Worcestershire. Two years later, at the age of 20, he was awarded his county cap, making him Yorkshire's youngest capped player. In 1937 scores of 161 against the MCC and centuries against Worcestershire and Kent gained him selection for England against New Zealand. He celebrated his selection in style hitting a superb 271 not out against Derbyshire at Sheffield, the first of five double hundreds for Yorkshire. Unfortunately, he made only 0 and 1 in his first Test, but in the second at Manchester he hit his maiden century, scoring 100 runs exactly. The following summer saw him stamp his name on English cricket against the seemingly invincible Australians. In the first Test at Nottingham he scored 100, and then in the fifth at the Oval he registered the greatest individual triumph by an English batsman, scoring 364 in an innings which lasted 13 hours and 20 minutes. The innings had overtaken Bradman's world record of 334 and is still the highest Test innings by an English batsman. Five Yorkshire players, Hutton, Bowes, Verity, Leyland and wicket-keeper Wood shared in England's greatest victory over Australia (an innings and 579 runs), with Hutton and Leyland adding 382 for England's second wicket, which is still a Test record for the second wicket for England.

In the winter of 1938–39 Hutton made the tour to South Africa, and the following summer he hit 12 centuries which included 196 and 165 not out against the West Indies, averaging 96 in the series. He also scored 280 not out against Hampshire at Sheffield, which was his highest score for Yorkshire.

Hutton was the supreme technician on all types of pitches and played the most handsome of strokes. His cover and off-driving in particular was at times quite brilliant and he never needed to hit the ball in the air. He was also an extremely valuable leg-break bowler at county level, and possibly should have bowled more.

When the war started in 1939, Hutton had a Test batting average of 67.25 from 21 innings. The loss of potentially the best six years of his cricketing career was one thing, but the physical disability he carried after badly injuring his left arm in a gymnasium accident was another. Three bone grafts were required to repair the damage and his left arm was weakened and two inches shorter than the right. However, such was Hutton's ability that he was able to make the technical adjustment necessary and there appeared to be no waning of his powers.

In 1947 he scored another 100 in his first Test at Leeds against South Africa and by 1950, with the retirement of Bradman, he became the most dependable batsman in world cricket. His ability to watch the ball right onto the bat, his perfect balance and skill in letting the ball come to him, finding the gaps and getting singles when he wanted, made him the number-one choice. His ability against the spinners was amply demonstrated against the West Indies in 1950, when he batted through England's first innings for 202 not out against Ramadhin and Valentine.

In Australia in the winter of 1950–51 he scored 533 runs at 88.83, which made him the batsman of the series, averaging more than double that of any other batsman on either side.

In 1952 Hutton became the first professional captain of England since Arthur Shrewsbury in 1886 and he brought to the role the pragmatism, caution and desire to win that always typified his cricket. He never lost a series as captain, beginning with the home Tests against India, and in the 1953 series against Australia he won the Ashes at the Oval for the first time since the 'Bodyline' tour of 1932–33, despite losing all five tosses. In 1954–55 he retained them in Australia after winning the series 3–1 (with the help of Tyson and Statham), becoming the first captain to win the Ashes and retain them. His record of 11 wins and four losses in 23 games was an excellent record. As a run-scorer for England, few were his superior, his 6,971 runs at 56.67 with 19 centuries places him high on a list with only Sutcliffe at 60.73 and Hobbs 56.94 comparable as opening batsmen. He is the only English batsman to carry his bat through a Test innings twice, with 202 against West Indies in 1950 and 156 against Australia in 1951.

He was a cricketing legend for Yorkshire and his first-class record of 40,140 runs with 129 centuries is exceeded only by Herbert Sutcliffe and Geoff Boycott; however, both had in excess of 200 more innings.

For Yorkshire he scored 24,807 runs at 53.54 with 84 centuries, took 154 wickets at 27.40 with four five-wicket hauls and held 278 catches.

Hutton retired in January 1956 and received a knighthood for his services to cricket.

Richard Anthony Hutton

RHB & RFM, 1962–76

Born: 6 September 1942, Pudsey.
Played for: Cambridge University, Yorkshire
      and Transvaal.
Test Matches: (5) 1971 Cap No. 450
Batting Career for England

I	NO	HS	Runs
8	2	81	219
AV	**100**	**50**	**Catches**
36.50	-	2	9

Bowling for England

Balls	Runs	Wkts	Av
738	257	9	28.55
Best	**5wl**	**10wl**	**Sr/Rate**
3–72	-	-	82.00

First-Class Career: (281 Matches) 1962–76
Batting

I	NO	HS	Runs
410	58	189	7,561
AV	**100**	**50**	**Catches**
21.48	5	29	216

Bowling

Balls	Runs	Wkts	Av
34,225	15,008	625	24.01
Best	**5wl**	**10wl**	**Sr/Rate**
8–50	21	3	54.76

The eldest son of England and Yorkshire legend Len Hutton, Richard Hutton was born in the West Yorkshire town of Pudsey. He attended Woodhall School near Wetherby before going to Repton School, where he developed his cricketing skills as an all-round player. He then went to Cambridge University and gained a Blue for cricket in each of the three years he was there.

In 1962 he made his debut for Cambridge against Essex and represented the Gentlemen versus the Players at Lord's. In the Cambridge team was Mike Brearley, later to be captain of Middlesex and

England, Tony Lewis, Glamorgan and England captain for a period, and all-rounder Tony Windows, who played for many years for Gloucestershire. The following summer Hutton took his best bowling figures in first-class cricket, 8 for 50 against Derbyshire, and scored 1,122 first-class runs at an average of 27.36. Altogether for Cambridge he scored 843 runs at 35.12, which included an innnings of 163 not out against Surrey at Guildford and a masterly 73 at Lord's in the Varsity match against Oxford University.

A tall man at 6ft 4in, Hutton used his height to good effect when either batting or bowling. He was generally an opening bowler of first-change or fast-medium, who was capable of seaming and swinging the ball, and as a batsman he favoured the front foot, using his height when playing his favourite driving shots. In addition he was a very fine slip fielder, where his sarcastic wit was often used to good effect.

He made his County Championship debut for Yorkshire against Lancashire in the Roses match at Old Trafford in 1962, and over the years he proved to a reliable third-seamer behind Fred Trueman and Tony Nicholson. In 1965 he took 62 first-class wickets at 19.38, which included 14 wickets in two successive matches against Somerset, taking 5 for 31 at Taunton and 5 for 28 at Hull.

In 1969 he took his best figures for Yorkshire, 7 for 39, once again against Somerset, this time at Headingley, and the following year he notched up his first century for the county (104) against Derbyshire at Bradford Park Avenue in the first match of the summer.

The following year a career best of 189 against the Pakistanis at Bradford earned him selection for the second Test playing against Pakistan at Lord's. A score of 58 not out helped him to retain his place for the third Test at Headingley, where he took a best of 3 for 72 in an England win by 25 runs. He kept his place for the three-match series against India, and in the last Test at the Oval he hit his top Test score of 81 and in the process shared a seventh-wicket partnership of 103 in 66 minutes with Alan Knott. However, he was not selected for Test duties again.

He was not in favour of Geoff Boycott becoming the Yorkshire captain in 1971 and the two had a rather frosty relationship which resulted in Hutton eventually leaving the county at the end of the 1974 season.

With Yorkshire he played in 208 matches, scoring 4,986 runs at an average of 20.18, with four centuries and took 468 wickets at 21.91 runs per wicket; he took five wickets or more on 17 occasions. He also held 160 catches.

After leaving Yorkshire Hutton decided to concentrate on his business commitments in stockbroking and accountancy. Also became heavily involved with the MCC, leading a team as player-manager to Bermuda in 1987. He was the editor of *The Cricketer* magazine between 1991 and 1998 and his son Ben was captain of Middlesex in 2005 and 2006.

Raymond Illingworth

RHB & OB, 1951–83

Born: 8 June 1932, Pudsey.

Played for: Yorkshire and Leicestershire.

Test Matches: (61) 1958–73 Cap No. 389

Batting Career for England

I	NO	HS	Runs
90	11	113	1,836
AV	100	50	Catches
23.24	2	5	45

Bowling for England

Balls	Runs	Wkts	Av
11,934	3,807	122	31.20
Best	5wl	10wl	Sr/Rate
6–29	3	-	97.82

First-Class Career: (787 Matches) 1951–83

Batting

I	NO	HS	Runs
1,073	213	162	24,134
AV	100	50	Catches
28.06	22	105	446

Bowling

Balls	Runs	Wkts	Av
117,866	42,023	2,072	20.28
Best	5wl	10wl	Sr/Rate
9–42	104	11	56.88

Although Ray Illingworth was born in Pudsey, it was with Farsley in the Bradford League that he began playing, and he was in their first team at the age of 15.

He first came to prominence when he scored 148 not out in a Priestley Cup match against Pudsey St Lawrence in 1949 when only 17 years of age. At that time he was a batsman who bowled medium pace, but he later turned very successfully to bowling off-spin, his first major figures being 5 for 5 against Saltaire in the Bradford League. He bowled a very accurate nagging line and length, and turned the ball appreciably in helpful conditions, while as a batsman he had a good defence and played on both sides of the wicket. If his team were in trouble he could be guaranteed to score runs and he was never better than in a crisis. He started his career with Yorkshire in impressive style, scoring 56 on his debut against Hampshire in the County Championship match at Headingley in August 1951. It was Ray's only first-team game of the '51 summer, but there was much to come from the young 19-year-old in future years.

Two years later Illingworth notched up his first century for the White Rose County in the opening Championship match of 1953, with 148 not out against Essex at Hull. His off-spin bowling was also developing fast and he completed a good season by taking 7 for 22 against Hampshire at Bournemouth.

The following summer he took 8 for 69 against Surrey at the Oval and in 1957 took a career best of 9 for 42 against Worcestershire at Worcester and 12 for 91 in the match. His bowling was now starting to take over from his batting, but nevertheless he still scored runs consistently. In 1959 he registered 1,726 runs at 46.64, which included four centuries and a career best of 162 against India at Bramall Lane. Three years later in 1962 he played a major part in one of Yorkshire's greatest ever County Championship victories. In a match against Hampshire at Bradford Park Avenue the south coast county needed just seven runs to win with five wickets left. Illingworth, turning his off-spin rapidly, took four wickets for no runs, Fred Trueman took the other and Yorkshire won by five runs.

In 1967 he had the remarkable bowling figures of 7 for 6 against Gloucestershire at Harrogate, and a year later he was the county's leading wicket-taker with 131 wickets at 14.36.

Twelve months later his career with Yorkshire was over. The county offered him a one year contract, he requested two, and he departed to Leicestershire as captain and Yorkshire had lost a player they could ill afford to. It was seen by many as one of the biggest mistakes that the county have ever made, one of several over the years, and arguably one of the worst.

Illingworth's career with Yorkshire had spanned 18 seasons (1951 to 1968) and he had scored 14,986 runs at 27.90, which included 14 centuries. He took 1,431 wickets at 18.73 (five wickets 79 times) and held 286 catches, mainly at gulley. In 1960 he was named one of *Wisden's* Five Cricketers of the Year, after a summer in which he had his best match figures of 15 for 123 (8 for 70 and 7 for 53) against Glamorgan at Swansea. In 1964, against Kent at Dover, he achieved the match double with an innings of 135 and took 14 for 101 (7 for 49 and 7 for 52).

With the Foxes he scored 5,341 runs at 29.51 and took 372 wickets at 20.29. As skipper he led them to the 1975 County Championship title for the first time in their history and won the Benson and Hedges One-Day Cup in 1972 and 1975, and the John Player Sunday League in 1974. He had a best score of 153 not out against Essex in 1969 and a bowling best of 8 for 38 against Glamorgan in 1976.

He made his England debut in 1958 against New Zealand at Manchester, and he captained England in 31 of his 61 Tests, losing only five. Illingworth's best performances for his country were 113 against West Indies in 1969 and 6 for 29 against India in 1967, both at Lord's. He bowled shrewdly at key moments in matches and in the 1967 series against India he took 20 wickets in the three Tests at an average of 13.3. His batting was always solid and determined, and he came in at either sixth or seventh in the order and helped build many partnerships in the middle order, such as the eighth-wicket partnership of 168 with Lancashire's Peter Lever against India at Manchester in 1971. However, his crowning glory as captain was on the 1970–71 tour to Australia when his leadership, assisted by Geoff Boycott's batting and John Snow's bowling, regained the Ashes and confirmed him as one of England's best ever captains. He is also the only England captain to go to Australia without the Ashes, return home with them and then retain them in the following series at home.

Illingworth later returned to Yorkshire as team manager from 1979 to 1983, including a season and a half as captain, and he was manager of England from 1994 to 1996.

He took 100 wickets in a season on 10 occasions, scored 1,000 runs in a season eight times and completed the 'double' on six seperate occasions in his second stay at Yorkshire. He is only the second Yorkshire-born cricketer to score in excess of 1,000 runs and take over 100 wickets in Test cricket, Wilfred Rhodes being the other, and his figures confirm him as one of England's best all-round cricketers of modern times.

Richard Keith Illingworth

RHB & SLA, 1982–2001

Born: 23 August 1963, Greengates, Bradford.
Played for: Worcestershire and Derbyshire.
Test Matches: (9) 1991–95 Cap No. 551

Batting Career for England

I	NO	HS	Runs
14	7	28	128
AV	**100**	**50**	**Catches**
18.28	-	-	5

Bowling for England

Balls	Runs	Wkts	Av
1,485	615	19	32.36
Best	**5wl**	**10wl**	**Sr/Rate**
4–96	-	-	78.15

First-Class Career: (376 Matches) 1982–2001

Batting

I	NO	HS	Runs
435	122	120*	7,027
AV	**100**	**50**	**Catches**
22.45	4	21	161

Bowling

Balls	Runs	Wkts	Av
65,868	26,213	831	31.54
Best	**5wl**	**10wl**	**Sr/Rate**
7–50	27	6	79.20

Richard Illingworth, a left-arm slow bowler, was unable to break into the Yorkshire Second XI and so decided to seek a career elsewhere. He moved to Worcestershire, playing a solitary game at the end of the 1981 season against Nottinghamshire at Collingham. With the bat he scored 29 runs, and although his four wickets cost him 167 runs, he nevertheless impressed the coach, Basil D'Oliveria, and was offered a contract for 1982.

Illingworth made his debut early in the season against Somerset at Worcester and he took the wickets of Peter Roebuck, Brian Rose and Ian Botham, finishing with 3 for 61. That season also saw the West Indies young cricketers touring England, and he was selected for the first Test at Northampton. In the Windies' first innings he took 4 for 46, which included two wickets with the last two balls of the first innings, and then took the wicket of Phil Simmons with his first ball in the second innings, thereby claiming a hat-trick. In the second innings he snared 6 for 36 and 10 for 82 in the match.

Worcestershire gave Illingworth an extended run in 1983 and he responded well, taking 48 wickets, including 5 for 24 against Somerset at Worcester, and he improved upon this total with 57 wickets in 1984.

The following season he took a career best of 7 for 50 against Oxford University in the Parks, and two years later notched up his maiden first-class century, when as nightwatchman he scored 120 not out of a total of 237 against Warwickshire at New Road, and he was awarded his county cap.

In the winter of 1988–89 he travelled to South Africa to play for Natal in the Currie Cup, but this was to be his only experience of overseas domestic cricket. He did make the following winter journey to Zimbabwe with the England A team and scored his second century, 106 at Harare, once again as nightwatchman.

In 1990 he had his most productive season, taking 75 wickets at 28.29, and was selected for the A team tour of Pakistan and Sri Lanka.

A year later he took 5 for 49 against Northamptonshire in a Sunday League game and was selected for the Texaco one-day international series against the West Indies a few days later. He had a fine debut, bowling 10 overs for only 20 runs and the wicket of Jeff Dujon, and he shared an unbroken last-wicket partnership of 23 with Mike Atherton to seal a thrilling one-wicket win.

Illingworth was then selected for the third Test at Trent Bridge and took the wicket of Phil Simmons (yet again) with his first ball in Test cricket, the first since Intikhab Alam in 1959–60. He also played in the following Test at Edgbaston, but in his two Tests had only four wickets to show for his 213 runs conceded.

Throughout his career he was never a big spinner of the ball, but he kept a good line and length and certainly at international level was more suited to one-day cricket than Test cricket. Indeed, he retained his place in the one-day side and went to New Zealand and Australia for the 1991–92 World Cup, and also to India and Pakistan for the following World Cup in 1995–96. In 25 matches in one-day internationals he took 302 wickets at 35.30, with a best of 3 for 33 against New Zealand at Albury.

In domestic cricket with Worcestershire he was the first bowler for the county to take a hat-trick in one-day cricket. In the Sunday League game against Sussex at Hove in 1993 he bowled Peter Moores and Tony Pigot and then he trapped Ed Giddins lbw with the last three balls of the Sussex innings.

Two years later he returned to Test cricket against the West Indies at Headingley, playing in four of the six Tests, in which he took his best Test figures of 4 for 96 at Trent Bridge. In the winter he toured South Africa, playing in three Tests and taking nine wickets at 20.77, but he was not selected for another Test.

In 1997 he took his best Championship figures, 7 for 79 and match figures of 10 for 147 against Hampshire at Southampton, and scored his fourth century, 112 against Warwickshire.

Having failed to win an extension to his contract at Worcestershire in 2001, he moved to Derbyshire and spent two years with the East Midland county, before being appointed to the first-class umpires' list in 2006.

Sir Stanley Francis Jackson

RHB & RMF, 1890–1907

Born: 21 November 1870, Chapel Allerton, Leeds.

Died: 9 May 1947, Knightsbridge, London.

Played for: Cambridge University and Yorkshire.

Test Matches: (20) 1893–1905 Cap No. 82

Batting Career for England

I	NO	HS	Runs
33	4	144*	1,415
AV	**100**	**50**	**Catches**
48.79	5	6	10

Bowling for England

Balls	Runs	Wkts	Av
1,587	799	24	33.29
Best	**5wl**	**10wl**	**Sr/Rate**
5–52	1	-	66.13

First-Class Career: (309 Match) 1890–1907

Batting

I	NO	HS	Runs
505	35	160	15,901
AV	**100**	**50**	**Catches**
33.83	31	76	195

Bowling

Balls	Runs	Wkts	Av
54,624	15,767	774	20.37
Best	**5wl**	**10wl**	**Sr/Rate**
8–54	42	6	70.57

'Jacko', as he was affectionately known, was one of the great amateur cricketers of the 'Golden Age'. Born at Chapel Allerton, near Leeds, Stanley Jackson showed remarkable batting prowess while at preparatory school, before he went to Harrow, where he was in the first XI for three years and appointed the captain in 1889. Interestingly, England's former Prime Minister Winston Churchill was his 'fag'.

Tall and impressively built, he proceeded to Cambridge University where he gained his Blue as a freshman, as he did in each of his four years there. He was captain in 1892 when he headed both the batting and bowling averages and maintained the role in 1893. In the Varsity match of 1893 he allowed one of his bowlers, C.M. Wells, to bowl a no-ball wide so that Oxford would save the compulsory follow-on. For Cambridge he played 35 matches, scoring 1,649 runs at 26.59 and took 153 wickets at 17.73.

Jackson made his debut for Yorkshire in 1890 against Lancashire at Huddersfield and played all his cricket under Lord Hawke, but he was destined, like Len Hutton, to captain his country but never his county.

At his best he was a brilliant all-rounder, a stylish attacking middle-order batsman, who combined natural timing with an appetite for on-driving and cutting. He was also a right-arm, medium-fast bowler who varied his pace considerably and used the off-cutter effectively.

In 1893, while playing for the Gents versus the Players at Lord's, he bowled unchanged in both innings with S.M.J. Woods, taking 12 for 77 and top scoring in the match with 63. In the same year he took his best first-class figures of 8 for 54 for Cambridge University against the Gentlemen of England at Fenners. He was in such convincing form that he was selected to play for England against Australia at Lord's, where he stroked a majestic 91 on debut. He followed this with his first century for his country, scoring 105 in 135 minutes in the next Test at the Oval, and it was the first in time in a Test match that a hundred had been completed with a hit over the boundary. He declined to play in the third Test at Old Trafford, preferring to play for Yorkshire against Sussex at Hove instead. It was felt that if there had not been the incident in the Varsity game and if he had not spurned the opportunity to play at Old Trafford, he would have been the England captain earlier in his career.

For Yorkshire he put in many fine performances: in 1895 he took 12 for 91 against Kent, which included 5 for 28 and 7 for 63, and two years later 12 for 80 against Hampshire, 6 for 19 and 6 for 61. Other outstanding performances included 5 for 8 against Lancashire and 5 for 12 against the Australians, which included four wickets in five balls. His best figures for Yorkshire were 7 for 42 against Middlesex at Leeds in 1898.

With the bat, his highest score for the White Rose County was 160 against Gloucestershire in 1898 at Sheffield, and in all he scored 1,000 runs in a season on 10 occasions, with his best season being 1899 (1,847 runs at 45.04). In 1898 he scored 1,442 runs and took 104 wickets, thus completing his only 'double'. For Yorkshire he only played regularly for four seasons, but he still scored 10,371 runs at 33.89, with 21 centuries, and took 506 wickets at 19.15.

In 1899 he scored 118 at the Oval, when he and Tom Haywood (137) shared a record partnership of 185 for the first wicket, and in 1902 'Jacko' scored a memorable 128 against Australia at Old Trafford. Three years later he was elected captain for the first time for the home series against Australia. He captained the side in all five Tests, won the toss each time, and scored two magnificent hundreds. His 144 not out at Leeds was his highest Test score and the first ever century in a Test at Headingley. At Manchester he scored 113 and totalled 492 runs in the series at 70.28. With the ball he took 13 wickets at 15.46 (which included figures of 5 for 52 at Nottingham); a return that no England captain has ever bettered.

Due to business and Parliamentary duties, Jackson never made an important tour abroad, although he did go to India with Lord Hawke's team in the winter of 1892–93.

His last season was in 1907 and in total he played 207 matches, scored 10.371 runs at 33,39 with 21 centuries, took 506 wickets at 19.15 with 25 five-wicket hauls and held 129 catches for Yorkshire.

Following his retirement from circket he served in the Boer war and was MP for the Howdenshire division of Yorkshire from 1915 to 1926. In 1922 he was appointed financial secretary to the War Office and the following year chairman of the Unionist party. In 1927 he went to India as Governor of Bengal, where he nearly fell victim to an assassination attempt while serving there during 1933.

He was also President of the MCC in 1921, served as a Test selector and was made President of Yorkshire County Cricket Club in 1939, a position he still held upon his death in 1947.

Paul William Jarvis

RHB & RFM, 1981–2000

Born: 29 June 1965, Redcar.

Played for: Yorkshire, Sussex and Somerset.

Test Matches: (9) 1988–93 Cap No. 527

Batting Career for England

I	NO	HS	Runs
15	2	29*	132
AV	**100**	**50**	**Catches**
10.15	-	-	2

Bowling for England

Balls	Runs	Wkts	Av
1,912	965	21	45.95
Best	**5wl**	**10wl**	**Sr/Rate**
4–107	-	-	91.04

First-Class Career: (215 Matches) 1981–2000

Batting

I	NO	HS	Runs
268	67	80	3,373
AV	**100**	**50**	**Catches**
16.78	-	10	67

Bowling

Balls	Runs	Wkts	Av
35,525	18,914	654	28.92
Best	**5wl**	**10wl**	**Sr/Rate**
7–55	22	3	54.30

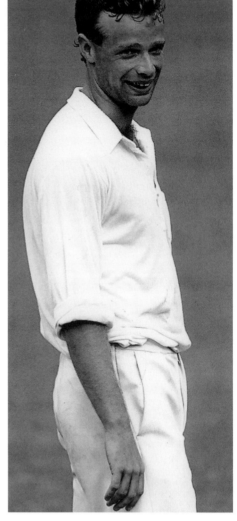

Born at Redcar and a member of Marske Cricket Club, Paul Jarvis captained their Junior team when they won the Lord Taverners Trophy in 1978.

In 1981, at the age of 16 years and 75 days, and after only five second XI games, he made his first-class debut for Yorkshire against Sussex at Hove in the last Championship match of the season. He is the youngest ever cricketer to appear in a first-class game for the White Rose County. The young right-arm fast bowler showed immense potential as a young player and was tipped for stardom at a very early age.

In the summer of 1982 he appeared in six first-class matches, while in the John Player Sunday League he created history by becoming the youngest player to take a hat-trick in the League when, against Derbyshire at the County Ground, he dismissed Kim Barnett, William Fowler and Bernard Maher, all clean bowled. He was also Yorkshire's second joint top wicket-taker with 15 wickets.

In 1985 he repeated the act, this time in the County Championship. Once again the opponents were Derbyshire at Queen's Park, Chesterfield, and Paul became the youngest ever player at 20 years of age to take a hat-trick in the Championship. At the end of the season he had snared 44 first-class wickets in 14 games.

The following summer he topped the Yorkshire bowling averages with 60 wickets at 22.20 in 15 games, which included his best bowling performance for the county, 7 for 55 against Surrey at Headingley (10 for 108 in the match). Earlier in the season against Middlesex at Lord's he had also taken 10 wickets in the match (5 for 45 and 6 for 47), which included six of the top seven batsmen. As a consequence he was awarded his county cap.

In 1987 he improved upon this by once again becoming Yorkshire's main strike bowler with 77 first-class wickets at 24.89, playing in 23 matches, which included 7 for 82 against Gloucestershire at Leeds. He also played a key role in the Benson and Hedges Cup-winning team, taking 4 for 43 in the Final against Northamptonshire at Lord's.

Although not very tall for a fast bowler at only 5ft 10in, he generated good pace from a relatively short run-up and tended to skid the ball through with a whippy action. Unfortunately, he suffered with various injuries, and he was probably over-bowled too much in the early part of his career.

The 1987 season's performances had helped secure him a place on England's tour to Pakistan and later to New Zealand and Australia. His debut came in Christchurch against New Zealand in February 1988, a match in which he took 3 for 73, followed by 3 for 128 at Auckland. He was dropped for the third Test at Wellington but was recalled for the home series against the West Indies. In the second Test at Lord's he bowled well, taking 4 for 107 and scoring 29 not out, and both scores, incidentally, were his best performances in Test cricket. However, a back strain ruled him out of the rest of the series, and although he was recalled against Australia in 1989, after two Tests and two very expensive wickets which cost 290 runs, he was dropped once more.

Jarvis, along with several others, decided to go on the 1989–90 rebel tour of South Africa, which saw him banned from Test cricket for three years. When the ban was lifted he was chosen to tour India and Sri Lanka in 1992–93, where he bowled with pace in the one-day series in India, winning the Man of the Match award at Bangalor with 5 for 35. His last Test appearance for England was at Colombo, where he took 3 for 90 in the match. Unfortunately, his was a Test career that had promised much but never really gathered momentum, partly due to niggling injuries. Indeed, that was also the case with Yorkshire, for after only four games in 1991 and eight in 1993 he was released by the county and joined Sussex for the start of the 1994 season.

For Yorkshire he took 449 wickets at 26.70 with 18 five-wicket hauls, scored 1,898 runs at 16.64, with a best of 80 against Northamptonshire at Scarborough in 1992, and he held 36 catches.

With Sussex he had a good first season (51 wickets) and won his second county cap, but in the following three summers he very rarely found full fitness. He left the south coast county in 1998 and ended his cricketing career with Somerset until the end of 2000. He did, however, prove he could occasionally be a force in one-day cricket, taking 5 for 55 for Somerset against Gloucestershire in the 1999 Natwest Final.

Roy Kilner

LHB & SLA, 1911–27

Born: 17 October 1890, Low Valley,
      Wombwell, Barnsley.
Died: 5 April 1928, Kendray, Barnsley.
Played for: Yorkshire.
Test Matches: (9) 1924–26 Cap No. 214
Batting Career for England

I	NO	HS	Runs
8	1	74	233
AV	**100**	**50**	**Catches**
33.28	-	2	6

Bowling for England

Balls	Runs	Wkts	Av
2,368	734	24	30.58
Best	**5wl**	**10wl**	**Sr/Rate**
4–51	-	-	98.66

First-Class Career: (413 Matches) 1911–27
Batting

I	NO	HS	Runs
540	55	206*	14,419
AV	**100**	**50**	**Catches**
29.72	17	81	264

Bowling

Balls	Runs	Wkts	Av
58,113	18,321	991	18.48
Best	**5wl**	**10wl**	**Sr/Rate**
8–26	47	10	58.64

Roy Kilner was one of the most popular players ever to appear for Yorkshire, winning acclaim wherever he went. A native of Low Valley, Wombwell, near Barnsley, he was the nephew of Irving Washington, who played for Yorkshire from 1900 to 1902, and the elder brother of Norman Kilner, who appeared for the county from 1919 to 1923 and later played over 300 games for Warwickshire.

    Kilner began his career with Mitchell Main at the age of 14 and made his debut for the county Second XI in 1910 before being allocated to Harrogate by Yorkshire. In 1911 he made his county debut against Somerset at Taunton, but it was another two years before he established for himself a regular spot in the team, scoring 1,586 runs at 34.47, with a debut century against Leicestershire at Headingley, which incidentally was his highest aggregate for any season. He again topped the 1,000 runs for the season in 1914 with 1,329, before he joined his Yorkshire colleagues Major Booth and Arthur Dolphin serving in World War One.

Prior to the conflict Kilner had been a batsman who bowled occasionally, but the death of his good friend Major Booth during hostilities and the sudden death of Alonzo Drake meant that he was thrust into an all-round capacity when the County Championship started again in 1919. Indeed, Kilner himself had been injured during the war, being severely wounded in the right wrist, though this did not affect his later cricket career.

The solid and chunky left-handed Kilner was renowned for his aggressive batting, and his off-side driving and strong pulling captured the crowds' interest, making him a huge favourite, but he could play a patient, dogged game if required. In 1920 he made his highest first-class score for Yorkshire, 206 not out against Derbyshire at Bramall Lane, and once more topped a 1,000 runs (1,316 at 36.55) with a hundred in both games against Northamptonshire, 166 at Northampton and 150 at Harrogate.

However, it was his bowling that was starting to gain attention and in 1922 he took 12 wickets for 142 in the first five games of the season. He then proceeded to take 5 for 14 against Nottinghamshire at Trent Bridge, 6 for 15 against Hampshire at Bournemouth and 11 for 51 in the match against Essex at Harrogate. In addition, he captured 5 for 38 off 37 overs against Middlesex at Lord's. He also took the first of four doubles for Yorkshire, scoring 1,198 runs at 27.22 and snaring 122 wickets at 14.73.

Though essentially a left-arm finger spinner, he would often deliver a chinaman and googly and it was this skill and variation of pace and flight even on hard wickets that made him a successful spin bowler.

In 1923 he took his best bowling figures for Yorkshire, 8 for 26 against Glamorgan at Cardiff, and the following year he made his Test debut against South Africa at Edgbaston, scoring 59 in England's win by an innings and 18 runs. He also captured his best aggregate of wickets in a match, 12 for 55 (5 for 18 and 7 for 37) against Sussex at Hove.

The following winter he was selected as a member of Arthur Gilligan's party to tour Australia, though he was only selected for the last three Test matches. However, he more than justified his inclusion with 17 wickets at only 20.29, and he was the only bowler who gave any support to the over-bowled Maurice Tate in England's 4–1 loss. At Adelaide in the third Test he took a personal best of 4 for 51 and in England's solitary win at Melbourne the following game he scored 74, his highest Test score, and took 5 for 70 in the match.

He toured the West Indies in the winter of 1925–26, and played the last of his nine Tests the following summer against Australia, taking 4 for 70 at Lord's.

Kilner was not only a man of charm, humour and generosity, he also had a marvellous sense of fun. When asked how he liked the battle of a Roses match he remarked that: 'What we want is no umpires and fair cheating all round.'

During the winter of 1927–28 he was engaged in a coaching capacity in India, but unfortunately he contracted typhoid fever and sadly died a few weeks later on his return to England. It is estimated that 100,000 people attended his funeral, lining the streets of Wombwell to pay their respects.

For Yorkshire he played 365 matches, scored 13,018 runs at 30.13, with 15 centuries, took 857 wickets at 17.13, with 39 five-wicket hauls, and held 231 catches.

James Charles Laker

RHB & OB, 1946–65

Born: 9 February 1922, Frizinghall.
Died: 23 April 1986, Putney, London.
Played for: Surrey and Essex.
Test Matches: (46) 1949–59 Cap No. 328

Batting Career for England

I	NO	HS	Runs
63	15	63	676
AV	100	50	Catches
14.08	-	2	12

Bowling for England

Balls	Runs	Wkts	Av
12,027	4,101	193	21.25
Best	5wl	10wl	Sr/Rate
10–53	9	3	62.32

First-Class Career: (450 Matches) 1946–65

Batting

I	NO	HS	Runs
548	108	113	7,304
AV	100	50	Catches
16.60	2	18	270

Bowling

Balls	Runs	Wkts	Av
101,352	35,791	1944	52.13
Best	5wl	10wl	Sr/Rate
10–53	127	32	52.13

After attending Saltaire School in Bradford, Jim Laker practised at pre-war nets at Headingley and was at that time a batsman who bowled fast-medium. At the age of 15 he played for his school and Saltaire in the Bradford League. He joined the army in 1941 and played on matting wickets in Cairo, where Jim Smith tried to persuade him to join Essex. When he returned to England he was billeted at Catford and joined the local club. A trial at Surrey followed and surprisingly Yorkshire, unaware of Laker's ability, consented to his registration. He played one match against the Combined Services in 1946 and was given his Championship debut a year later. He immediately topped the Surrey averages and was fourth in the county averages with 66 wickets at 16.65.

Laker was the absolute master of control, accuracy, flight and guile, the complete slow bowler and was consequently selected for the tour to the West Indies in 1948. In his first Test at Barbados he took 7 for 103 in the second innings, which included 6 for 25 in nine overs. He took 18 wickets at 30.44 in the four Tests, and *Wisden* suggested that undoubtedly he was the find of the tour.

However, in the summer of 1948 he suffered at the hands of the strongest Australian batting team to visit England. He had started the series with a fine knock of 63 and was easily England's top scorer; he also took three early wickets – Morris, Barnes and Miller. However, after that he was ineffective, as indeed he was in the second Test. Dropped for the third, he returned for the fourth at Leeds, but bowled poorly and his 14 wickets cost him 59.35 runs each.

In 1949 he scored the first of his two centuries for Surrey, including 100 against Cambridge University at Guildford, and took 100 Championship wickets at 17.79. Twelve months later he took a further 142 wickets at 14.45 and also took 8 for 2 for England against The Rest at Bradford, but he was not selected for the 1950–51 tour to Australia.

Laker returned to the Test scene in the summer of 1951, taking 14 wickets at 14.85 against the touring South Africans and playing in the 1952 series against India. In 1953 he played in three of the five Tests against the Australians when England regained the Ashes under Len Hutton, taking 4 for 75 in the second innings in the vital win at the Oval, the only result of the series. However, once more he was not chosen for the 1954–55 return series in Australia, with the selectors of the opinion that off-spinners were of little use on the hard Australian wickets. In the summer of 1954 he registered his highest first-class score, 113 against Glamorgan at the Oval, his second century for Surrey. He continued to be a tremendous bowler for Surrey, and his partnership with Tony Lock, along with Alec Bedser and Peter Loader, helped Surrey to win seven consecutive Championships from 1952 to 1958.

However, the highlight of his career was to be the year 1956. It all started in May when he took 10 for 88 as Surrey beat the Australians by 10 wickets to become the first county to defeat them in 44 years. In the three Tests before Old Trafford he had taken 20 wickets at only 13.2, but at Manchester he became the first bowler to take over 17 wickets in a single Test when he completely bemused the Australians. In the first innings he took 9 for 37, and on a drying pitch on the last afternoon he completed the most outstanding bowling performance in the history of the game as he took all 10 wickets for 53 runs to return a match analysis of 19 for 90, a feat unlikely ever to be equalled. In the series he took 46 wickets at 9.60, and only Syd Barnes with 49 against South Africa in 1913–14 has bettered his return.

There are a few that felt that Laker was a one-series wonder, but nothing could be further from the truth. Of all spin-bowlers to take in excess of 150 wickets in Test cricket, only two have career averages of less than 25 runs per wicket – Clarrie Grimmett (216 wickets at 24.22) and currently Muttiah Muralitharan. Take out the 1956 Ashes series and Laker's return is 147 wickets at 24.89. He averaged less than 20 runs per wicket against Australia (18.27), New Zealand (12.47), Pakistan (19.50) and South Africa (19.56), and just 23.63 against India. It was only against the West Indies where his wickets were more expensive at 30.44.

For Surrey he played 309 matches, scored 5,531 runs at 17.44, with two centuries, took 1,395 wickets at 17.37, with 93 five-wicket hauls, and held 223 catches.

Laker ended his career with Essex after Trevor Bailey persuaded him to join them and he played 30 matches as an amateur from 1962 to 1964.

The one slight on Laker's reputation is that in the period between his first Test and his last England were involved in 99 Tests, but he played in only 46 of them. For such a great bowler, the selectors seemed to have little faith in him until 1956. Fred Trueman once remarked that, 'when he was really spinning the ball you could actually hear his fingers click as he delivered.' Perhaps Len Hutton gave the most fitting tribute to him when even before the Ashes series of 1956 he nominated Laker as the best off-spinner on all types of wickets that he had ever seen.

Edric 'Eddie' Leadbeater

RHB & LB, 1949–58

Born: 15 August 1927, Lockwood,
　　　Huddersfield.
Played for: Yorkshire and Warwickshire.
Test Matches: (2) 1951–52 Cap No. 367
Batting Career for England

I	NO	HS	Runs
2	0	38	40
AV	**100**	**50**	**Catches**
20.00	-	-	3
Balls	**Runs**	**Wkts**	**Av**
289	218	2	109.00
Best	**5wl**	**10wl**	**Sr/Rate**
1–38	-	-	144.50

First-Class Career: (118 Matches) 1949–58
Batting

I	NO	HS	Runs
138	36	116	1,548
AV	**100**	**50**	**Catches**
15.17	1	3	74

Bowling

Balls	Runs	Wkts	Av
16,509	7,947	289	27.49
Best	**5wl**	**10wl**	**Sr/Rate**
8–83	11	2	57.12

Eddie Leadbeater was one of a rare breed of Yorkshire bowlers – a leg-spinner, the type of which the county did not trust in the 1950s. At only 17 years of age, Leadbeater played as a professional for Almondbury in the Huddersfield League, and, although not a massive spinner of the ball, he gave it plenty of air, while he used the top-spinner to good effect as well. He was always a useful late-order batsman and a brilliant fielder in any outfield position.

　　Having followed the usual route into the Yorkshire team, via the second XI, he made his first-class debut for Yorkshire in 1949 at Grace Road, Leicester, taking 5 for 158 in the match and playing in three games that season.

　　In 1950 he became a regular in the team, playing in 23 of the 28 games, taking 87 wickets at 26.64, including a career best of 8 for 83 against Worcestershire at New Road (10 for 155 in the match), the best innings figures by a Yorkshire leg-spinner. He also took a career best match aggregate of 11 for 162 against Nottinghamshire at Trent Bridge (6 for 96 and 5 for 66).

The following summer Leadbeater took a further 81 wickets at 24.18, which included a best of 7 for 131 against Nottinghamshire at Trent Bridge yet again, and 6 for 40 against Cambridge University at Fenners. He may well have taken many more wickets that season, but he only bowled just over half the overs that Appleyard and Wardle bowled and was well behind them both in the pecking order. During the season he also scored his highest score for Yorkshire, 91 against Nottinghamshire at Bramall Lane, Sheffield, sharing a sixth-wicket partnership of 127 with Ted Lester (118).

In the winter of 1951–52 he was a surprise selection for the MCC tour to India, Pakistan and Ceylon, when he replaced the injured 'Dusty' Rhodes. However, he was not a success, playing in only two Tests against India, where he took two wickets for 218 runs, with a best of 1 for 38 at the Brabourne Stadium. He scored 40 runs, with a best of 38 at Eden Gardens. It was thought that he had modified his action a little for this series, pushing the bowl through much quicker, but he failed to make an impact and he was never the same bowler again.

On his return to Yorkshire he was rarely used, taking only 25 wickets at 38 runs per wicket, and his last game for the club, against Gloucestershire at the County Ground, Bristol, was a reflection of his form at that time – a pair and no wickets in the match.

For Yorkshire he played a total of 81 matches, scored 898 runs at 13.81 and took 201 wickets at 28.14, which included seven five-wicket hauls, and held 49 catches.

In 1957 he joined Warwickshire, making his Bears debut against Leicestershire at Edgbaston, and he played regularly in 1958 after Eric Hollies had retired. In all he played 27 first-class matches for Warwickshire in the two seasons he was with them, taking just 52 first-class wickets at 25.50. He did, however, score his only first-class century against Glamorgan at the Courtaulds Ground, Coventry, when, going in as nightwatchman, he made 116 and shared a second-wicket stand of 209 with Fred Gardner.

After leaving Edgbaston, he returned to Huddersfield to play League cricket and by 1981 he had taken 1,712 wickets. The teams he played for at this time were Liversedge (Central Yorkshire League), Pudsey St Lawrence (Bradford League) and Royton (Central Lancashire League).

Walter Scott Lees

RHB & RFM, 1896–1911

Born: 25 December 1875, Sowerby Bridge.
Died: 10 September 1924, West Hartlepool, Durham.
Played for: Surrey and London County.
Test Matches: (5) 1905–06 Cap No. 149
Batting Career for England

I	NO	HS	Runs
9	3	25*	66
AV	100	50	Catches
11.00	-	-	2

Bowling for England

1,256	467	26	17.96
Best	5wl	10wl	Sr/Rate
6–78	2	-	48.30

First-Class Career: (364 Matches) 1896–1911
Batting

I	NO	HS	Runs
522	76	137	7,642
AV	100	50	Catches
17.13	2	17	125

Bowling

Balls	Runs	Wkts	Av
69,778	30,008	1,402	21.40
Best	5wl	10wl	Sr/Rate
9–81	97	20	49.77

Walter Lees was born at Sowerby Bridge, near Halifax, and although not a truly great bowler, he was certainly a very good one and was a Surrey regular from 1896 to 1911.

He played his early cricket in Halifax, but joined Surrey after answering an advertisement by Surrey County Cricket Club to become a member of the groundstaff. In 1896, at the age of 20, he made his debut for Surrey, and the following season took a hat-trick against Hampshire at Southampton where he took 78 wickets very economically.

In 1898 he bowled unchanged with Thomas Rushby in both innings against Lancashire at Old Trafford. In the winter of that year he was engaged to play and coach in Argentina and was attached to three clubs: Buenos Aires, Hurlingham and Lomas, and Belgrano.

In the following three seasons he was at his peak, extracting plenty of zip from the pitch with his fast-medium pace bowling, while hard wickets suited him better than wet ones.

In the summer of 1904 he was picked for the Players versus the Gentlemen at the Oval, and against London County at the Oval he took five wickets for seven runs in 42 balls, his victims including Archie MacLaren, William Murdoch, Leslie Poidevin and the great W.G. Grace. That season also saw him take five wickets for seven runs in 55 balls against Hampshire, also at the Oval.

The following year he took 193 wickets at an average of 18.01, (which included 184 wickets for Surrey) and also included his best bowling figures of 9 for 81 against Sussex at Eastbourne. He also scored his maiden first-class century (130) against Hampshire at Aldershot, with his 100 coming up in only 60 minutes, and his highest first-class score (137) came against Sussex at the Oval in 1906.

He was a more than useful batsman, with a good eye, and he played many bold attacking shots. In 1905 he also took 168 wickets (154 for Surrey) and was named one of *Wisden's* Five Cricketers of the Year in 1909.

Meanwhile he had been chosen by the MCC for the winter tour to South Africa under the leadership of Plum Warner. It was a disastrous tour for the English team as they lost the series 4–1, with the leg-spin quartet of Scharz, Faulkner, Vogler and White being almost unplayable on their matting wickets. However, for Walter Lees it was a good tour. In the first Test at Johannesburg he took 5 for 34 in the first innings and 8 for 108 in the match, and took his best return for England at the same venue in the third Test with 6 for 78 and 9 for 163 in the match. In the five Test series he took 26 wickets at 17.96, with a strike rate of a wicket every 48 balls, and was by far England's best bowler.

Surprisingly, England never selected him again, but at county level he continued to take his 100 wickets a season, with 135 more in 1907 and 128 in 1909.

In 1906 he also featured well in the annual Players versus Gentlemen games at Lord's, taking six wickets and scoring 51 runs on the last day, when facing the fast men (his fellow colleagues at Surrey, Neville Alexander Knox and Walter Brearley) with great assurance. Indeed, he showed more confidence than many of the recognised batsmen.

When he retired in 1911 he had taken 1,331 wickets for Surrey at 21.44, which places him eighth on the all-time Surrey list. He also scored 7,237 runs at 17.23 and held 118 catches for the county.

He died in West Hartlepool in 1924 at the age of 49.

Peter Lever

RHB & RFM, 1960–76

Born: 17 September 1940, Todmorden.
Played for: Lancashire and Tasmania.
Test Matches: (17) 1970–75 Cap No. 447

I	NO	HS	Runs
18	2	88*	350
AV	**100**	**50**	**Catches**
21.87	-	2	11

Bowling for England

Balls	Runs	Wkts	Av
3,571	1,509	41	36.80
Best	**5wl**	**10wl**	**Sr/Rate**
6–38	2	-	87.09

First-Class Career: (301 Matches) 1960–76
Batting

I	NO	HS	Runs
314	66	88*	3,534
AV	**100**	**50**	**Catches**
14.25	-	11	106

Bowling

Balls	Runs	Wkts	Av
45,997	20,377	796	25.59
Best	**5wl**	**10wl**	**Sr/Rate**
7–70	28	2	57.78

A product of Todmorden, Peter Lever attended the local grammer school before being signed by Lancashire on a special registration in 1960. He made his debut that year against Cambridge University at Old Trafford, playing in five matches that season. In the early 1960s competition for places in the Lancashire attack was keen, with the likes of Brian Statham, Ken Higgs and Colin Hilton, and it was not until 1963 that he took his first 50 wickets in the Championship, while two years later he gained his county cap.

As a batsman he was improving all the time, and a year later he scored his highest first-class score for Lancashire, 83 against Essex at Colchester. He had also become an aggressive fast-medium bowler and in 1969 he snared 6 for 49 at Lord's against Middlesex and grabbed a hat-trick against Nottinghamshire at Old Trafford. As at Lancashire, he faced stiff competition for an England place, competing with John Snow, David Brown and his Lancashire colleague Ken Higgs, but in 1970 he was called-up by the England selectors to face the Rest of the World XI, who had taken the place of South Africa after they had been banned from playing Test cricket because of apartheid. The games, of course, were unofficial Tests, but he made an immediate impact taking 7 for 83 in 33 overs in their first innings and included star batsmen Graham Pollock, Gary Sobers, Eddie Barlow, Mushtaq Mohammad, Clive Lloyd and Mike Proctor among his victims. This magnificent performance prompted the selectors to choose him for the winter tour to Australia in 1970–71.

He missed the first Test at Brisbane but made his Test debut at Perth, where he had to battle into the Freemantle Doctor, with John Snow bowling with the breeze. While Snow took the wickets in the six-match series, he finished with 31, Lever with 13 wickets at 33.76 was a perfect foil and certainly contributed to England regaining the Ashes.

On the New Zealand leg of the tour, in the second Test at Auckland, he scored 64 in a record seventh-wicket stand of 149 with Alan Knott, and the two repeated the performance against Pakistan in the first Test at Birmingham with a seventh-wicket partnership of 159, Lever's share being 47. In the second half of the summer he confirmed his ability with the bat, notching up his highest first-class score of 88 not out in 227 minutes in a record eighth-wicket partnership of 168 with Ray Illingworth against India at Old Trafford.

In the winter of 1971–72 he went to play for Tasmania in the Sheffield Shield and returned the following summer to a benefit at Lancashire which raised £7,000.

With the ball he was always at his best when he pitched the ball up far enough to allow it to swing and seam and he remained an integral part of England's attack until 1975. On the winter tour of 1974–75 to Australia and New Zealand he took a personal best of 6 for 38 against Australia at Melbourne (which included a spell of four wickets for five runs) to seal an England win by an innings and four runs.

In New Zealand in the first Test at Auckland he bowled a bouncer which Ewen Chatfield deflected into his left temple. Chatfield collapsed with a hairline fracture of the skull and his heart stopped beating for several seconds. Indeed, only heart massage and mouth-to-mouth resuscitation by the MCC physiotherapist Bernard Thomas saved his life.

Peter also played 10 one-day internationals, including the 1975 World Cup in which he took 11 wickets. Unfortunately, he had started to have back problems by that time, which hastened his retirement in 1976, having taken 716 wickets at 24.64 and scored 3,073 runs at 13.59 for the Red Rose County.

On retirement he was invited to become the Lancashire coach and he held the position until the end of 1986, when he and manager Jack Bond were sacked after the team lost in the Natwest Final to Sussex and finished third from bottom of the County Championship.

Maurice Leyland

RHB & SLA, 1920–48

Born: 20 July 1900, New Park, Harrogate.
Died: 1 January 1967, Scotton Banks,
    Harrogate.
Played for: Yorkshire.
Test Matches: (41) 1928–38 Cap No. 237

Batting Career for England

I	NO	HS	Runs
65	5	187	2,764
AV	**100**	**50**	**Catches**
46/06	9	10	13

Bowling for England

Balls	Runs	Wkts	Av
1,103	585	6	97.50
Best	**5wl**	**10wl**	**Sr/Rate**
3–91	-	-	183.83

First-Class Career: (686 Matches) 1920–48

Batting

I	NO	HS	Runs
932	101	263	33,660
AV	**100**	**50**	**Catches**
40.50	80	154	246

Bowling

Balls	Runs	Wkts	Av
29,012	13,659	466	29.31
Best	**5wl**	**10wl**	**Sr/Rate**
8–63	11	1	62.25

Maurice Leyland, as he was always known (although he was christened Morris), was one of Yorkshire's best ever middle-order batsmen and one of England's favourite left-handers. Born in Harrogate, he was the son of a former League professional who became groundsman at Headingley, and he graduated to the Yorkshire team via Moorside of the Lancashire League.

Strongly built with a high grip, he was a powerful stroke-player and one of the finest square cutters of a ball to play for the county. He relished a battle and was an ideal man in a crisis, whether batting for Yorkshire or for England. He was also an unorthodox left-arm slow bowler who bowled chinamen and googlies out of the back of his hand, similar to another great Yorkshire left-arm slow bowler, Johnny Wardle. In addition he was an outstanding fielder, with a safe pair of hands.

He made his debut for Yorkshire against Essex in 1920 and was capped in 1922. A year later he scored 1,088 runs and in 1924 scored his first century for Yorkshire with 133 not out in the Roses match against Lancashire. The summer of 1927 saw him score the first of five double centuries, 204 not out against Middlesex at Bramall Lane, and in 1928 he registered 1,783 First-Class runs and was selected as one of *Wisden's* Five Cricketers of the Year. In the same year he played his first game for England against the West Indies and within 12 months he had hit his maiden Test century (137) against Australia at the MCG, his only Test of the 1928–29 tour.

The following summer he notched up 294 runs at an average of 42 against the touring South Africans, which included 102 at Lord's, and in 1930 he hit 1,814 runs, which included a magnificent 211 not out against Lancashire. During the winter tour of South Africa he took his best Test bowling figures, 3 for 91, and had now become an integral part of England's Test side.

During the 1930s he toured Australia twice, the first time in 1932–33, when he was part of Jardine's 'bodyline tour', and then again in 1936–37, when he scored 441 runs at 55.12, which included 126 at Brisbane and 111 not out at Melbourne. His record against Australia both home and away was excellent. Of his 41 Test matches, he played in 20 against the Aussies, in which he scored 1,705 runs at 56.83, while in his final Test in 1938 he scored 187 (his highest Test score), sharing a second-wicket partnership of 382 with Len Hutton, thus achieving a unique record of a century in his first and last Test against them. In Test cricket only Wally Hammond and Herbert Sutcliffe achieved better Test match figures and his final tally of 2,764 runs at 46.06 places him in the top tier of England's best ever batsmen.

In 1933 he amassed 2,196 runs for Yorkshire at an average of 54.90, which included 210 not out against Kent, 192 against Northamptonshire and seven centuries during the season. A year later he was awarded a much deserved benefit, which realised £3,648, a good sum in those days.

His highest ever score for Yorkshire was 263 against Essex at Hull in 1936 and his best bowling figures were 8 for 63 against Hampshire at Huddersfield in 1938. In addition, he took a hat-trick against Surrey at Sheffield in 1935 and claimed 204 catches for the county. He was an outstandingly consistent batsman, who scored over 1,000 runs in each of 17 successive seasons (1922 to 1939), including 2,000 on three occasions.

After the war he played a full season, helping Yorkshire to their 12th Championship of his career, before retiring to become a much respected coach, which was mainly due to his cheerful nature. Known for his humour, he once remarked when asked how to combat pace bowling with the remark 'none of us like fast bowlers, only some of us don't let on'. There were other pearls of wisdom, such as when Len Hutton made a duck on his Test debut and Leyland told him, 'At least tha's started at bottom'. Another was when Yorkshire batsman Arthur Mitchell told the legendary cricket writer Neville Cardus that his writing was too flowery, Leyland was reputed to have said, 'Well nobody could say that about thy batting Arthur'.

For Yorkshire Leyland scored 26,180 runs in 548 games at an average of 41.03, with 62 centuries, he took 409 wickets at 27.08, which included 10 five-wicket hauls, and he held 204 catches.

Frank Anderson Lowson

RHB & OB, 1949–58

Born: 1 July 1925, Bradford.
Died: 8 September 1984, Pool-in-
    Wharfedale.
Played for: Yorkshire.
Test Matches: (7) 1951–55 Cap No. 360
Batting Career For England

I	NO	HS	Runs
13	0	68	245
AV	**100**	**50**	**Ct/St**
18.84	-	2	5

First-Class Career: (277 Matches) 1949–58
Batting

I	NO	HS	Runs
449	37	259*	15,321
AV	**100**	**50**	**Ct/St**
37.18	31	72	190

Bowling

Balls	Runs	Wkts	Av
30	31	0	-
Best	**5wl**	**10wl**	**Sr/Rate**
-	-	-	-

Frank Lowson was the son of a footballing father of the same name and attended Bradford Grammer School, playing in the first XI at the age of 11. He began his League career with Bowling Old Lane, and after playing five second XI games in 1948, he was given a first-class debut in the third game of the season at Fenners against Cambridge University, where he made 2 and 78 not out in the second innings. Within weeks of his debut he impressed, with a score of 64 in a Test trial. Although he had come late to first-class cricket at 23 years of age, he soon made up for it, scoring 1,678 runs in his debut season with a best of 104 against Middlesex at Bramall Lane, Sheffield. The aggregate was the highest from a Yorkshire batsman in his debut season, with the exception of Herbert Sutcliffe, who notched up 1,839 in 1919.

The following season he made his highest aggregate number of runs for a season with 2,152 at an average of 42.19, which included five hundreds, the best being a stylish 141 not out against Northamptonshire at Headingley, after already making 91 in the first innings.

Lawson was a patient and technically correct opening batsman, who probably modelled his methods on those of the great Len Hutton, with whom he opened the batting for Yorkshire during most of his career. He was particularly strong on the on-side, but he could cut well and his cover driving was both stylish and a joy to watch when he was on form.

In 1951 he scored 76 not out, carrying his bat in a total of 218 against the MCC at Lord's and was given his Test baptism against South Africa at Leeds making a useful 58, and he was then chosen for a gruelling five month MCC winter tour of India, Pakistan and Ceylon. Lowson played in four of the five Tests against India and made his highest Test score (68) in his first Test in the second innings at Delhi. On tour he made over 1,000 first-class runs at an average of 44 runs per innings, but could only average 18.12 in the Tests. Indeed, *Wisden's* review of the tour said: 'Lowson possessed more strokes and looked the most accomplished batsman in the team, but he had an unfortunate time in the Tests. His skill could not be denied and he seemed an England batsman all over, the only doubt being the question of temperament.'

Unfortunately, the tour marked the end of Lowson's Test career and he made only one further appearance, replacing his county colleague Willie Watson at Headingley against the 1955 touring South Africans. That time he made only 5 and 0 and he never got another chance.

Throughout the 1950s he remained a consistent batsman, scoring well in excess of 1,000 runs per season, and in 1954 he notched up his second highest aggregate, 1,719 runs, including six centuries, the highest of which was 165 against Sussex at Hove.

At the end of the 1958 season, Yorkshire, having endured the least successful period in its history, the committee and new captain Ronnie Burnett decided to go with a policy of youth and so dispensed with the services of several senior players including Lowson, Johnny Wardle and Bob Appleyard.

In 1959 Lowson received a testimonial, which realised £2,500. His Yorkshire career saw him score 13,897 runs at an average of 37.23, which included 30 centuries, which included a career best of 259 n.o against Worcestershire at Worcester in 1953. He also took 180 catches. His last game for the county was against Derbyshire at Chesterfield in July 1958.

After leaving Yorkshire he went back to League cricket, playing as a professional with Brighouse in the Bradford League from 1959 to 1963. In the latter season he became the fourth player to reach 1,000 runs in a Bradford League season, while he also played for Bradford and Bingley. Sadly, he died at the age of 59 from cancer.

George Gibson Macauley

RHB & RFM/OB, 1920–35

Born: 7 December 1897, Thirsk.
Died: 13 December 1940, Sullom Voe,
　　Shetland Islands.
Played for: Yorkshire.
Test Matches: (8) 1922–33 Cap No. 211

Batting Career for England

I	NO	HS	Runs
10	4	76	112
AV	100	50	Catches
18.66	-	1	5

Bowling for England

Balls	Runs	Wkts	Av
1,701	662	24	27.58
Best	5wl	10wl	Sr/Rate
5–64	1	-	70.87

First-Class Career: (468 Matches) 1920–35

Batting

I	NO	HS	Runs
460	125	125*	6,056
AV	100	50	Catches
18.07	3	20	373

Bowling

Balls	Runs	Wkts	Av
90,102	32,440	1,837	17.65
Best	5wl	10wl	Sr/Rate
8–21	126	31	49.04

A native of Thirsk, George Macauley was educated at Barnard Castle School, was later employed as a bank clerk and played club cricket for Thirsk Victoria, Wakefield and Ossett. He also played professional football for the latter.

　Macaulay, a young, tearaway fast bowler, made his debut for Yorkshire against Derbyshire at Bramall Lane in 1920 at the age of 22, but he was soon influenced by George Hirst to reduce his pace and work on the swing, seam and cut of his bowling. He did so to such great affect that he became two bowlers in one, opening with the new ball and later changing to his off-breaks, which turned appreciably on a wicket to give him some help. He was also one of the most aggressive bowlers to play for the county, never once admitting defeat, and he was an outstanding close-to-the-wicket fielder, particularly off his own bowling. As a batsman, although not a genuine all-rounder, he played many vital innings and hit three centuries for the county.

In his first full season in 1921 Macauley hit his first and highest century for Yorkshire, 125 not out against Nottinghamshire at Trent Bridge and took 101 first-class wickets, including 6 for 10 against Warwickshire at Edgbaston and 6 for 3 against Derbyshire at Hull, finishing fifth in the national bowling averages.

From 1922 to 1926 he was one of the most feared and respected bowlers in the country, never finishing outside of the top five bowlers in the County Championship averages. Among his 130 wickets in 1922 he captured 12 for 76 against Gloucestershire at Dewsbury, (7 for 47 and 5 for 29), 6 for 12 against Glamorgan at Cardiff and also notched up his second century, 101 not out against Essex at Harrogate, adding an unbroken partnership of 192 for the eighth-wicket with Wilfred Rhodes (108 not out).

In the winter he was selected for the tour of South Africa under George Mann, making his debut at Cape Town in the second Test, where he took a wicket with his first ball in Test cricket, finishing with 5 for 64 in the second innings and scoring the winning run in a one-wicket victory for England. In the series he took 16 wickets in four Tests at 20.37.

In the summer of 1923 he snared 163 first-class wickets, including the hat-trick against Warwickshire at Edgbaston. Just a year later he topped the County Championship averages with 159 wickets at only 11.73 and 184 wickets in total, including 12 for 40 against Gloucestershire at Gloucester (5 for 19 and 7 for 21), while he was also named one of *Wisden's* Five Cricketers of the Year.

The summer of 1925 was his best in first-class cricket, with 211 wickets at 15.48, and a year later he took his best aggregate of wickets in a match with 14 for 92 against Gloucestershire (6 for 49 and 8 for 43), which was one of 31 times that he took 10 or more wickets in a match, a figure only exceeded by Rhodes and Hirst. He also scored his highest Test score, 76 in his only appearance against Australia, at Headingley when he and George Geary (35 not out) shared a match-saving ninth-wicket stand of 103.

Bowling in tandem with Emmott Robinson (8 for 65), he took 12 for 50 (7 for 17 and 5 for 33) to bowl out Worcestershire at Leeds in 1927, and four years later he received a much deserved benefit of £1,633.

A career best of 8 for 21 against India at Harrogate in 1932 was followed by another outstanding season when he took 141 wickets, including 7 for 9 against Northamptonshire in only 14 overs at Kettering and 12 for 49 (7 for 28 and 5 for 21) against Lancashire in the Roses match at Old Trafford, which included a hat-trick and four wickets in five balls. He played the last of his eight Test matches for England against the West Indies, taking 4 for 57 at Lord's. For a bowler of his ability it was scant reward, for he never got the chance to tour Australia, but his abrasive and outspoken nature may well have contributed to this on some occasions.

Unfortunately, an injury to his spinning finger when attempting to hold a return catch in the match against Leicestershire at Headingley in 1934 hastened Macaulay's retirement. He left Yorkshire at the end of the following season after playing 445 matches for the county, scoring 5,717 runs at 17.97, capturing 1,774 wickets at 17.22, including 125 five-wicket hauls, and holding 361 catches.

He then proceeded to play League cricket in Wales and Lancashire, before becoming the professional at Todmorden in 1938 and 1939. In the 1938 Worsley Cup Final against Ramsbottom, Todmorden were bowled out for only 74 and a dejected dressing room assumed the match was over. But not for Macaulay, as he tore in to such an extent that Ramsbottom routed for just 47 and he finished as Man of the Match, taking 9 for 10 in 13 overs.

In 1940 he joined the RAF (he had served in the Royal Field Artillery in World War One), but contracted pneumonia while on duty in the Shetland Islands and died in December of the same year in Sullom Voe.

Anthony McGrath

RHB & RM, 1995–to date

Born: 6 October 1975, Bradford.

Played for: Yorkshire.

Test Matches: (4) 2003 Cap No. 614

Batting Career for England

I	NO	HS	Runs
5	0	81	201
AV	100	50	Catches
40.20	-	2	3

Bowling for England

Balls	Runs	Wkts	Av
102	56	4	14.00
Best	5wl	10wl	Sr/Rate
3–16	-	-	25.5

First-Class Career: (198 Matches) 1995–to date

Batting

I	NO	HS	Runs
333	25	188*	11,475
AV	100	50	Catches
37.25	27	55	144

Bowling

Balls	Runs	Wkts	Av
7,338	3,728	109	34.20
Best	5wl	10wl	Sr/Rate
5–39	1	-	67.30

Anthony McGrath was an outstanding schoolboy cricketer, not only captaining the Yorkshire Schoolboys from Under-13 through to Under-16, but was also skipper of the England Under-17 team. He played for the Under-19s, opening the batting with Marcus Trescothick, and was selected for the A tour to the West Indies in 1994–95 and Pakistan in 1995–96.

He displayed good form in the Yorkshire Second XI in seasons 1994 and 1995, scoring 815 runs at 62.69 (a high score of 218 not out against Surrey at Elland) in the former and 1,144 at 67.29 in the latter, with a high score of 151 against Somerset, once more at Elland.

He made his first-class debut for the county at the beginning of 1995 against Glamorgan at Bradford Park Avenue, opening the batting with Michael Vaughan and contributing 36 in the second innings after a debut 0 in the first.

Indeed, McGrath's early career was as an opening batsman, but as the years have gone on he has established himself as a middle-order batsman of substance and reliability. Always at his best when playing his shots, when on form his driving was a joy to watch, and he found an ideal spot at number three in the Yorkshire batting line up. In addition to his batting, he was a more than useful medium-pace bowler, with movement through the air and off the pitch.

In 1996 he notched up nearly 1,000 runs for the county (909), scoring his maiden century for Yorkshire, 101 against Kent at Canterbury, and followed this with 137 against Hampshire at Harrogate where he and skipper David Byas amassed 272 for the fourth wicket.

Over the following four summers his career stagnated somewhat, his best being in 1999 with 831 runs, but fortunately his bowling helped him maintain a place in the team. In the meantime, to help rediscover his form he wintered in Australia, playing club cricket in Melbourne and Perth.

In 2002 he was back on top and played the type of cricket everyone knew him capable of. He scored 803 runs and took 18 wickets at 27.66, which placed him top of the Yorkshire bowling averages. In addition he hit a magnificent 165 against Lancashire in the Roses match at Headingley, and together with Darren Lehmann (187) put on 317 for the third wicket. He also won the Man of the Match award in the quarter-final of the Cheltenham and Gloucester Trophy against Essex at Chelmsford with 72 not out, while in the Final he took 1 for 37 off nine tight overs and scored 46 not out in a fifth-wicket winning partnership of 103 with Matthew Elliott to help clinch Yorkshire's victory.

At the beginning of 2003, with Darren Lehmann taking a sabbatical for a year, Yorkshire surprisingly handed McGrath the captaincy. After a useful start to the season an injury to Andrew Flintoff left the England selectors searching for a replacement and McGrath was their choice. He had a splendid debut against Zimbabwe at Lord's, scoring 69 while batting at number seven and taking 3 for 16 with the ball, his best Test figures to date. In the second Test at Chester-Le-Street he top scored with 81 (his best to date), again from number seven in an England victory by an innings. Two further Tests followed later that summer against South Africa, but 51 runs from three innings was not sufficient for him to keep his place. However, as he was still a fringe member of the England set-up, albeit the one-day side, Yorkshire decided to appoint Craig White as the new captain for 2004.

In one-day international cricket he has appeared in 14 matches so far, with a highest score of 52 against South Africa at Old Trafford and a bowling best of 1 for 13 against the West Indies at Trent Bridge. He had a superb season in 2004, making 1,425 runs for Yorkshire at 59.37, and in 2006 he hit a further 1,293 runs, averaging over 60 (61.57). However, he became somewhat disillusioned by the direction that the county was taking and contemplated leaving. Fortunately, Darren Gough's appointment as the new captain for 2007 and the signings of Jacques Rudolph and Younis Khan convinced him to stay. As it was he had another fine season, just failing to notch up 1,000 runs with a total of 931, which included a career best of 188 not out against Warwickshire at Edgbaston.

With Yorkshire just avoiding relegation from the First Division of the County Championship at the end of 2008 and Darren Gough retiring, the county turned to McGrath once again and appointed him as skipper for the 2009 season.

Joseph William Henry Makepeace

RHB & LB, 1906–30

Born: 22 August 1881, Middlesbrough.
Died: 19 December 1952, Spital Bebington, Cheshire.
Played for: Lancashire.
Test Matches: (4) 1920–21 Cap No. 186
Batting Career for England

I	NO	HS	Runs
8	0	117	279
AV	**100**	**50**	**Ct/St**
34.87	1	2	-

First-Class Career: (499 Matches) 1906–30
Batting

I	NO	HS	Runs
778	66	203	25,799
AV	**100**	**50**	**Ct/St**
36.23	43	140	194

Bowling

Balls	Runs	Wkts	Av
4,043	1,971	42	46.92
Best	**5wl**	**10wl**	**Sr/Rate**
4–33	-	-	96.26

Joseph William Henry 'Harry' Makepeace was one of 11 'double' internationals to play both Test cricket and Association football for England. Born in Middlesbrough, Makepeace (having played Schoolboy football in Liverpool, with Bootle Amatuers) was already a professional footballer, playing for Everton from 1902 before he joined the Lancashire staff in 1906. Indeed, he had already played football for England as a hard-tackling, aggressive wing-half against Scotland in April 1906 and had won a FA Cup-winners' medal with Everton when they beat Newcastle United 1–0, also in April that year. He gained three further England caps against Scotland in 1910, Wales and Scotland in 1912 and won a League Championship medal with Everton in 1915. He is the only 'double' international to win a FA Cup-winners' medal and First Division Championship medal in football and to win a County Championship medal (Lancashire 1926, 1927, 1928 and 1930) and four Test caps (1920–21) for England at cricket.

Makepeace made his debut for Lancashire against Everton at Leyton in 1906, scoring 49 opening the innings with Archie MacLaren, and he earned a reputation as a patient right-hand batsman with an immaculate defence, who relied on technique and timing to score the majority of his runs. He was reputably one of the best players on bad pitches during his era, and he was also noted for his brilliant fielding at cover and as being a useful leg-spin bowler.

In 1911 he was Lancashire's outstanding batsman with 1,623 Championship runs at an average of 38 per innings, and the following year, in partnership with Albert Henry Hornby against Nottinghamshire at Trent Bridge, he engaged in opening stands in each innings of 141 and 196.

In 1913 he took the best bowling figures of his career, 4 for 33 against Warwickshire at Old Trafford and carried his bat for the first time, scoring 39 out of 88 against Kent at Maidstone. He also scored over a 1,000 Championship runs in the 1921 season.

World War One interrupted his sporting career, but immediately afterwards he carried his bat making 71 out of 185 against Cambridge University at Fenners, and once again notched up over 1,000 runs for the season.

Eventually, he received a long awaited Test call-up, when he was selected for the tour to Australia under Johnny Douglas's team in 1920–21. The tour proved to be a disaster for England for they lost all five Tests. Makepeace, however, did reasonably well, scoring 279 runs at 34.87, which included a maiden Test century (117) at Melbourne in the fourth Test. In doing so he created a record which still stands today, that of being the oldest player (he was 39 years and 173 days) to score a maiden Test hundred.

Harry did not get another call-up, partly because of his age but also because he was now competing for an opening position with Hobbs and Sutcliffe. However, back with Lancashire he continued to churn out the runs and in 1922 he and his opening partner Charlie Hallows shared a partnership of 270 against Worcestershire at Worcester. The county also granted him a benefit match against Surrey, which realised £2,110.

A year later, also against Worcestershire, he scored his highest first-class score (203) and he also notched up a second double hundred, 200 not out against Northamptonshire at Liverpool. He carried his bat yet again for 39 out of 208 against Nottinghamshire at Trent Bridge and scored over 2,000 runs for the season at an average of 50.80.

Three years later the county won the Championship, the first of three successive years. It was Makepeace's best season, scoring 2,340 runs at an average of 48.75, with a highest score of 180 in the last match of the season against Nottinghamshire at Old Trafford out of a total of 454, a match which clinched the Championship for the Red Rose County for the first time since 1904.

One of the cornerstones of Lancashire's success had been the opening partnership of Harry and Charlie Hallows. They were a perfect combination, with the forceful left-handed Hallows complementing the correct and watchful Makepeace.

The last of his centuries came on his 48th birthday, and when he retired in 1930 he had scored 25,207 runs for Lancashire at an average of 36.37, with 42 hundreds and 42 wickets, and 194 catches. Only Cyril Washbrook and John and Ernest Tyldesley have scored more runs for the county.

When he ended his playing days, he was appointed county coach in 1931 and remained in the position for 20 years. When he finally retired at the age of 70 he was made an honorary life member of Lancashire County Cricket Club.

Neil Alan Mallender

RHB & RMF, 1960–96

Born: 13 August 1961, Kirk Sandall, Doncaster.
Played for: Northamptonshire, Otago and Somerset.
Test Matches: (2) 1992 Cap No. 556

Batting Career for England

I	NO	HS	Runs
3	0	8	2.66
AV	**100**	**50**	**Catches**
2.66	-	-	0

Bowling for England

Balls	Runs	Wkts	Av
449	215	10	21.50
Best	**5wl**	**10wl**	**Sr/Rate**
5–50	1	-	44.90

First-Class Career: (345 Matches) 1980–96

Batting

I	NO	HS	Runs
396	122	100*	4,709
AV	**100**	**50**	**Catches**
17.18	1	10	111

Bowling

Balls	Runs	Wkts	Av
53,215	24,654	937	26.31
Best	**5wl**	**10wl**	**Sr/Rate**
7–27	36	5	56.70

Neil Mallender is one of a number of northern-born cricketers who began their cricket career with Northamptonshire, having slipped through the Yorkshire net. A right-arm fast-medium bowler, who was always at his best when running in and pitching the ball up, he improved as his career progressed. He was only 19 years of age when he arrived at the County Ground in 1980, having caught the eye on a tour of the West Indies with England's young cricketers, and made an immediate impression, mostly with the bat. A year later, however, he topped the county's bowling averages and claimed 3 for 35 from 10 overs in the Natwest Trophy Final against Derbyshire. Earlier in the season he had taken 5 for 34 against Middlesex in the John Player Sunday League. In August he took his best Championship figures of the season, 6 for 37 off 23 overs against his native Yorkshire at Wellingborough, despite Northamptonshire losing by six wickets.

In 1982 Mallender produced several fine performances, the best of them against Derbyshire as he took a best of 7 for 41 at Wantage Road. Two years later he took 7 for 37 against Worcestershire in the second round of the Natwest Trophy.

In the winter of 1983 he journeyed to New Zealand to play club cricket for Kaikoria and for Otago in the State competition. Indeed, he spent many winters there (from 1983–84 to 1992–93) playing for Otago, so much so that he became something of a local. He captained the state for two years (1990–91 and 1991–92) and his swing and seam bowling was ideal for New Zealand conditions, which meant he generally featured near the top of the bowling averages in every season that he played. Indeed, his best first-class figures were in January 1985 when he took 7 for 27 against Auckland at Eden Park. He also scored his only first-class century, 100 not out against Central Districts in the 1991–92 competition, when he played purely as a batsman, and he was awarded the rare honour of a testimonial, not ususally given to overseas players.

He twice came close to selection for England in 1983–84 and 1991–92 when he narrowly missed out as England searched for replacements to their injury-hit squad.

Mallender won his county cap for Northamptonshire in 1984 but left the county at the end of the 1986 season to join Somerset. His decision not to seek a new deal with Northamptonshire at the end of 1986 was partly due to the lifeless pitches at Wantage Road.

In 1992, at the age of 30, he was called upon by England to play against Pakistan on a seaming Headingley pitch – it was a selection based on 'horses for courses'. It certainly paid off, for he took 5 for 50 and 8 for 123 in the match, helping to win the game for England by six wickets and thereby ensuring his selection for the final Test of the series. Unfortunately, he found conditions much harder at the Oval where he took 2 for 93 off nearly 29 overs, and as a result he was overlooked for the tour to India and Sri Lanka and was never selected again.

Meanwhile he produced some consistent spells with Somerset, taking 46 wickets in his first season, with the only hat-trick of his career against the Combined Universities at Taunton in the Benson and Hedges Cup. He earned a richly deserved benefit in 1994, but then left to return to Northamptonshire after playing 118 games for Somerset, taking 329 wickets at 25.78, with a best of 7 for 61, and scoring 1,461 runs at 17.81, with a top score of 87 not out.

Unfortunately, his return to Wantage Road was plagued by injuries, which restricted him to Just 10 appearances in two seasons and his contract was not renewed.

In his two spells for Northamptonshire he took 326 wickets at 31.90 and scored 1,367 runs at 12.77.

He remained in the game and was appointed to the umpires list in 1999, officiating in 22 one-day internationals between 2000 and 2003 and in three Test matches in 2003–04. He was elected a member of the Elite Panel in February 2004.

Arthur Mitchell

RHB & OB, 1922–45

Born: 13 September 1902, Baildon Green.
Died: 25 December 1976, Bradford.
Played for: Yorkshire.
Test Matches: (6) 1933–36 Cap No. 271
Batting Career for England

I	NO	HS	Runs
10	0	72	298
AV	**100**	**50**	**Catches**
29.80	-	2	9

Bowling for England

Balls	Runs	Wkts	Av
6	4	0	-
Best	**5wl**	**10wl**	**Sr/Rate**
-	-	-	-

First-Class Career: (426 Matches) 1922–45
Batting

I	NO	HS	Runs
593	72	189	19,523
AV	**100**	**50**	**Catches**
37.47	44	98	438

Bowling

Balls	Runs	Wkts	Av
523	327	7	46.71
Best	**5wl**	**10wl**	**Sr/Rate**
3–49	-	-	74.71

A native of Baildon Green, Bradford, Arthur 'Ticker' Mitchell earned his nickname from his constant chattering when play was in process. In his early career he played for several Bradford area clubs, among them Bailden Green, Tong Park and Saltaire, before joining Yorkshire, making his debut in 1922 against Glamorgan at Headingley at the age of 19 and scoring 29 out of a stand of 69 with Edgar Oldroyd.

A solid top-order batsman, with a tight defensive technique, he occasionally carried caution to the extreme and was not the most attractive batsman to watch. However, when it was needed he could play powerful driving shots and could force shots off his legs. As a fielder he was only average when he first joined the county, but he improved so much that he became one of the best close-to-the-wicket fieldsmen in the country, either at short leg, gulley or in the slips.

He found it difficult at first to break into the strong Yorkshire batting line up, but in 1928 he registered 1,320 first-class runs at 50.38 and was also awarded his county cap. Ironically, his highest first-class score for the county had come two years earlier when he hit 189 against Northamptonshire at Northampton.

In 1930 he was seventh in the national averages, scoring 1,633 runs with a top score of 176 against Nottinghamshire, including five centuries. Upon Percy Holmes's retirement he was promoted to open the batting, and in the 1933 season he topped the batting averages with 2,300 runs at 58.97, which included four successive centuries, with a highest score of 158 against the MCC in a purple patch of 508 runs from 30 August to 7 September.

In the winter of 1933–34 he was selected for the tour of India under Douglas Jardine, and although he scored 47 at Calcutta in the second Test, 114 runs at 22.80 was a poor return by his standards.

The following summers of 1934 and 1935 saw him register 1,854 and 1,530 runs respectively, and in the latter he was chosen to play in the third Test at Headingley as a last minute replacement for his Yorkshire colleague Morris Leyland who had lumbago. He scored 58 in the first innings and followed this with an innings of 72, which proved to be his highest score in Test cricket, opening the batting with Derbyshire's Denis Smith. He played in the following Test at the Oval, scoring 40 in his only innings in the match, and played his last Test match 12 months later against India at Lord's.

The winter of 1935 saw Yorkshire tour Jamaica under Paul Gibb's leadership and Mitchell not only topped the batting averages but also the bowling averages, taking a career best of 3 for 49 against Jamaica at Sabina Park, Kingston. He continued to score runs consistently for Yorkshire during the 1930s and was a vital member of a team which won seven Championship titles during this period. For the county he passed the 1,000 runs per season mark on 10 occasions and in 401 first-class games he scored 18,189 runs at 37.81, which included 39 centuries. He also took five wickets at 58.20 and held 406 catches.

On his retirement in 1945 he became a professional with Bowling Old Lane, and also played for Hunslet and Undercliffe in the early 1950s. However, it was as the first full-time county coach that he made a further contribution to Yorkshire cricket. For over 25 years the well-respected Mitchell, along with Morris Leyland, developed the future cricketers of the county. He did not suffer fools gladly, was often blunt with his comments and left none of the young players under his command in any doubt as to what he expected of them. He eventually passed over the reins to Doug Padgett, and sadly he died on Christmas Day in Bradford at the age of 74.

Frank Mitchell

RHB & RFM, 1894–1912

Born: 13 August 1872, Market Weighton.
Died: 11 October 1935, Blackheath, Kent.
Played for: Cambridge University, Yorkshire,
London County, Transvaal and
South Africa.
Test Matches: (5) 1898–99 Cap No. 115 (2
Tests for England, 3 for SA)
Batting Career for England and South Africa

I	NO	HS	Runs
10	0	41	116
AV	**100**	**50**	**Ct/St**
11.60	-	-	2

First-Class Career: (198 Matches) 1894–1912
Batting

I	NO	HS	Runs
304	19	194	9,117
AV	**100**	**50**	**Ct/St**
31.98	17	38	146/2

Bowling

Balls	Runs	Wkts	Av
1,596	828	35	23.65
Best	**5wl**	**10wl**	**Sr/Rate**
5–57	1	-	45.60

Frank Mitchell, born at Market Weighton, was one of the finest all-round sportsmen in the early years of the 20th century. A hard-hitting, aggressive batsman, he was well known for his attacking off-side strokes, and he scored at a fast rate whenever possible. He was also a more than useful right-arm medium-pace bowler.

He was educated initially at St Peter's School in York and he captained the school team for two years before moving to Brighton, where he took employment as a schoolmaster for another two years. In 1894 he went to Caius College, Cambridge, where he made his first-class debut against C.I. Thornton's XI at Fenners. In the same season he came to the attention of Yorkshire captain Lord Hawke when he scored 75 and 92 against Yorkshire and captured his best bowling figures in first-class cricket with 5 for 57 against Surrey at the Oval. He also made his Yorkshire debut against Nottinghamshire at Trent Bridge.

Twelve months later, after touring North America, he returned to captain Cambridge, and he caused huge controversy in the Varsity match against Oxford in 1896 when he instructed one of his bowlers, E.B. Shine, to give extra runs so that Oxford would not be required to follow-on. There was uproar at Lord's, with booing and demonstrations in the crowd, but the action rebounded on Mitchell as Oxford eventually won the match by four wickets. Needless to say, the following-on bar was raised to 150 runs three years later.

At Cambridge he not only won Blues for cricket, but also for rugby and shot put. He captained the university's rugby team, and later he played for Blackheath and won six caps for England at rugby in 1895 and 1896 as a forward, in addition to keeping goal for Sussex at football.

After leaving Cambridge in 1897 he was selected to tour South Africa with Lord Hawke's team in the winter of 1898–99, and he made his Test debut at Johannesburg with a score of 24 and 1. In the second Test at Cape Town he scored 18 and 41 in the second innings, which proved to be his highest Test score.

On his return he played the season of 1899 for Yorkshire, scoring 1,678 runs, which included three centuries, the first of which was against Gloucestershire when he hit a hundred in only 130 minutes. He followed this with 194 against Leicestershire at Grace Road, his highest score in first-class cricket, and 121 against Middlesex in a four-hour innings.

Mitchell then returned to South Africa with the Yorkshire Dragoons, with whom he fought in the Second Boer War, a conflict which saw him miss the entire 1900 county cricket season.

In 1901 he was back playing for Yorkshire and had an outstanding season, finishing top of the batting averages with 1,801 runs at 46.17, which included seven centuries. It also saw a magnificent run of form with consecutive scores of 100, 100, 4 not out, 106, 12, 162 and 52. During the run his 162 was his highest score of the season and was made against Warwickshire at Edgbaston. He repeated the act against the Midlands county with 116 at Bradford. In the same year he also appeared for the London County.

His time in South Africa fostered a love of the country and he returned there in 1902 to act as Sir Abe Bailey's secretary, while also playing cricket for Transvaal. He did, however, return to England in 1904 as captain of a South African touring team and while in the country he played his last games for Yorkshire, in one of which he scored 63 against Oxford University in the Parks.

In 1912 he again captained the South African team to England, this time for the triangular tournament with Australia. He played once against England and twice against Australia, and the first Test at Old Trafford was his first Test match for 13 years and 53 days. He thus has the unique distinction of being the only Test cricketer to have played for two countries against three other countries, for England against South Africa and for South Africa against England and Australia.

In World War One he returned to active duty, rose to the rank of Lieutenant Colonel in the West Riding Regiment and was mentioned in despatches. He later followed a career as a sports journalist and wrote the *Badminton Book on Rugby Football* and several books on cricket and military affairs. He died at the age of 63 in Blackheath, Kent.

Martyn Douglas Moxon

RHB & RM, 1981–97

Born: 4 May 1960, Stairfoot, Barnsley.
Played for: Yorkshire and Griqualand West.
Test Matches: (10) 1986–89 Cap No. 520
Batting Career for England

I	NO	HS	Runs
17	1	99	455
AV	**100**	**50**	**Ct/St**
28.43	-	3	10

Bowling for England

Balls	Runs	Wkts	Av
48	30	0	-
Best	**5wl**	**10wl**	**Sr/Rate**
-	-	-	-

First-Class Career: (317 Matches) 1981–97
Batting

I	NO	HS	Runs
541	47	274*	21,161
AV	**100**	**50**	**Catches**
42.83	45	116	218

Bowling

Balls	Runs	Wkts	Av
2,650	1,481	28	52.89
Best	**5wl**	**10wl**	**Sr/Rate**
3–24	-	-	94.60

Martyn Moxon was another product of the Barnsley and Yorkshire Boys system and was also ably coached by his father Derek. He played cricket with Monk Bretton, Barnsley and Bowling Old Lane in the Bradford League.

Although he held the bat high in his stance, he was a classical driver of the ball and was technically correct when playing off the front or back foot. He also had the key elements required of an opening batsman, patience and concentration. He was also a part-time medium-pace bowler and an excellent fielder, either at slip or in the front of the wicket. He made a sensational start to his Yorkshire career, scoring 116 on his debut against Essex at Headingley, and he followed this with 111 against Derbyshire in the next match at Abbeydale Park, Sheffield, thus becoming the first Yorkshire batsman to score centuries in his first two Championship matches.

Labelled the new Geoff Boycott, it was an unfair tag for the quiet and unassuming young batsman and it was not surprising that his form dipped a little in the next two years. In his early career he

did, in fact, open the batting with Boycott; however when Boycott was removed from the Yorkshire scene he established a much longer opening partnership with Ashley Metcalf, sharing 21 century partnerships.

In 1983 he scored a superb 153 in his first Roses match at Headingley, and the following season he scored 1,016 first-class runs at 36.28, with two centuries, and was awarded his county cap.

In 1984 he was selected for the Lord's Test against the West Indies, but a cracked rib sustained in the county match at Northampton meant that his Test debut had to be put on hold. Indeed, at various times he suffered from broken fingers, and, unfortunately for him, this mostly occured when he was in good form.

In the winter of 1984–85 he was chosen for the tour of India and Sri Lanka, but the death of his father meant he had to miss the early part of the tour. However, he returned for the one-day internationals, making his debut in the fourth game at Nagpur where he top scored with 70, his highest score in one-day internationals.

He eventually made his Test debut against New Zealand in 1986, making a sound 74, but like many others at the time he found Richard Hadlee a handful. On the tour of New Zealand in the winter of 1987–88 he played two innings of great skill and headed the England averages. At Auckland he scored a superb 99 and was denied a maiden Test century by an umpiring mistake. Early in his innings he had swept spinner John Bracewell for three, but umpire McHarg signalled leg byes, although Bracewell later admitted that Moxon had hit it. In the next Test at Wellington he was 81 not out in England's first innings until rain washed out the remainder of the match. Although he played two Tests against the West Indies in 1988 and was recalled for the Nottingham Test against Australia in 1989, scores of 0 and 18 meant that he was not given another chance.

In the following two summers, Moxon had the best seasons of his career. In 1990 he scored 1,621 runs at 49.12, which included the first of five double hundreds, 218 not out against Sussex at Eastbourne, while a year later he notched up his best aggregate of runs, 1,669 at 46.36, which included three centuries, with a highest of 200 against Essex at Castle Park, Colchester. By then he had taken over the captaincy and he held the role from 1990 to 1995. His last season in charge saw an eighth-place finish in the Championship and was the highest position the team achieved.

In 1993 he had a benefit season which raised £103,000, and he was named as one of *Wisden's* Five Cricketers of the Year. During the following summer he notched up his highest first-class score, 274 not out, against Worcestershire at Worcester, and in 1996, in the opening Championship match of the season, he took part in the highest post-war opening stand for Yorkshire with 362 alongside Michael Vaughan (183) when they played against Glamorgan at Sophia Gardens, Cardiff.

For Yorkshire he scored 18,973 first-class runs at 43.71 with 41 centuries, took 22 wickets at 55.13 and held 190 catches. In one-day cricket he notched up 4,128 runs at 30.58 with three centuries and a highest score of 141 not out against Glamorgan at Cardiff. He also took 21 wickets at 41.33 and took 46 catches.

Upon retiring in 1997 he became Director of Coaching at Yorkshire, before moving on to coach Durham in 2001. He was also chosen to coach the England A team against Bangladesh and New Zealand in the winter of 1999–2000. In March 2007 he resigned from Durham and returned to his native county as the club's Director of professional cricket.

Christopher Middleton Old

RHB & RFM, 1966–85

Born: 22 December 1948, Middlesbrough.
Played for: Yorkshire, Northern Transvaal and Warwickshire.
Test Matches: (46) 1972–81 Cap No. 455

Batting Career for England

I	NO	HS	Runs
66	9	65	845
AV	**100**	**50**	**Catches**
14.82	-	2	22

Bowling for England

Balls	Runs	Wkts	Av
8,858	4,020	143	28.11
Best	**5wl**	**10wl**	**Sr/Rate**
7–50	4	-	61.94

First-Class Career: (379 Matches) 1966–1985

Batting

I	NO	HS	Runs
463	91	116	7,756
AV	**100**	**50**	**Catches**
20.84	6	27	214

Bowling

Balls	Runs	Wkts	Av
57,822	25,127	1,070	23.48
Best	**5wl**	**10wl**	**Sr/Rate**
7–20	39	2	54.03

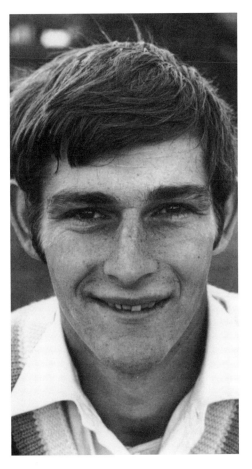

One of five Middlesbrough-born Test players, Chris Old was a natural all-round cricketer, who probably should have achieved more on the highest stage of the game.

A product of Acklam Hall Grammer School, and the younger brother of Warwickshire cricketer and rugby union international Alan Old, he captained Durham Boys and played for England Schools. He made his Yorkshire debut at the age of 17 against Hampshire at Portsmouth in 1966, but it was not until 1969, when he replaced the retired Fred Trueman, that he gained a regular place in the side, in the process becoming the opening bowling partner for Tony Nicholson. It was a season in which he matured quickly with the ball, taking 57 first-class wickets for Yorkshire at 18.61, with a best of 7 for 20 against Gloucestershire in his home town of Middlesbrough and took 11 for 46 in the match. It was also his best bowling performance in first-class cricket and he was awarded his county cap.

Old had an easy, rhythmical action, and he used his 6ft 3in frame to extract pace and bounce from the pitch. As a batsman, it it is probably fair to say that he underachieved. He was a left-hander with a good basic technique and he was a powerful hitter, who favoured the straight boundaries when in form. However, he did have a weakness against short-pitched bowling which restricted his scoring opportunities at the top level. But though he had limitations with the bat, he was still a fine fielder, either at slip or in the outfield.

In 1970 he was selected for two of the unofficial Tests against the Rest of the World, but unfortunately he suffered the first of many knee and back injuries and underwent surgery on his knees in 1970 and 1971.

In the winter of 1972–73 he was selected for the Test series in India and Pakistan where he took 15 wickets at 31.26, and he followed this with 5 for 113 against New Zealand in his first home Test at Lord's in 1973. The following summer in the second Test against India at Lord's he took 4 for 67 and 5 for 21, while in the six Tests that summer against India and Pakistan he took 25 wickets at 22.92. In total he took 72 wickets at 18.97, his best season with the ball, and in addition he scored his first century for Yorkshire, 116 against India at Bradford, his highest first-class score.

Despite the problems with his knees and back, he continued to bowl long spells for England, particularly overseas. In the centenary Test in Australia in 1977 he took 7 for 143 in 53 overs in the match, and in the winter tour of New Zealand he bowled 30 eight-bowl overs in the first innings, taking 6 for 54. In the summer of 1978 he took his best figures in Test cricket, 7 for 50 against Pakistan on the opening day of the first Test at Edgbaston, taking four wickets in five balls.

While his highest score in Test cricket was his 65 at the Oval in 1974, his 29 runs in a partnership of 67 with Ian Botham at Headingley in 'Botham's Test' of 1981 was more significant.

For Yorkshire he continued to score runs and take wickets, and in the summer of 1976 he took 7 for 42 against the West Indies at Sheffield and he scored 112 against Northamptonshire at Wantage Road. A year later, against Warwickshire at Edgbaston, he blasted the first 100 out of his final score of 107 in just 37 minutes. However, the game which probably gave him the most satisfaction was the Roses match at Old Trafford in 1978 in which he scored 100 not out, sharing a partnership of 105 with Howard Cooper for the ninth wicket, and took 9 for 85 (4 for 38 and 5 for 47) in a Yorkshire victory by 10 wickets.

In the winters of 1981–82 and 1982–83 he played for Northern Transvaal in South Africa, but in 1983 he was replaced as captain of Yorkshire by Ray Illingworth (he was appointed in 1981) and he departed the county to join Warwickshire.

For Yorkshire he scored 4.785 runs at 23.22 in 222 matches, took 647 wickets at 20.72, with 24 five-wicket hauls, and took 131 catches. In one-day cricket his 192 wickets for Yorkshire was then a county record.

He spent two years at Edgbaston, played 47 matches and scored 911 runs at 21.18 with a best of 70 against Worcestershire at Edgbaston in 1984, and he took 120 wickets at 29.96, with a best of 6 for 46 against Yorkshire at Headingley in the same year. He then moved to play for Northumberland in the Minor Counties League in seasons 1986 and 1987.

On retirement he moved to Cornwall and opened a fish and chip restaurant in Praa Sands and also tutored coaching courses in Falmouth.

Douglas Vernon Padgett

RHB & RM, 1951–71

Born: 20 July 1934, Dick Hill, Bradford.
Played for: Yorkshire.
Test Matches: (2) 1960 Cap No. 401
Batting Career for England

I	NO	HS	Runs
4	0	31	51
AV	**100**	**50**	**Catches**
12.75	-	-	-

Bowling for England

Balls	Runs	Wkts	Av
12	8	-	-
Best	**5wl**	**10wl**	**Sr/Rate**
-	-	-	-

First-Class Career: (506 Matches) 1951–71
Batting

I	NO	HS	Runs
806	67	161*	21,124
AV	**100**	**50**	**Catches**
28.58	32	97	261

Bowling

Balls	Runs	Wkts	Av
586	216	6	36.0
Best	**5wl**	**10wl**	**Sr/Rate**
1–2	-	-	97.66

Bradford-born Douglas Padgett played for Bradford League club Idle at the age of only 13 in 1947. A true sportsman, he went on to captain Bradford Boys at cricket and football, while he also played cricket for Yorkshire Boys, North of England Boys and the Yorkshire Federation.

After making his debut for the second XI in 1950, he made his first-class debut a year later against Somerset at Taunton, scoring 25 not out in a Yorkshire victory by an innings and three runs. At the time he was Yorkshire's youngest ever first-class cricketer at 16 years and 321 days, a record he held for 30 years until it was beaten by Paul Jarvis (16 years and 75 days) in 1981.

After his national service had ended he was one of a new generation of Yorkshire batsmen in the early 1950s, alongside Brian Close, Brian Stott and Ken Taylor. Padgett was a stylish and technically correct batsman with a sound defence, ideal for the number three position which he occupied for most of his career. His execution of the late cut was as good as any of his contemporaries and was a joy to watch. He established himself in the team in 1955 when he scored 571 first-class runs at 27.10, scoring his first century for the county with 115 against Warwickshire at Edgbaston, when he shared a second-wicket partnership of 228 with Vic Wilson (132 not out).

A year later he passed 1,000 runs in a season for the first time, scoring 1.046 at 27.52, which included 107 against Scotland, but it was not until 1959 that he finally achieved fame for the county. In all matches he notched up 2,158 runs at 41.50, his best aggregate of runs for a season, which included four centuries and his highest first-class score of 161 not out against Oxford University in the Parks. However, he left his most famous innings until the last Championship match of the season, playing against Sussex at Hove. Yorkshire needed to score 215 runs in only 105 minutes if they were to win the County Championship title for the first time in 10 years. Padgett, along with Brian Stott, plundered the Sussex attack to the tune of 141 runs in just over an hour and Yorkshire reached their target with only minutes to spare; Padgett made a sublime 79 and Stott 96.

The following season he was rewarded with selection for the fourth Test against South Africa at Old Trafford, but he made only 5 and 2 in his two innings. Retained for the next Test, he did slightly better scoring 47 runs in the match with a top score of 31. He was selected for the MCC tour to New Zealand in the winter of 1960–61 and batted well enough, but he was not selected for a representative match and was not involved on the international scene again.

However, he remained a valued member of a Yorkshire team that won six further Championship titles, scoring over 1,000 runs in a season on 12 occasions – every year from 1959 to 1970, with the exception of 1963. For Yorkshire he scored 20,306 first-class runs at 28.85, with 29 centuries, took six wickets at 34.66 and took 250 catches.

After he retired from first-team cricket he captained the Yorkshire Second XI and also played League cricket for Bowling Old Lane in the Bradford League and Marske in North Yorkshire, for whom he scored over 1,000 runs in 1973.

He was appointed chief coach of Yorkshire at the end of the 1971 season, a position he fulfilled until the 1999 season, and it was Padgett who recommended the county sign a young Michael Vaughan.

Edmund Peate

LHB & SLA, 1879–87

Born: 2 March 1855, Holbeck, Leeds.
Died: 11 March 1900, Newlay, Horsforth, Leeds.
Played for: Yorkshire.
Test Matches: (9) 1881–86 Cap No. 32

Batting Career for England

I	NO	HS	Runs
14	8	13	70
AV	**100**	**50**	**Catches**
11.66	-	-	2

Bowling for England

Balls	Runs	Wkts	Av
2,096	682	31	22.00
Best	**5wl**	**10wl**	**Sr/Rate**
6–85	2	-	67.61

First-Class Career: (209 Matches) 1879–87

Batting

I	NO	HS	Runs
312	88	95	2,384
AV	**100**	**50**	**Catches**
10.64	-	3	132

Bowling

Balls	Runs	Wkts	Av
45,916	14,515	1,076	13.48
Best	**5wl**	**10wl**	**Sr/Rate**
8–5	94	27	42.67

Edmund 'Ted' Peate, although born in Holbeck, Leeds, moved to Yeadon and started as a fast bowler with the Treloar's cricket clowns, before moving to Batley and Carlisle (Cumberland). He then turned professional at Manningham in Bradford, where he changed to bowling slow left-arm.

In 1879 he took 17 wickets for 33 runs and scored 25 not out in his first match for the Yorkshire Colts, before making his first-class debut for the county against Nottinghamshire at Trent Bridge, taking 2 for 31 in 39 overs. Shortly afterwards, in his third game for Yorkshire, he captured 12 for 77 against Kent at Bramall Lane (6 for 39 and 6 for 38) and finished the season with 75 wickets at 12 runs per wicket. The following year he repeated the feat, this time at Mote Park, Maidstone, taking 12 for 108 (5 for 47 and 7 for 61), while in the Roses match at Old Trafford he captured a further 14 wickets. At the end of his second season he had taken 131 wickets at 11.55 and was easily Yorkshire's best bowler.

Peate was the first in a line of five great slow left-arm bowlers for Yorkshire (he was followed by Peel, Rhodes, Verity and Wardle), and although he was not a prodigious spinner of the ball he maintained an immaculate line and length, with variations in flight and pace, and he could be deadly when the pitch offered him grip. Lord Hawke wrote that 'he had the most perfect action of any man I have seen deliver a ball'. Indeed, many of his contemporaries maintained he was superior to both Bobby Peel and Wilfred Rhodes, while his career average of 12.57 runs per wicket is the lowest of any Yorkshire bowler to have taken in excess of 500 wickets.

In the summer of 1881 he was again Yorkshire's outstanding bowler, taking 133 wickets at 12.26, which included 28 wickets in two games, 14 for 77 (6 for 47 and 8 for 30) against Surrey at Fartown, Huddersfield, and 14 for 130 (6 for 61 and 8 for 69) against Sussex at Hove. These were performances which earned him a trip to Australia for the first and only time under the captaincy of Alfred Shaw. Along with his Yorkshire colleague Willie Bates he was England's most successful bowler on tour, with both men taking 30 First-Class wickets and Peate snaring 11 in the Tests. He made his Test debut at the MCG in the first Test but took his best figures in the third Test at Sydney, with a return of 8 for 58 after capturing 5 for 43 in the Australian first innings.

On his return to England in the season of 1882 he had his most outstanding aggregate of wickets with 165 for Yorkshire at 11.13 and 214 first-class wickets for only 11.52 each. Among his career highlights were his performances at Bramall Lane where he took 7 for 31 against the Australians and 12 for 95 (4 for 63 and 8 for 32) against Middlesex. He also played in the only Test against Australia at the Oval, when with only eight runs needed to win he took a heave at a ball from Harry Boyle and was bowled, thereby losing England the match and giving Australia their first victory in this country. Naturally, he was cast as the villain and, despite taking a creditable 8 for 71 in the match, his overall performance was something he had to live with for the rest of his life. At the other crease was Charles Studd, who was playing in his first Test, and Peate's excuse for the shot he played was, 'I couldn't trust Mr Studd with the bowling' – one of the most famous quotes in cricket history.

During that season he also took a hat-trick against Kent at Sheffield, and in the following season he recorded his best first-class bowling figures of 8 for 5 against Surrey at Holbeck, Leeds. In 1884 he took a second hat-trick against Gloucestershire at Moreton-in-the-Marsh and recorded his highest score in first-class cricket, 95 against Surrey at Dewsbury. He also played in four further Tests against Australia, gaining his best figures in Test cricket, 6 for 85 in the second Test at Lord's. His last appearance was at Old Trafford in 1886.

However, over the next few years he started to drink heavily, his weight increased and his general health deteriorated, and after taking only 39 wickets in 1887 Yorkshire dispensed with his services. Lord Hawke said that it was one of his saddest tasks, but records suggest that Peate bore no ill feeling towards Hawke and both men communicated with each other afterwards.

For Yorkshire he played 154 matches in his nine seasons with the county, scored 1,793 runs at 10.86, held 97 catches, but more importantly he took 794 wickets at an amazing 12.57 runs per wicket.

He later played League cricket for Skipton, but within three years he had died from pneumonia, at the age of only 45.

Robert Peel

LHB & SLA, 1882–99

Born: 12 February 1857, Churwell.
Died: 12 August 1941, Morley.
Played for: Yorkshire.
Test Matches: (20) 1884–96 Cap No. 50

Batting Career for England

I	NO	HS	Runs
33	4	83	427
AV	100	50	Catches
14.72	-	3	17

Bowling for England

Balls	Runs	Wkts	Av
5,216	1,715	101	16.98
Best	5wl	10wl	Sr/Rate
7–31	5	1	51.64

First-Class Career: (433 Matches) 1882–99

Batting

I	NO	HS	Runs
689	66	210*	12,191
AV	100	50	Catches
19.44	7	48	214

Bowling

Balls	Runs	Wkts	Av
87,711	28,442	1,775	16.20
Best	5wl	10wl	Sr/Rate
9–22	123	33	49.41

Born at Churwell, near Leeds, Bobby Peel first played for the county in 1882 and made his debut against Surrey at Bramall Lane, taking 9 for 129 in 92 overs. As Ted Peate was the main left-arm slow bowler at the time, Peel kept his place in the team due to his aggressive batting and his brilliant fielding in the cover area. He succeeded Peate in 1888, and in his career he went on to take 1,775 wickets at 16.20, which included 123 five-wicket hauls. In 1889 he was named as one of *Wisden's* cricketers of the year.

He was a master of line and length, and, according to A.C. MacLaren, the Lancashire and England captain, he was the best bowler at exploiting a batsman's weakness. MacLaren also added that it was his wonderful judgement, his cleverness and natural ability that in his opinion made Peel the best left-arm spinner of his era. It was some tribute, coming from a man who had under his leadership at Old Trafford the great Johnny Briggs. Peel also had a quicker, medium-paced ball in his locker and on a helpful wicket he was virtually unplayable. His batting was useful, with seven first-class hundreds to his name and a best of 210 not out for Yorkshire against Warwickshire at Edgbaston in 1896 in a partnership of 292 with Lord Hawke (166). In the same year he achieved the 'double', scoring 1,206 runs at 30.15 and taking 128 wickets at 17.50.

After only two years in the Yorkshire team he was selected for the tour to Australia in the winter of 1884–85, and in the first Test at Adelaide he took 3 for 68 and 5 for 51 as England strolled to an eight-wicket win. In the solitary Test of 1888 at Sydney he and George Lohmann bowled Australia out for 42 and 82, with Peel taking 5 for 18 and 5 for 40 on a sticky wicket. On Australia's fifth visit to England in the summer of that year he tormented them even further, taking 4 for 36 and 4 for 14 at Lord's, while at Manchester, in the deciding Test of the series, he destroyed them with 7 for 31 and 4 for 37. In the three-match series he snared 24 wickets at a staggering average of 7.54. In all he toured Australia on four seperate occasions, his other two tours being 1891–92, where he hit his highest Test score of 83 in the third Test at Adelaide, and 1894–95, where he was responsible for England's dramatic victory at Sydney. With Australia chasing only a further 64 to win on the last day and with everything seemingly lost, a few of the England team, including Bobby Peel, drank heavily to drown their sorrows. However, upon waking up in the morning and seeing that it had rained substantially overnight Peel quickly became sober and demanded the ball from captain Andrew Stoddart, with the now famous words, 'Give me the ball, Mr Stoddart and I'll get t'boogers out before loonch!' Get them out he did, taking 6 for 67, and he was ably assisted by Lancashire's Johnny Briggs with 3 for 35. Together they saw England home by 10 runs, two minutes before lunch.

In his final Test at the Oval, in 1896, his second innings figures of 6 for 23 saw the Aussies routed for only 44, and victory went to England by 66 runs. In only 20 Test matches he took 105 wickets, at a average of only 16.81 runs per wicket, making him one of the most successful bowlers ever in Ashes contests.

For Yorkshire his best return was 9 for 22 against Somerset in 1895, the year of his highest aggregate, 155 wickets at 14.92.

Unfortunately, in 1897 his career came to an abrupt end. After taking 8 for 53 against Kent at Halifax, a few weeks later, in the match against Middlesex at Bramall Lane, he appeared on the pitch the worse for drink. George Hirst had put him back to bed in their hotel room before he had left for the match and told Yorkshire's skipper Lord Hawke that Peel was unwell and had stayed in the hotel. However, Peel made his way to the ground and appeared on the field, refusing to leave. After he was escorted off the field by Lord Hawke, he never played for the White Rose County again. The irony of it was that on the same ground where he had made such a great start to his Yorkshire career, he was to leave it in disgrace. In the following years Peel and Hawke made up, and he never lost contact with his native county, assisting George Hirst in the early 1920s with coaching.

For Yorkshire he played 318 matches, took 1,311 wickets at 15.74, with 100 five-wicket hauls, scored 9,322 runs at 19.91, with six centuries, and held 141 catches.

He continued playing, returning to his roots as a professional with Churwell and appeared for an England XI against Joe Darling's Australians at Truro, two years after the Bramall Lane incident, tormenting the Aussies for the last time by taking five wickets. He later played for Accrington in the Lancashire League, and also for Morley.

On his retirement from cricket he kept the Commercial Hotel in Churwell, and lived to the ripe old age of 84.

Liam Edward Plunkett

RHB & RFM, 2003–to date

Born: 6 April 1985, Middlesbrough.
Played for: Durham.
Test Matches: (9) 2005–to date Cap No. 628

Batting Career for England

I	NO	HS	Runs
13	2	44*	126
AV	**100**	**50**	**Catches**
11.45	-	-	3

Bowling for England

Balls	Runs	Wkts	Av
1,538	916	23	39.82
Best	**5wl**	**10wl**	**Sr/Rate**
3–17	-	-	66.86

First-Class Career: (68 Matches) 2003–to date
Batting

I	NO	HS	Runs
102	21	74*	1,591
AV	**100**	**50**	**Catches**
19.64	-	6	37

Bowling

Balls	Runs	Wkts	Av
10,432	6,423	202	31.79
Best	**5wl**	**10wl**	**Sr/Rate**
6–74	5	-	51.60

Although born in Middlesbrough, Liam Plunkett joined Durham Academy. Such was his progress that he played junior international cricket with the England Under-19 team on the tour to Australia in 2002–03 and at the Under-19 World Cup in Bangladesh in 2003–04. He graduated to the Durham first XI and made his County Championship debut against Yorkshire at the end of May 2003, taking 5 for 53 in the first innings and 2 for 21 in the second, thereby steering Durham to a 167 run victory. He played seven games in his debut season, taking 19 wickets at 35.36, deputising mainly for Steve Harmison and the injured Mark Davies.

The following summer he continued to improve and took a career best to date, 6 for 74 against Hampshire at Chester-Le-Street, and in 2005 he was Durham's leading wicket-taker, with 51 wickets at 30.84 and a best of 5 for 34.

A right-arm, fast-medium bowler, Plunkett extracted plenty of bounce from firm wickets, and his batting was also improving as he scored a career best (so far) of 74 not out against Somerset at Stockton in 2005.

In the winter of 2005 he was selected for the England one-day international and Test squads touring Pakistan in November and December. Due to an ankle injury to Simon Jones he made his Test debut at Lahore, taking 2 for 125 in an innings defeat for England. In December of 2005 he came on as a super-sub in his first ODI against Pakistan, replacing the injured Kevin Pietersen. As it was he finished as England's best bowler by taking 3 for 31, and was involved in the run out of Shoaib Akhtar. England went on to win the match by 42 runs.

In the second ODI, a few days later, England had collapsed to 138 for 8, but Plunkett notched up his first international half-century (56) and played with Vikram Solanki in a record ninth-wicket 100 partnership.

He was then included in the tour to India in 2006 and played in the second Test at Mohali, replacing Ian Blackwell in the team. Unfortunately, he was not impressive, taking only one wicket and scoring just one run in his two innings, and he was replaced by James Anderson for the following Test. However, he was still only 20 years of age and was considered by most to be a bowler of the future.

When Sri Lanka toured England in 2006, injuries to Steve Harmison, James Anderson and Simon Jones gave him the opportunity of another Test start. In the second Test at Edgbaston he took 3 for 17, his best figures to date, which included a double-wicket maiden in his first over of the day when he dismissed Michael Vandort and Mahela Jayawardene. He was then selected for England's 2006–07 Ashes series but did not get to play a Test. However, he did get a chance in the one-day games and took 3 for 54 in nine overs against New Zealand in Perth. Plunkett followed this in the next game against Australia in February 2007 at Sydney by taking 3 for 34 off 9.5 overs, which included the wickets of Adam Gilchrist (first ball) and Michael Clarke. Altogether he took 12 wickets in the series, including 3 for 43 in the second Final against Australia as England took home the trophy 2–0.

He was also part of England's World Cup squad that played unsuccessfully in the West Indies, but he did not display the form he had in Australia.

Unfortunately, several injuries slowed his progress, but he took 40 first-class wickets in 2007, while in the winter he played for Nashua Dolphin in South Africa. In 2008 he took 29 wickets and played a part in Durham's first ever Championship title.

Steven John Rhodes

RHB & WK, 1981–2004

Born: 17 June 1964, Bradford.
Played for: Yorkshire and Worcestershire.
Test Matches: (11) 1994–95 Cap No. 566
Batting Career for England

I	NO	HS	Runs
17	5	65*	294
AV	**100**	**50**	**Ct/St**
24.50	-	1	46/3

First-Class Career: (440 Matches) 1981–2004
Batting

I	NO	HS	Runs
618	166	124	14,839
AV	**100**	**50**	**Ct/St**
32.82	12	72	1139/124

Bowling

Balls	Runs	Wkts	Av
6	30	0	-
Best	**5wl**	**10wl**	**Sr/Rate**
-	-	-	-

Steve Rhodes, born in Bradford, was the son of the former Nottinghamshire wicket-keeper Billy, who played 36 matches for them between 1960 and 1964. The young Rhodes first appeared for Yorkshire in 1981, making his first-class debut against Sri Lanka at Abbeydale Park, Sheffield, and at the age of 17 years and 28 days he was the youngest 'keeper to play for the county. Unfortunately for Rhodes, his opportunities were very much limited due to being understudy to the Yorkshire captain David Bairstow. By the end of 1984 he had played only three first-class games, in which he had registered his highest score of 35 against Somerset at Middlesbrough, and it was no surprise when he asked for his release at the end of the season.

In 1985 he joined Worcestershire and he was arguably one of their best ever signings at New Road. He made his debut on the opening day of the season against Middlesex and played 97 consecutive matches, missing only two in 1989 when he was selected for the England Texaco Squad.

He was awarded his county cap in 1986 and was selected for the England A tour to Sri Lanka that winter. Indeed, he may well have played for the England Test team much earlier than he did as he was selected for the tour to India in 1988–89 which was cancelled for political reasons.

At his best he was a fine attacking batsman, whose driving and square cutting were of the highest order. As a wicket-keeper he was agile and athletic and he was as good an all-rounder 'keeper as any of his contemporaries.

In 1988, against Sussex at Kidderminster, he took nine catches in the match, equalling the Worcestershire record of Hugo Yarnold, who caught five and stumped four against Hampshire in 1949. During the season he notched up his maiden century for Worcestershire against Derbyshire at Derby, scoring 108 in 154 minutes out of a partnership of 192 with captain Phil Neale for the sixth wicket, which included a six and seven fours. Earlier in the season he had shared another sixth-wicket partnership of 265 (a Worcestershire record) off 274 balls with Graham Hick against Somerset at Taunton, which saw Hick's magnificent 405 not out and Rhodes scoring 56.

He also played an important part in the Worcestershire team that won the Sunday League in 1987 and 1988, and the County Championship in 1988 and 1989. In 1988 he took 78 dismissals (70 catches and eight stumpings). Three years later, once again at Kidderminster, he shared a record Worcestershire eight-wicket partnership of 184 against Derbyshire with Stuart Lampitt, as they saved the match for Worcestershire, with Rhodes scoring 90 and Lampitt 93. In the same year he notched up his highest one-day score, 105 against Lancashire at Old Trafford.

In 1994 he scored an impressive century against the touring New Zealanders at New Road and was selected for his first Test against the Kiwis at Trent Bridge, replacing Jack Russell. He had a good first Test and scored 49, with six catches in a resounding England win by an innings and 90 runs. He kept his place for the second half of the summer against the touring South Africans, where in the second Test at Headingley he recorded his highest Test innings of 65 not out. He was also named as one of *Wisden's* Five Cricketers of the Year.

In the winter of 1994–95 he went to Australia as the number-one 'keeper, but only 72 runs in 10 innings in a losing England team meant that his Test days were over.

In the following summer he hit 122 not out against Young Australia at Worcester and scored 1,018 runs, his best-ever season. A year later, in 1996, he was awarded a benefit, while in 1999 he reached the milestone of 1,000 dismissals in first-class cricket.

The season of 2002 saw him share a third record partnership for a wicket, this time the seventh (256 runs scored), with David Leatherdale against Nottinghamshire at Trent Bridge.

Towards the end of the 2004 season he took over as county captain for a brief period when Ben Smith resigned during a match against Northamptonshire.

He retired from playing at the end of the season and was appointed head coach following the departure of Tom Moody. He was then appointed Director of Cricket/First XI Coach for the start of the 2006 season, and still holds the record dismissals for the county (1,263), with 1,139 catches and 124 stumpings.

Wilfred Rhodes

RHB & SLA, 1898–1930

Born: 29 October 1877, Kirkheaton.
Died: 8 July 1973, Branksome Park, Dorset.
Played for: Yorkshire.
Test Matches: (58) 1899–1930 Cap No. 121

Batting Career for England

I	NO	HS	Runs
98	21	179	2,325
AV	**100**	**50**	**Catches**
30.19	2	11	60

Bowling for England

Balls	Runs	Wkts	Av
8,231	3,425	127	26.97
Best	**5wl**	**10wl**	**Sr/Rate**
8–68	6	1	64.81

First-Class Career: (1110 Matches) 1898–1930

Batting

I	NO	HS	Runs
1,534	237	267*	39,969
AV	**100**	**50**	**Catches**
30.82	58	197	765

Bowling

Balls	Runs	Wkts	Av
185,799	70,322	4,204	16.73
Best	**5wl**	**10wl**	**Sr/Rate**
9–24	287	68	44.20

Wilfred Rhodes was a true cricketing legend, not only of Yorkshire but of England, the likes of which will never be seen again. Like his county colleague George Hirst, he too came from the village of Kirkheaton and initially played for Galashiels in Scotland as a professional. When Yorkshire sacked Bobby Peel they had to choose between two left-arm slow bowlers, Wilfred Rhodes and Albert Cordingley from Bradford. For the opening game of the 1898 season both were included in the party to play the opening encounter against the MCC. After net practise, Rhodes was selected and took figures of 6 for 33 in the match. Retained for the next game against Somerset at Bath, he returned a match analysis of 13 for 45 (7 for 24 and 6 for 21) and a star was born. So much so that in his debut season in first-class cricket he took 154 wickets at an average of 14.60, which is still the most wickets in a debut season. This immediately brought him recognition as one of *Wisden's* Five Cricketers of the Year. Not only could he spin the ball prodigiously, but he could also deceive the best batsmen in the country with his flight, length and guile, and was possibly at this time the best slow bowler in the world.

Twelve months later Rhodes played his first game for England against Australia at Nottingham where he took 4 for 58 and 3 for 60 in a drawn Test. He also returned his best figures in cricket, taking 9 for 28 against Essex at Leyton in the Championship and then 9 for 24 for C.I. Thornton's XI against the Australians at Scarborough.

In 1900 he became the first Yorkshire bowler to take over 200 wickets in a season (240 at 12.72), with a best of 8 for 23 against Hampshire at Hull. Incredibly, his tally of wickets included eight wickets in an innings on five occasions and seven wickets on seven occasions. The following summer, Rhodes, still only 23 years of age, repeated the act with 233 wickets at 15.00, with a best of 8 for 53 against Middlesex at Lord's.

In 1902 the Australians visited once again and in a compelling five-match series England won the last Test at the Oval by one wicket, when Rhodes, batting at number 11, joined George Hirst to knock off the 15 runs required to win. In the series he took 22 wickets at 15.27, including 7 for 17 in the first Test at Birmingham, (still a Test record at Edgbaston) and 5 for 63 in the only Test played at Bramall Lane in Sheffield.

He continued to take wickets in abundance for Yorkshire, with 174 in 1902 and 169 in 1903, and was selected for the tour to Australia in the winter of 1903–04, where they retained the Ashes by three Tests to two. In the series Rhodes took 33 wickets at 17.69 (still a best average for an England bowler taking in excess of 30 wickets in a series in Australia). In the first Test at Sydney he shared in a record 10th-wicket partnership of 130 with R.E. Foster in England's first innings, Rhodes contributing 40 not out, and in the second Test at Melbourne he took 7 for 56 in the first innings and then a Test best of 8 for 68 in the second. His match figures of 15 for 124 still remain a record for a Melbourne Test.

The following summer Rhodes's batting had improved so much that he registered his first 1,000 runs in a season for Yorkshire (1,251), a feat he was to accomplish on 17 occasions for his county and 20 times in all. Not a player renowned for his style, he had a good technique but reportedly only two or three strokes; although they were enough for him to score nearly 40,000 first-class runs and 58 centuries. His best season with the bat was 1911 when he scored 2,261 runs at 38.32, while his highest score was 267 not out against Leicestershire at Headingley. He also scored 201 against Somerset at Taunton in 1905 and carried his bat through the innings on two occasions for Yorkshire (98 not out of a total of 184 against MCC at Lord's in 1903, and 85 not out from a total of 152 against Essex at Leyton in 1910).

For England his highest score was 179 at Melbourne in 1911–12, when he and Jack Hobbs put together a first wicket stand of 323, which remains England's record first-wicket partnership against Australia. In the first Test at Sydney in December 1911 he became the only batsman in Test history to bat in all positions from number one to 11, a unique record unlikely to be equalled.

His bowling took a backward step until after World War One, but he remained good enough to help bowl out Australia at the Oval in 1926, taking 6 for 79. He played his last Test at Kingston, Jamaica, in April 1930 at the age of 52 years and 165 days, which meant his Test career lasted a total of 31 years and 315 days.

He is the only man to have taken in excess of 4,000 first-class wickets (4.204), made the highest number of first-class appearances (1,110) and Championship appearances (763), taken 100 wickets a record 23 times, achieved 16 doubles, and the first to score 2,000 runs and take 100 wickets in Test cricket.

For Yorkshire he played 883 matches, scored 31,075 runs, with 46 centuries, took 3,598 wickets at 16.01, with 252 five-wicket hauls, and held 586 catches.

Fittingly, Rhodes took a wicket with his first ball in first-class cricket and will surely go down in history as one of the greatest all-round cricketers that the game has ever known.

Derek Shackleton

RHB & RMF, 1948–69

Born: 12 August 1924, Todmorden.

Died: 27 September 2007, Canford Magna, Dorset.

Played for: Hampshire.

Test Matches: (7) 1950–63 Cap No. 350

Batting Career for England

I	NO	HS	Runs
13	7	42	113
AV	**100**	**50**	**Catches**
18.83	-	-	1

Bowling for England

Balls	Runs	Wkts	Av
2,078	768	18	42.66
Best	**5wl**	**10wl**	**Sr/Rate**
4–72	-	-	115.44

First-Class Career: (647 Matches) 1948–69

Batting

I	NO	HS	Runs
852	197	87*	9,574
AV	**100**	**50**	**Catches**
14.61	-	20	221

Bowling

Balls	Runs	Wkts	Av
158,856	53,303	2,857	8.65
Best	**5wl**	**10wl**	**Sr/Rate**
9–30	194	38	55.60

'Shack', as he was known, was born in Todmorden on the Yorkshire/Lancashire border, but neither county chased him even though he played League cricket in the area. He was essentially a batsman who bowled leg-spin, while he was also on the staff of Burnley Football Club as a goalkeeper for a time. He joined the army in 1942, entering the Pioneer Corps, and played cricket and football. A Hampshire coach saw him playing and he was given a trial, first as a batsman but he then started bowling medium-pace seam and was signed as an all-rounder. He made his debut for Hampshire in 1948, taking 21 wickets, and a year later he took over 100 wickets (92 in the Championship at 26.00) and scored 914 runs, which included 87 not out against Essex, his highest score in first-class cricket. He was also awarded his county cap, and Hampshire had found a bowler who was to serve them loyally for the next 20 years.

The following year Shackleton took five wickets in nine balls against Leicestershire at Grace Road and was selected by England for the third Test against the West Indies at Trent Bridge, scoring 42 on his debut, which was to be his highest score in Test cricket. In the winter of 1951–52 he was selected for the tour of India but, although bowling accurately at Delhi in the first Test (1 for 76 off 29 overs), he lacked penetration on the slow Indian wickets and disappeared from Test cricket for next 12 years.

In the summer of 1952 he bowled unchanged for the first time with Vic Cannings through both Kent innings, a rare feat in which Shackleton took 12 for 67 and Cannings 8 for 55, while Kent were destroyed for 32 and 91 respectively. His county record continued to improve and he took 150 wickets at 20.46 in 1953, including 9 for 77 against Glamorgan at Newport. He improved that two years later with 159 wickets, including an outstanding match analysis of 14 for 29 against Somerset at Weston-super-Mare. In the first innings he took 8 for 4, his figures being 11.1 overs, seven maidens, four runs and eight wickets, and in the second innings he took a mere 6 for 25.

In the latter part of the 1950s and early 1960s he bowled more overs than any other bowler in the country; this included 144 wickets at 15.69 in 1957, 161 at 15.32 in 1958, 9 for 59 against Gloucestershire at Bristol also in 1958, while he received a benefit that year which realised £5,000. The next two years saw him take a further 254 wickets at below 20 runs apiece, and in 1959 he was chosen as one of *Wisden's* Five Cricketers of the Year.

In 1960 he took his best return in first-class cricket with 9 for 30 against Warwickshire at Portsmouth. His captain Colin Ingleby-Mackenzie called on him to bowl with Warwickshire on 196 for 4 and only 45 minutes left for play. He conceded a four to secure the new ball and then proceeded to take six wickets in 26 deliveries without conceding a run to give Hampshire a remarkable win.

In 1961 Shackleton bowled in excess of 9,000 balls with 158 wickets at 19.09. On 12 occasions he took five or more wickets in an innings, and none was more crucial than in the Derbyshire second innings in the penultimate match at Bournemouth. Derbyshire were set by 252 to win in 192 minutes, but 'Shack' was at his best and in half an hour he grabbed 4 for 8 and 6 for 39 in the innings to clinch Hampshire's very first Championship title.

The following summer he took 172 wickets and was the last bowler to bowl 10,000 balls in a season. Only J.T. Hearne and Maurice Tate as seam bowlers have bowled as many in a season.

In 1963 he was recalled to the England team for the series against the West Indies, playing in four of the five Tests, taking 15 wickets at 34.53, including his best Test figures of 4 for 72 at Lord's. Twelve months later, just short of his 40th birthday, he was the first bowler in the country to take 100 wickets, finishing with 138 at 19.98 each.

Throughout his career he was never more than medium-fast, but his strengths lay in his immense variations of swing, seam and cut coupled with relentless accuracy. Indeed, it was said that if he bowled a long hop or half volley then the Hampshire committee held an emergency meeting.

From 1949 until he retired at the end of 1968 he took 100 wickets in 20 consecutive seasons, a feat beaten only by the great Wilfred Rhodes and even he did not do so for 20 consecutive seasons.

Although officially retired, he returned for one Championship match a year later, a week before his 45th birthday. Sussex were visiting, and, opening the bowling as usual, he returned figures of 2 for 37 and 5 for 58 from nearly 48 overs. In all he played 583 matches for Hampshire, scored 8,602 runs at 14.43 and took 2,669 wickets at 18.23, with 190 five-wicket hauls.

After his retirement he was coach and groundsman at Cranford School in Dorset from 1969 to 1979, and played Minor County cricket for Dorset between 1971 to 1974. He also had a short stint as a first-class umpire from 1979 to 1981, and his son Julian played 48 matches for Gloucestershire from 1971 to 1978.

Philip John Sharpe

RHB & OB, 1958–76

Born: 27 December 1936, Shipley, Bradford.
Played for: Yorkshire and Derbyshire.
Test Matches: (12) 1963–69 Cap No. 416
Batting Career for England

I	NO	HS	Runs
21	4	111	786
AV	**100**	**50**	**Ct/St**
46.23	1	4	17

First-Class Career: (493 Matches) 1958–76
Batting

I	NO	HS	Runs
811	78	228	22,530
AV	**100**	**50**	**Ct/St**
30.73	29	111	617

Bowling

Balls	Runs	Wkts	Av
302	197	3	65.66
Best	**5wl**	**10wl**	**Sr/Rate**
1–1	-	-	100.66

Philip Sharpe was another Bradford-born youngster who attended Bradford Grammar School, before furthering his education at Worksop College, where he excelled at many sports, particularly cricket. He captained the team in his final year, scoring 1,251 runs at an average of 113.00, with seven centuries, two double hundreds and a top score of 240 not out against Wrekin School in 1956, which is still a school record. The previous season he had also notched up an unbeaten 202 for the Yorkshire Federation team against Nottinghamshire, and also top scored in both innings for the Rest against Southern Schools at Lord's.

He played League cricket for Pudsey St Lawrence and then Bradford from 1955 to 1957, while he made his first-class debut for the Combined Universities against Warwickshire at Edgbaston in 1956. He made his Yorkshire debut against Sussex at Worthing in 1958, making an unbeaten 56 in a second innings total of only 106, in a match that Yorkshire lost by 114 runs. A week later at Bramall Lane, Sheffield, opening the batting with Ken Taylor, he notched up his first century for Yorkshire 141 against Somerset.

However, the position where he scored most of his runs was number three in the batting order, and in 1960 he made 1,000 first-class runs for the first time (1,039 at 32.46), with his highest score for Yorkshire, 203 not out, against Cambridge University at Fenners. He also hit a fine 152 against Kent at Bramall Lane out of a final score of 315.

Two years later Sharpe amassed his highest aggregate for a season when he scored 2,201 runs for Yorkshire at 40.75, which included seven centuries, the highest of which was 138 against Somerset at Taunton. He also held 70 catches at slip, which equalled the Yorkshire record set by John Tunnicliffe in 1901.

In 1963 he was named as one of *Wisden's* Five Cricketers of the Year and was selected for his debut Test match against the West Indies at Edgbaston, scoring 85 not out in the second innings and batting at number six. In the winter of 1963–64 he was part of the MCC squad which toured India and played in the first Test at Madras, making 27 and 31 not out. Although he averaged 46.23 in his 21 Test innings, and scored four half-centuries against the West Indian quicks, he never held down a regular place in the team and his only century for his country was the 111 he scored at Trent Bridge in the second Test against New Zealand in 1969, his last series in Test cricket.

As a batsman he favoured the hard, fast pitches where he could use his favourite shots, the cut and pull, to best advantage, but he was also a fine driver of the ball when he was batting well.

However, while he was one of the mainstays of Yorkshire's batting in the 1960s, his value to the team was increased by his wonderful catching ability. Without question he was one of the best slip fielders that the game has ever known, and he can easily be compared with greats such as Bobby Simpson, Wally Hammond, Frank Woolley and his Yorkshire predecessor John Tunnicliffe. Sharpe's great asset was his concentration and ability to catch the ball at the last possible minute when it would

appear that the ball had gone past him, whereupon he would nonchalantly place it in his trouser pocket.

For Yorkshire he scored 17,685 runs at 29.72 with 23 centuries, and held 525 catches – only Tunnicliffe, Rhodes and Close have taken more.

In 1975 he moved to Derbyshire and spent two years with the East Midland county, scoring 2,031 runs in 40 matches at 29.43, and holding 47 catches with four centuries. His time there also saw a career best first-class score of 228 against Oxford University in the Parks in 1976.

In 1977 he joined Norfolk, playing Minor County cricket until 1981, while he also played for Manningham Mills in the Bradford League, scoring over 1,000 runs in 1977 before joining the Yorkshire committee as a member for York.

Today he is still involved with the county and organises overseas tours for cricket enthusiasts.

Arnold Sidebottom

RHB & RFM, 1973–91

Born: 1 April 1954, Shawlands, Barnsley.
Played for: Yorkshire and Orange Free State.
Test Matches: (1) 1985 Cap No. 512

Batting Career for England

I	NO	HS	Runs
1	0	2	2
AV	**100**	**50**	**Catches**
2.00	-	-	-

Bowling for England

Balls	Runs	Wkts	Av
112	65	1	65.00
Best	**5wl**	**10wl**	**Sr/Rate**
1–65	-	-	112.00

First-Class Career: (228 Matches) 1973–91

Batting

I	NO	HS	Runs
263	62	124	4,508
AV	**100**	**50**	**Catches**
22.42	1	-	63

Bowling

Balls	Runs	Wkts	Av
30,657	14,558	596	24.42
Best	**5wl**	**10wl**	**Sr/Rate**
8–72	23	3	51.40

The father of current Test bowler Ryan, Arnie Sidebottom was a Barnsley and Yorkshire Schoolboy cricketer, who captained Yorkshire Boys and went on to play for the English Schools Cricket Association team. He was also a very good footballer and joined Manchester United as an amateur in 1971, turning professional in 1972. A central-defender, he was a strong header of the ball and helped United to win the Second Division Championship in 1974–75. He made 16 appearances for United before being transferred to Huddersfield Town (56 games), and he later played for Halifax Town (21 games in 1978).

As a cricketer he played League cricket for Barnsley Cricket Club and followed the usual route into the Yorkshire first team, playing briefly in the second XI in 1971 and 1972, before making his first-class debut against Gloucestershire at the Winget Ground, Gloucester. On debut he made 1 run and took 3 for 61 with the ball.

Sidebottom was an all-round cricketer; he could bat anywhere, had a solid technique and was a more than useful medium-fast bowler. He was capable of exploiting conditions that suited him, could swing and seam the ball and in his later years he developed a very fine off-cutter. It was for his bowling that Yorkshire needed him most, but it took him some time to develop and it was not until 1980 that he gained a regular place on the side. In that season he played 20 first-class games, scoring 284 runs and snaring 42 wickets at 22.90. He had a best of 7 for 18 against Oxford University in the Parks, with 10 for 30 in the match and 11 for 64 against Kent at Abbeydale Park, Sheffield (6 for 30 and 5 for 34) in the second innings. He was also awarded his county cap, a fitting reward for such a good season.

In 1982 he went on the rebel tour of South Africa, a party led by Graham Gooch, which earned him a three-year Test ban. He also played for the Orange Free State in South Africa in 1982–83. In county cricket he topped the Yorkshire bowling averages, with 47 first-class wickets at 19.12. The following summer he improved on this tally with 62 wickets at 24.80 and in 1985 was a surprise call-up for the third Test at Trent Bridge against Australia. Unfortunately for him, his debut was marred by injury and he broke down after bowling 18 overs, although he did manage a Test wicket – that of nightwatchman leg-spinner Bob Holland. Sidebottom himself admitted afterwards that the selection had come too late in his career.

Injuries continued to be a problem for him, with these being in the main shin splints, but in 1986 he took a career best of 8 for 72 against Leicestershire at Acklam Park, Middlesbrough.

In 1989 he had his best season for the county, taking 68 wickets at 23.38, which included five five-wicket hauls and one 10-wicket haul – 10 for 111 against Middlesex on a seaming wicket at Headingley.

The previous season he had recieved a well deserved benefit match which produced £103,240. His last game for the White Rose County was in September 1991, a Joshua Tetley Festival semi-final against Derbyshire at Scarborough.

He retired at the end of the season after playing 216 matches, with 4,243 runs at 22.33, which included one century, 124 against Glamorgan at Sophia Gardens, Cardiff, in 1977 when he added 144 for the last wicket with Arthur Robinson (30 not out). He also took 558 wickets at 24.82, with 22 five-wicket hauls, and held 60 catches.

He then moved into coaching with the Yorkshire Academy and in 2000 he succeeded Doug Padgett as senior coach. His 30-year association with Yorkshire ended in 2003 when he fell victim to new management structures and he now coaches pupils in football and cricket at the Woodhouse Grove School near Bradford.

Ryan Jay Sidebottom

LHB & RFM, 1997–to date

Born: 15 January 1978, Huddersfield.

Played for: Yorkshire and Nottinghamshire.

Test Matches: (18) 2001–to date Cap No. 604

Batting Career for England

I	NO	HS	Runs
27	10	31	266
AV	**100**	**50**	**Catches**
15.64	-	-	5

Bowling for England

Balls	Runs	Wkts	Av
4,272	1,952	76	25.68
Best	**5wl**	**10wl**	**Sr/Rate**
7–47	5	1	56.20

First-Class Career: (126 Matches) 1997–to date

Batting

I	NO	HS	Runs
163	48	54	1,361
AV	**100**	**50**	**Catches**
11.83	-	1	45

Bowling

Balls	Runs	Wkts	Av
22,236	10,371	410	25.29
Best	**5wl**	**10wl**	**Sr/Rate**
7–47	17	2	54.20

Ryan Sidebottom, the son of former Yorkshire all-rounder Arnie, played his early cricket in the Huddersfield League before making his debut in 1997 against Leicestershire at Grace Road, taking 3 for 71 in Leicestershire's only innings. The following summer the left-arm seam bowler proved he could bat as well, scoring 54, his highest first-class score to date, against Glamorgan at Sophia Gardens, Cardiff, which, coincidentally, was also the ground where his father notched up his highest score (124) 19 years earlier.

In 1999 and 2000 he was the winner of the NBC Denis Compton award and in the latter year he finished as the leading domestic bowler, taking 24 wickets in only six matches at 12.5 runs per wicket, and was among the nominations for the Young Cricketer of the Year award by the Cricket Writers' Club. He had his share of injuries that season, but in the winter he toured the West Indies with England A, snaring 16 wickets at an average of 16.81.

The following summer an injury to his Yorkshire colleague Matthew Hoggard gave Sidebottom the opportunity to win his first Test cap against Pakistan at Leeds. Unfortunately, he failed to take a wicket in 20 overs and although he bowled tidily he was dropped from the Test scene for a further six years. However, he did play in two ODIs against Zimbabwe that October but was not overly impressive, taking just two wickets for 84 runs off 14 overs.

Back in county cricket he had an excellent season in 2002, taking 41 wickets at 29.02, and he was Yorkshire's leading wicket-taker with a best of 5 for 60 against Leicestershire at Scarborough. He was slowly learning the art of swinging the ball back into the right-hand batsman, but after taking 35 wickets in 2003, with a Yorkshire best of 7 for 97 against Derbyshire at Leeds, he decided to quit the White Rose County. His father Arnie, who had been in charge of the second team, also left at the same time. Ryan had taken 163 wickets at an average of 25.12 and joined nearby Nottinghamshire in time for the start of the 2004 season.

In his first three years at Trent Bridge he took 130 wickets at 25.81, confirming him as one of the most consistent seam bowlers in the country. In the process he helped Nottinghamshire to win the County Championship in 2005, their first for 18 years, since the days of Hadlee and Rice, and Ryan was named their Player of the Year.

Internationally he had been left out in the cold, one of the reasons being Duncan Fletcher's obsession with raw pace, but when Peter Moore took over as the new coach in 2006 he was given another chance at Test level. Once again Ryan replaced an injured Matthew Hoggard for the second Test against the West Indies at Headingley and responded brilliantly by taking 8 for 86 in a match that England won by an innings and 283 runs. Needless to say, he kept his place in the side and 16 wickets at 19.68 in the series confirmed that the selectors were right to recall him. In the process he took his first five-wicket haul when he claimed 5 for 88 at Chester-Le-Street.

Although he only took eight wickets at 37.87 in the following series against India, he was still selected for the winter tours to Sri Lanka and New Zealand. In Sri Lanka he was impressive with the white ball in the one-day series, taking the Man of the Match award as England won the tournament, but it was in New Zealand where he really came of age as a Test bowler.

In the three-match series he totally dominated the batsmen, taking 10 for 139 at Hamilton, 6 for 141 at Wellington and finally 8 for 130 at Napier, which included a Test best of 7 for 47 in the first innings and a hat-trick in the process. In the series his 24 wickets at 17.08 was the most for an England bowler in a three-Test series in New Zealand and his performances won him the Man of the Series award.

He continued his grip on the New Zealand batsmen in the return series in England, taking 17 wickets at 20.47, which confirmed him as one of England's leading Test bowlers in the summer of 2008.

Christopher Eric Wilfred Silverwood

RHB & RF, 1993–to date

Born: 5 March 1975, Pontefract.

Played for: Yorkshire and Middlesex.

Test Matches: (6) 1996–2002 Cap No. 583

Batting Career for England

I	NO	HS	Runs
7	3	10	29

AV	100	50	Catches
7.25	-	-	2

Bowling for England

Balls	Runs	Wkts	Av
828	444	11	40.36

Best	5wl	10wl	Sr/Rate
5–91	1	-	75.27

First-Class Career: (178 Matches) 1993–to date

Batting

I	NO	HS	Runs
234	47	80	2,962

AV	100	50	Catches
15.83	-	9	41

Bowling

Balls	Runs	Wkts	Av
29,083	15,394	570	27.00

Best	5wl	10wl	Sr/Rate
7–93	25	1	51.00

Chris Silverwood, educated at Garforth Comprehensive School near Leeds, was a YTS scholar at Yorkshire and made his second XI debut at the beginning of 1992 against a Young England XI at Headingley. He was also a member of the cricket academy at Bradford.

Silverwood made his first-class debut for the Tykes versus Hampshire at Southampton in 1993, taking 1 for 19, but he failed to score in his innings, in what was his only first-class game of the season. He did, however, play in several one-day games.

The following season he played a further eight first-class matches, taking 26 wickets at 31.96, but injury problems (the first of many to come his way) blighted his progress somewhat in 1995.

His breakthrough came in the summer of 1996, when he played 16 Championship matches, snaring 47 wickets at 30.68, with a best of 5 for 72 against Worcestershire at New Road and 5 for 78 against

Gloucestershire at Bristol towards the end of the season. He was also awarded his county cap, was voted the Cricket Writers' Young Cricketer of the Year, and was selected for the England tour of Zimbabwe and New Zealand.

In Zimbabwe he made his debut at Bulawayo taking 4 for 71 in the match, but then he had to wait a further three years until his next chance on the tour to South Africa in 1999–2000.

Silverwood's bowling had now gathered momentum, and his pace had increased to such an extent that on his day he was as quick as any English qualified bowler in the Championship. He also possessed an exciting bouncer and a lively out-swinger. Indeed, the former English bowling coach Bob Cottam said that when conditions suited him, he believed him to be as fast as the great South African pace-bowler Allan Donald.

He had a good season with Yorkshire in 1997, taking his first 50-wicket haul in the Championship (58 at 20.06), which included his best first-class bowling figures of 7 for 93 in Kent's first innings at Headingley, and match figures of 12 for 148.

The seasons of 1998 and 1999 brought him 107 wickets, and in the latter his tally of 59 at 20.40 was his best for the White Rose County. It also earned him an England recall for the tour of South Africa in the winter of 1999–2000, due, in the main, to an injury to Dean Headley. His second England cap was at Port Elizabeth and in the fourth Test at Cape Town he took his best figures for his country, 5 for 91.

To date he has played only one further Test, when he was flown out to Perth for the third Test in November 2002. He only bowled four overs for 29 runs in the match, when he injured his ankle and took no further part in the match or the series.

Twelve months previously he played a part in Yorkshire's first County Championship title since 1968, and in August 2002 he was a member of the team which won the Cheltenham and Gloucester Trophy at Lord's, when they beat Somerset by six wickets.

Unfortunately, injuries continued to come his way and in the following four seasons he played a little more than half (37) of 64 Championship games. In 2005 he hit his highest first-class score for Yorkshire (80) against Durham at Chester-Le-Street.

At the end of the summer he decided to leave his native county and team up with Middlesex, having taken 427 wickets at 27.62, scored 2.369 runs at 16.22 and held 30 catches in 131 matches for Yorkshire.

In his first season at Lord's he took a Championship season best of 61 wickets at 25.22, but since 2007 he has once again been plagued by injuries, thereby restricting his Middlesex appearances.

Frank Smailes

LHB & RM/OB, 1932–48

Born: 27 March 1910, Ripley, Harrogate.
Died: 1 December 1970, Starbeck, Harrogate.
Played for: Yorkshire.
Test Matches: (1) 1946 Cap No. 313

Batting Career for England

I	NO	HS	Runs
1	-	25	25
AV	**100**	**50**	**Catches**
25	-	-	-

Bowling for England

Balls	Runs	Wkts	Av
120	62	3	20.66
Best	**5wl**	**10wl**	**Sr/Rate**
3–44	-	-	40.00

First-Class Career: (269 Matches) 1932–48

Batting

I	NO	HS	Runs
349	43	117	5,892
AV	**100**	**50**	**Catches**
19.25	3	24	154

Bowling

Balls	Runs	Wkts	Av
41,008	17,114	822	20.81
Best	**5wl**	**10wl**	**Sr/Rate**
10–47	41	6	49.88

A pupil of Pocklington Grammer School, Frank Smailes began playing for Ilkey Cricket Club at the age of 16 and then followed his elder brother George to Harrogate, before becoming a professional for Forfarshire in 1931 and then returning to play for Brighouse in 1933. He was a 6ft tall, all-round cricketer, who bowled right-arm medium-pace with a high classical action. He also had an exceptional command of line and length and could swing the ball either way. Later in an innings he could change to bowling off-spin when the pitch offered him turn. With the bat, the left-handed Smailes could hit the ball very hard from a position in the late or middle-order.

He made his first-class debut for Yorkshire in 1932 against Oxford University in the Parks, but it was not until 1934 that he established himself in the Yorkshire team, due mainly to an injury to George Macaulay. He took his chance very effectively, taking 105 wickets at 20.33 with a best of 6 for 56 against Kent, when he swung the ball alarmingly. The following summer he had fewer opportunities to play, but still took 96 wickets at 20.62, with 7 for 47 against Sussex at Hove his best. With the bat he scored 654 runs at 18.68, including a best of 89 against Sussex at Headingley, when he shared a eighth-wicket partnership of 180 with Wilf Barber who went on to make 191.

In 1936 he had his best season with the ball, taking 130 first-class wickets at 17.54, with a best of 7 for 24 against Worcestershire at Leeds. It was a season which included nine five-wicket hauls. He was also involved in a ninth-wicket partnership of 167 with Hedley Verity (89) against Somerset at Bath.

Smailes, now the principal all-rounder, had become an integral member of the Yorkshire side of the 1930s, a team which, under the leadership of Brian Sellers, won seven County Championships from 1930 to 1939.

In 1937 he scored his maiden first-class century against Warwickshire (109), and he also contributed to another partnership, this time 125 for the seventh wicket against Kent at Bradford with skipper Brian

Sellers (109). To confirm his all-round ability he took 5 for 16 in the same match.

In the following summer he had his most outstanding season, scoring 1,002 runs, with a career best of 117 against Glamorgan at Cardiff. In addition he took 113 wickets at 20.84 with 14 for 103 in the return game against Glamorgan at Hull, thus achieving the 'double' for the first and only time. To complete a memorable season he also took 7 for 24 against Scotland at Harrogate and then 6 for 92 and 4 for 45 against Bradman's Australians at Bramall Lane, Sheffield, when rain, for once, came to the aid of the Aussies and saved them from a possible defeat.

He was one of 13 players selected for the third Test against Australia at Old Trafford, but the rain intervened once again and the game was abandoned without a ball being bowled. However, in 1946 he did make a solitary appearance for England, against India at Lord's, scoring 25 in his only innings and taking 3 for 44 in the Indian second innings. He was now 36 years of age and, but for the war, he would probably have played many more games for his country.

In the same season he joined an elite list of Yorkshire bowlers when he took 10 for 47 against Derbyshire at Bramall Lane (14 for 58 in the match), joining Alonzo Drake and Hedley Verity as the only bowlers to have obtained a maximum in an innings.

His last first-class game for Yorkshire was against the MCC at Scarborough in September 1948, a year in which he was awarded a well-earned benefit that realised £5,104.

For Yorkshire he scored 5,686 runs at 19.14, with three centuries, took 802 wickets at 20.68, with 39 five-wicket hauls, and held 153 catches.

On his retirement from first-class cricket he became a professional with Walsall in the Staffordshire League and involved himself more in the family business of cattle dealing. He was also the licensee of the Sportsman's Arms at Wath, near Ripon in North Yorkshire.

Gerald Athur Smithson

LHB & RM, 1946–56

Born: 1 November 1926, Spofforth, Harrogate.
Died: 6 September 1970, Abingdon, Berkshire.
Played for: Yorkshire and Leicestershire.
Test Matches: (2) 1947–48 Cap No. 330

Batting Career for England

I	NO	HS	Runs
3	0	35	70
AV	**100**	**50**	**Catches**
23.33	-	-	-

First-Class Career: (200 Matches) 1946–56

Batting

I	NO	HS	Runs
333	27	169	6,940
AV	**100**	**50**	**Catches**
22.67	8	31	131

Bowling

Balls	Runs	Wkts	Av
94	117	1	117.00
Best	**5wl**	**10wl**	**Sr/Rate**
1–26	-	-	94

Born at Spofforth, near Harrogate, Gerald Smithson first played for Yorkshire immediately after World War Two. In 1946 he appeared for the second XI when he scored 252 runs at 21.00. He made his County Championship debut the same season, making a solitary appearance against Essex at Harrogate and scoring 16 in his first innings.

The following year the left-handed, middle-order batsman registered his maiden century for the county in his second game of the season, scoring 107 not out in the second innings against Surrey at Bradford Park Avenue. In the Roses game against Lancashire at Bramall Lane he made a thrilling 98 before lunch, and he followed this by notching up his highest first-class score, 169 against Leicestershire at Grace Road, contributing to partnerships of 196 with Len Hutton and then 147 with captain Norman Yardley. At the end of the summer he had notched up 810 runs at 38.57 and was awarded his county cap. He was also selected in the MCC party to tour the West Indies, which led to the issue being debated in the House of Commons. Smithson had been conscripted into the coal mines at Askern Colliery rather than into the Services, and only after his case had been discussed in Parliament was he granted permission to join the party. He played in two Tests at Bridgetown and Port of Spain, making 70 runs in total. Unfortunately, a severe arm injury sustained on tour meant that he missed the entire 1948 season.

During the next two years Smithson failed to rediscover his previous form and played only 26 first-class matches for Yorkshire, scoring 454 runs at 19.91, and decided to seek a special registration for Leicestershire for the season of 1951. His last game for the White Rose County was against Scotland at Edinburgh in July 1950. For Yorkshire he scored 1.449 runs in 39 matches at 26.34, with two centuries, took one wicket at 84.00 and held 21 catches.

The move to Leicestershire paid dividends for him, for in his debut season at Grace Road he notched up 951 runs at an average of 20, which included a brilliant 105 in 90 minutes against Kent at Leicester that contained a six and 15 fours, and indeed he was awarded his county cap on the strength of that performance.

The following year the graceful left-hander, who was also a fine all-round fielder, had his best season with the East Midlands county, notching up 1,351 runs at 27.57, which included his highest score for the Foxes, 111 not out against Essex.

He just failed to register 1,000 runs in seasons 1953 and 1954, but he had a poor summer in 1955 and was released from his contract at the end of the 1956 after scoring 615 runs. His last first-class match for Leicestershire was against Northamptonshire at Wantage Road, Northampton, in August 1956. He had scored 5,305 runs for the county at an average of 22.10 and had held 110 catches.

It was a career that had promised much, but he never fulfilled the potential that many, including his former captain at Yorkshire Norman Yardley, believed he had.

Upon leaving Leicestershire he played Minor County cricket with Hertfordshire from 1957 to 1962 and served as a professional cricket coach, first at Caterham School and then at Abingdon School, where he was also the head groundsman.

He died suddenly at his home in Abingdon, Oxfordshire, on 6 September 1970 at the age of only 43.

Graham Barry Stevenson

RHB & RMF, 1973–87

Born: 16 December 1955, Ackworth.
Played for: Yorkshire and Northamptonshire.
Test Matches: (2) 1979–81 Cap No. 485
Batting Career for England

I	NO	HS	Runs
2	1	27*	28
AV	**100**	**50**	**Catches**
28.00	-	-	-

Bowling for England

Balls	Runs	Wkts	Av
312	183	5	36.60
Best	**5wl**	**10wl**	**Sr/Rate**
3–111	-	-	62.40

First-Class Career: (188 Matches) 1973–87
Batting

I	NO	HS	Runs
229	34	115*	3,965
AV	**100**	**50**	**Catches**
20.33	2	16	73

Bowling

Balls	Runs	Wkts	Av
26,680	14,075	488	28.44
Best	**5wl**	**10wl**	**Sr/Rate**
8–57	18	2	54.67

Graham Stevenson was one of the most gifted young players to grace the Yorkshire scene. A fine right-arm, fast-medium bowler, with an easy natural action, he could be very quick when in the mood and swung and seamed the ball when conditions suited. In the field he had a tremendous throw and there were very few who could land the distance that he did. As a batsman he had enormous power and was as good a striker of the ball as any player of his era, including Ian Botham. Indeed, there was a distinct comparison between 'Stevo' and Botham in terms of all-round ability, but Botham had the consistency and confidence to go on and perform at the highest level. Stevenson, unfortunately, did not, and so a wonderful talent never strutted the world stage like he should have. Like Botham in his younger days, he too spent time in Australia, playing League cricket in Melbourne.

A product of Geoff Boycott country, Stevenson scored a century for Ackworth Second XI at the age of 14, before moving on to play for Hemsworth and Barnsley Cricket Clubs respectively. Indeed, Boycott played an early part in young Stevenson's development, arranging nets at Headingley for him.

Stevenson performed creditably with the second XI in 1972 and he was given his county debut against Middlesex at Bradford Park Avenue, in the last Championship game of the 1973 season, taking 3 for 50 in the match. However, it was not until 1976 that he became a regular in the Yorkshire team, when he scored 442 runs at 27.62, with a highest score of 83 against Derbyshire at Chesterfield, but he took only 23 wickets at 32.83. A year later he took 10 wickets in a match for the first time, with figures of 10 for 139 (4 for 57 and 6 for 82) against Glamorgan at Cardiff, and he finished the season with 69 wickets at 25.68

In the Roses match at Headingley in 1978 he destroyed Lancashire's first innings, taking 8 for 65 in only 12.1 overs, and in the return match at Old Trafford he repeated the act with 5 for 61 and 3 for 57, while during the season he was awarded his county cap.

Two years later he took his best figures for Yorkshire, 8 for 57 against Northamptonshire at Leeds, and also took 7 for 48 at Trent Bridge against Notts, which included a spell of 5 for 0. He also scored the first of two centuries for the county, hitting 111 against Derbyshire at Chesterfield.

By then he had started to get niggling injuries, though in the last Championship match of 1981 at Scarborough he took another seven-wicket haul, this time 7 for 46 against Northamptonshire.

With the bat he could be immensely destructive, and it was a surprise that he only hit two hundreds in his career. The second was at Edgbaston in 1982, when he and Geoff Boycott shared a 10th-wicket partnership of 149 (still a county record), Stevenson hammering 115 not out and Boycott, who had opened the innings, chipped in with 79. However, his most ferocious hitting was in a Sunday League game at Middlesbrough in 1984, when he smashed 81 not out off just 29 balls against Somerset, an innings which included 10 sixes.

He was selected to tour Australia and India in 1979–80, and although he did not play a Test match in Australia he did play in the one-day games, making a stunning debut at Sydney. With the ball he took 4 for 33 and then, when England needed 35 off 30 balls to win with only two wickets remaining, he struck 28 not out, and along with Yorkshire colleague David Bairstow he silenced the barrackers on the hill in seeing England home to victory. On the Indian leg of the tour he made his Test debut in the Jubilee Test at Bombay, scoring 27 not out (his best Test score), and he then took 2 for 59 with the ball. However, he only played one more Test, on the tour to the West Indies in the fourth Test at St Johns, when he took 3 for 111 off 33 overs, his best Test figures.

In 1986 he was released by Yorkshire, surprisingly without a benefit, and played one first-class game for Northamptonshire.

For Yorkshire in 177 first-class matches he took 464 wickets at 28.56, with 17 five-wicket hauls, scored 3,856 runs at 20.84 and held 73 catches.

Herbert Sutcliffe

RHB & RM, 1919–45

Born: 24 November 1894, Summerbridge, Harrogate.
Died: 22 January 1978, Cross Hills.
Played for: Yorkshire.
Test Matches: (54) 1924–35 Cap No. 215
Batting Career for England

I	NO	HS	Runs
84	9	194	4,555
AV	**100**	**50**	**Catches**
60.73	16	23	23

First-Class Career: (754 Matches) 1919–45
Batting

I	NO	HS	Runs
1,098	124	313	50,670
AV	**100**	**50**	**Catches**
52.05	150	229	473

Bowling

Balls	Runs	Wkts	Av
993	563	14	40.21
Best	**5wl**	**10wl**	**Sr/Rate**
3–15	-	-	70.92

One in a long list of Yorkshire's great batsmen, Herbert Sutcliffe scored more first-class runs than any other Yorkshire-born batsman in a career which spanned over 20 years. Although born at Summerbridge, near Harrogate, he moved to Pudsey in 1909 as a boy and played for both of the town's clubs, Pudsey St Lawrence and Pudsey Britannia, as well as the West of Scotland.

World War One delayed his entry into county cricket until he was 24 years of age, when, after demobilisation from a commission in the Green Howards, he was given a place in the Yorkshire team. In 1919, his first season in county cricket, he scored 1,839 runs, a record for a debut season, which included five centuries, the highest score being 174 against Kent. He topped the Yorkshire averages and was voted one of *Wisden's* Five Cricketers of the Year. He also formed a first-wicket partnership with Percy Holmes that was to become the finest in county cricket.

Although he scored 1,393 and 1,235 runs respectively in seasons 1920 and 1921, which included four centuries, it was not until 1922 that he scored over 2,000 runs in a first-class season. It was then that he was truly counted among the best batsmen in the country. It was a season which also saw him score the first of 16 double hundreds, with 232 against Surrey, and he also scored 2,000 runs for the next 14 seasons (an unbeaten record).

Sutcliffe opened the batting for the first time with Jack Hobbs for the Players versus the Gentlemen at Scarborough, and further success in 1923 earned him selection a year later for England against South Africa at Birmingham. He made 64 on his debut in his only innings of the Test, but in the second at Lord's, he and Hobbs produced a stand of 268, of which Sutcliffe scored 122, the first of 16 Test centuries. In 38 Test innings the pair averaged 87.81 for the first wicket, the highest average of opening partnerships to add 1,000 runs together, and 15 of those 38 stands went for more than 100 runs and only four for less than 10. Surprisingly, two of those were in the fifth Ashes Test of the 1924–25 series, when Hobbs was run out for a duck in the first innings and Sutcliffe followed suit in exactly the same way in the second.

In that first Test series against South Africa he averaged 75.55. Immediately, it was to Australia where he averaged 81.55 after scoring 115 at Sydney in the first Test in 1924–25, 176 and 127 at Melbourne in the second and 143 at Melbourne in the fourth. His average did not dip below 70 until his 20th Test at Durban in 1928 and it was still 65.87 at the end of the bodyline series in 1932–33. By this time Sutcliffe was 38 years of age, but he played on for another two years, scoring 471 runs at 36.23 in his final 11 Tests.

Herbert never averaged less than 50 in a series against Australia, who were then the toughest opponents in world cricket. His performances in the six Test series against them were 28 Tests, 2,741 runs, eight centuries and an average of 66.85. Indeed, his highest Test score was 194 against Australia at Sydney in December 1932. He made 16 in total and the lowest batting average he had in Test cricket was his final figure of 60.73, fourth best of all those to play at least 30 innings and still the best by an English batsman.

Sutcliffe's two most famous innings were played on sticky wickets in Ashes Tests, one in 1926 and the other in 1928–29, and both, almost inevitably, were played in tandem with Hobbs. At the start of the third day of the fifth Test at the Oval, England were 0 for 49 after Australia had already gleaned a first-innings lead of 22. It rained all night and the sun came out early in the morning, making the wicket very sticky, yet Hobbs made 100 and Sutcliffe 161, enabling England to win the match by 289 runs. In the 1928–29 series the wicket at the MCG was even worse when England were set 332 to win, a seemingly hopeless task. Yet Sutcliffe batted nearly all day, made 135 and England won by three wickets.

For Yorkshire his performances were just as legendary and he scored a record number of runs, 38,558 at 50.20, recorded the most hundreds in a season (12 in 1932), and he also took the record for the most runs in a season with 2,883 (average of 80.08) in 1932. The same year he hit his highest ever score of 313 against Essex at Leyton, when he and Percy Holmes (224 not out) compiled 555 for the first wicket, which is still the highest partnership for any wicket in the County Championship.

During his career, which began in 1919 and ended in 1945, he scored 50,670 first-class runs at 52.05, with 150 centuries, 112 for Yorkshire, and only one other batsman (Geoff Boycott with 103) has scored in excess of 100 centuries for the county. He never knew a season of failures, except by the standard of his own astonishing peaks, and at the zenith of his career he scored 16,255 runs in five years. This was the true measure of his mastery over all the world's best bowlers, and his artistry and efficiency in difficult conditions became legendary in his lifetime. Herbert Sutcliffe would surely grace any best-ever England XI.

Kenneth Taylor

RHB & RM/LB, 1953–68

Born: 21 August 1935, Primrose Hill, Huddersfield.

Played for: Yorkshire and Auckland.

Test Matches: (3) 1959–64 Cap No. 395

Batting Career for England

I	NO	HS	Runs
5	0	24	57
AV	**100**	**50**	**Catches**
11.40	-	-	1

Bowling for England

Balls	Runs	Wkts	Av
12	6	0	-
Best	**5wl**	**10wl**	**Sr/Rate**
-	-	-	-

First-Class Career: (313 Matches) 1953–68

Batting

I	NO	HS	Runs
524	36	203*	13,053
AV	**100**	**50**	**Catches**
26.74	16	68	150

Bowling

Balls	Runs	Wkts	Av
10,628	3,763	131	28.72
Best	**5wl**	**10wl**	**Sr/Rate**
6–75	1	-	81.12

Ken Taylor was a fine all-round sportsman, who excelled at both cricket and football. Born in Huddersfield, he played for Huddersfield, Yorkshire and England Schools at cricket and was a regular member of the Yorkshire Second XI by the age of 15, scoring 386 runs and taking 17 wickets in his first season in 1951.

A confident and fluent batsman, Taylor was a fine straight driver of the ball, which owed much to the narrowness of the ginnels where he batted as a child. In addition, he was noted for his excellence at playing the late cut shot, and was a fine player of spin bowling, having had plenty of practise in the schoolyard when he faced his teacher Colin Garthwaite, an ex-Cleckheaton professional. He was also a much underrated bowler of accurate medium-pace seamers, who often broke many a stubborn partnership for his captains, Vic Wilson and Brian Close. His fielding was brilliant, particularly at cover point, where he was one of the best of his generation, as well as having a magnificent throw.

His first season of Championship cricket came in 1953 when he made his debut against Northamptonshire at Headingley. However, he did not become a regular in the Yorkshire team until 1956, when he notched up 738 runs at 29.52, which included his first century of 168 not out against Nottinghamshire at Trent Bridge when he opened the batting with Frank Lowson.

The following year he repeated the feat against the East Midlands county, scoring 140 not out in an opening partnership of 230 with Brian Stott (114), the first of three double century partnerships between the pair. Indeed, this was the first of many fast-scoring partnerships between the two during the next six years or so, and there can have been very few that ran so many quick singles as Taylor and Stott. During the 1957 season Taylor was also awarded his county cap.

In 1959 he scored a 1,000 runs for the first time (1,306 at 27.21), with a top score of 144 against Derbyshire at Queen's Park, Chesterfield, and he took 27 wickets at 23.44, with bests of 3 for 8 off eight overs against Surrey at the Oval and then 4 for 25 in the return match at Bradford Park Avenue.

In 1961 he had his best season for Yorkshire and amassed 1,494 runs at 34.74, which included four centuries and a top score of 203 not out against Warwickshire at Edgbaston (his highest First-Class score). He also had his best bowling figures, 6 for 75 off 44 overs against Lancashire in the Roses match at Old Trafford, a game Yorkshire won by 10 wickets.

In the same year he played the first of his three Test matches for England, being selected for the first two Test matches at Nottingham and Leeds. In three innings he opened the batting with Arthur Milton, but he scored only 33 runs, with a highest score of 24, his highest in Test cricket, and he disappeared from the Test arena for another five years. He reappeared again for England in 1964 against Australia after scoring 160 for Yorkshire against them at Bramall Lane. However, he made only 9 and 15, batting in the middle order in the Headingley Test, and he did not get another chance.

In 1968, his final year with Yorkshire, he was granted a benefit which realised £6,301, and he later played Minor County cricket for Norfolk from 1972 to 1974.

For Yorkshire he scored 12,864 runs at 27.37, with 16 centuries, took 129 wickets at 28.52 and held 146 catches.

Taylor was also a fine footballer. He played for Yorkshire Amatuers, Huddersfield Town and Bradford City from 1953 to 1966, making 301 League appearances and scoring 15 goals, which included four goals from centre-forward in a match against West Ham United. He also played for the England Under-23 team.

After his retirement Ken coached both cricket and football in New Zealand and South Africa and became an Art Master at Gresham School in Holt, Norfolk, having previously studied art at the Slade School of Fine Art in London. He has had books published on his cricketing portraits, and he is the father of Nicholas Taylor who played eight matches for Yorkshire in the 1980s.

Dr Patrick George Thornton

LHB & SLA, 1887–1911

Born: 24 December 1867, Skipton.
Died: 31 January 1939, Kensington, London.
Played for: Scotland, Yorkshire, Middlesex, MCC, Transvaal, Europeans and Ceylon.
Test Matches: (1) 1902–03 Cap No. 53

Batting Career For South Africa

I	NO	HS	Runs
1	1	1*	1
AV	**100**	**50**	**Catches**
1	0	0	1

Bowling for South Africa

Balls	Runs	Wkts	Av
24	20	1	20.00
Best	**5wl**	**10wl**	**Sr/Rate**
1-20	0	0	24.00

First Class Career: (42 matches) 1891–1903

Batting

I	NO	HS	Runs
67	11	161	1,263
AV	**100**	**50**	**Catches**
22.55	1	4	13

Bowling

Balls	Runs	Wkts	Av
1,969	1,007	32	31.46
Best	**5wl**	**10wl**	**Sr/Rate**
5-20	1	0	61.50

Born in Skipton, North Yorkshire, George Thornton was educated at Skipton Grammar School and Edinburgh University, where he gained his doctorate.

Thornton made his cricket debut for the Gentlemen of Scotland against the Gentlemen of Canada in July 1887, scoring 14 not out in his only innings and taking 10 for 103 (4 for 60 and 6 for 43) with the ball. He played three further matches for Scotland before playing London club cricket for Hampstead Cricket Club with Andrew Stoddart, the England captain and Middlesex player. Indeed, it was Stoddart who recommended him to Yorkshire, and he made his White Rose County debut in August 1891 against Kent at Maidstone but suffered the embarrassment of a pair and failed to take a wicket in either innings.

George only played three matches for Yorkshire, all as an amateur, scoring 21 runs at 5.25, with a top score of 16 versus Kent, and taking two wickets at 37.00.

In 1893 he decided to play his cricket in the south of England with Middlesex, making his debut against Kent. Two years later he notched the first of four first-class half-centuries (67 not out) versus Somerset at Lord's.

Dr Patrick was a hard hitting left-handed batsman, who incidentally played in spectacles, who was also a more than useful slow to medium left-arm bowler and a safe and reliable fielder. He continued to play periodically for both Middlesex and the Marylebone Cricket Club for the following six years with a limited amount of success.

In May 1895 he took his one and only five-wicket haul (5 for 20) and 9 for 72 in the match against Gloucestershire at Lord's which included the wicket of W.G. Grace, whom he clean bowled.

The following season he notched his only first-class century (161) for Middlesex against Gloucestershire also at the game's headquarters, and in the following three years he registered two further scores in excess of fifty, (56 against Yorkshire in 1897) and 85 not out for the MCC against Leicestershire in May 1898.

For Middlesex he played 33 games scored 977 runs at 22.20, took 29 wickets at 28.75 and held nine catches.

Thornton, a general medical practitioner, was one of the first to volunteer for service in the Boer War and he was made head of the Government Hospital in Pretoria, and he spent the following nine years in the country, mainly in Transvaal. He played some games for Transvaal, though not at a first-class level, and indeed his first contact with South African cricket had been in 1894 when he was a member of the MCC and Ground team, captained by W.G. Grace, which was beaten by the first South African touring team by 11 runs at Lord's in a match which was all over in a single day.

He remained in South Africa after the war and became one of Transvaal's most successful club cricketers, so much so that when the Australians toured in 1902–03 he was selected for the first Test without having appeared in first-class cricket in the country. He was given little chance to make his mark in what was to be his only Test match, scoring one not out, batting at number 10 and bowling four overs to take 1 for 20, his victim being Warwick Armstrong. He also held one catch. The match marked the end of his first-class career of 42 matches in which he scored 1,263 runs at 22.55, captured 32 wickets at 31.46 and held 13 catches.

After spending nine years in South Africa, he took up an appointment in Ceylon and was Superintendant of the Colombo General Hospital from 1909 to 1920.

In December 1909 he toured Bangalore and Madras with the Europeans and two years later represented an All Ceylon XI against the Marylebone Cricket Club at Colombo and was one of five batsmen who failed to score, having been bowled by Frank Foster.

He later became the President of Colombo Cricket Club and his son, Patrick Alban Thornton, appeared on six occasions for Ireland between 1927 and 1929 and played two games for Border in the Currie Cup in South Africa in the season of 1933–34.

Frederick Sewards Trueman

RHB & RFB, 1949–69

Born: 6 February 1931, Stainton.
Died: 2 July 2006, Skipton.
Played for: Yorkshire and Derbyshire.
Test Matches: (67) 1952–65 Cap No. 369

Batting Career for England

I	NO	HS	Runs
85	14	39*	981
AV	**100**	**50**	**Catches**
13.82	-	-	64

Bowling for England

Balls	Runs	Wkts	Av
15,178	6,625	307	21.58
Best	**5wl**	**10wl**	**Sr/Rate**
8–31	17	3	49.44

First-Class Career: (603 Matches) 1949–69

Batting

I	NO	HS	Runs
713	120	9,231	104
AV	**100**	**50**	**Catches**
15.57	3	26	439

Bowling

Balls	Runs	Wkts	Av
99,701	42,154	2,304	18.30
Best	**5wl**	**10wl**	**Sr/Rate**
8–28	126	25	43.27

Throughout the history of Test cricket, England have arguably only produced half a dozen great fast bowlers and Frederick Sewards Trueman would probably be number one.

He was born at Stainton, the son of a miner, who was also a useful League cricketer himself. The young Fred did not need any encouragement to take up the game and at 17 years of age he was taken to the nets at Bramall Lane, Sheffield. He went on the Yorkshire Schools tour of the South of England and made his debut for Yorkshire against Cambridge University at Fenners in May 1949, without ever having played a second team game.

When he was a young bowler he was often wild and erratic, but genuinely fast. With experience he completely mastered the art of quick bowling and into his repertoire came a superb off-cutter, bowled at medium fast, and a yorker and bouncer as good as any of his contempories'. To all of that,

Trueman is applauded off the field by his teammates.

he had strength, stamina, determination and the most beautiful classical action, making him the most complete fast bowler of his era.

A month after his debut he took 8 for 70 at Lord's against The Minor Counties, but an injury against the touring New Zealanders ended his first summer for Yorkshire.

In 1951 he captured 90 wickets at 20.57, which included 8 for 68 and 8 for 53 in the two county games against Nottinghamshire and Northamptonshire at Sheffield, while in the latter game he recorded his first Yorkshire hat-trick (the first of four, to equal George Macauley's county record).

The following summer, while serving in the RAF, he was rather surprisingly given his Test debut against India at Leeds, returning 3 for 89 and 4 for 27, and incredibly he reduced India to 0 for 4 with three wickets in eight balls. Eight wickets in the next Test at Lord's were followed by the eclipse of the Indians at Old Trafford when he snared 8 for 31 in their first innings, which incidentally were his best Test figures. In four Tests he had taken 29 wickets at 13.31, and his impact on English cricket was such that he was voted the Young Cricketer of the Year and selected as one of *Wisden's* Five Cricketers of the Year. Not only had England unearthed the fast bowler they had been searching for years, but so had Yorkshire.

Throughout most of the 1950s Yorkshire had to settle for second place in the Championship behind Surrey, but Trueman remained the spearhead, taking 129 wickets in 1954, 140 in 1955 and 104 in 1959. For England during this period he went on the tour to the West Indies in 1953–54, but rumours that he was hard to handle and too outspoken meant that he was not selected for the tours to Australia in 1954–55 and South Africa in 1956–57. However, he did play at home and one of his greatest performances was at Leeds in 1961, when against Australia he took 5 for 58 in the first innings and then 6 for 30 in the second, as he bowled off-cutters at various speeds, snaring 5 for 0 in a spell of 24 balls. Two years later, against Frank Worrell's champion West Indies team, he took 34 wickets at 17.47, which included 5 for 74 and 7 for 44 at Edgbaston in the third Test.

In 1964 against Australia in the fifth Test at the Oval he took 4 for 87 in their only innings and when Neil Hawke edged a catch to Colin Cowdrey at second slip he became the first bowler to take 300 Test wickets.

Incredibly, between his first and last Test Trueman only played 67 out of 120 Tests. It was amazing that the selectors could leave him out so often, but England's loss was Yorkshire's gain, and he became an important factor in Yorkshire winning the County Championship seven times during his career. For the White Rose alone he took 1,745 wickets at 17.12, with a best of 8 for 28 against Kent at Dover in 1954. His Yorkshire stats also include 97 five-wicket hauls and 6,852 runs at 15.12, which included two centuries, with a highest score of 104 against Northamptonshire in 1963. In addition, he was a superb close-to-the-wicket fielder who made 325 catches.

Perhaps the most fitting tribute to Trueman comes from John Arlott in his book *Fred: Portrait of a Fast Bowler*. The chapter entitled 'In his Pomp' captures a tremendous competitor and a master of his craft. 'At times he was lit by the fire of greatness', wrote Arlott of his subject. 'The most stirring memories of him recall days when, in the face of completely discouraging opposition, conditions and state of the game, over-bowled and ill-supported, he tried harder than any captain could fairly ask and sometimes succeeded beyond the bounds of reasonable possibility.'

Trueman always liked to call himself 'the finest fast bowler who ever drew breath', and on statistics alone he was not far off. Of all the fast bowlers to have taken in excess of 300 Test wickets, only Malcolm Marshall (20.94) and Curtly Ambrose (20.99) have better averages and only Marshall (46.76) a better strike rate.

In July 2006 he passed away peacefully at his home in the Yorkshire Dales, but his place in English cricket and Yorkshire in particular will likely remain unchallenged forever.

George Ulyett

RHB & RF, 1873–93

Born: 21 October 1851, Pitsmoor, Sheffield.
Died: 18 June 1898, Pitsmoor, Sheffield.
Played for: Yorkshire.
Test Matches: (25) 1877–90 Cap No. 11
Batting Career for England

I	NO	HS	Runs
39	0	149	949
AV	**100**	**50**	**Catches**
24.33	1	7	19

Bowling for England

Balls	Runs	Wkts	Av
2,627	1,020	50	20.40
Best	**5wl**	**10wl**	**Sr/Rate**
7–36	1	-	52.54

First-Class Career: (533 Matches) 1873–93
Batting

I	NO	HS	Runs
922	40	199*	20,629
AV	**100**	**50**	**Catches**
23.38	18	99	365

Bowling

Balls	Runs	Wkts	Av
31,043	13,113	650	20.17
Best	**5wl**	**10wl**	**Sr/Rate**
7–30	23	3	47.75

'Happy Jack', as he became known, was one of Yorkshire's greatest all-round cricketers in the last quarter of the 19th century. A Sheffield man by birth, he followed his brother Jack into the Pitsmoor team at the age of 16 and later played as a professional at the Old Horton Road ground in Bradford from 1871 to 1873. In the latter year he made his debut for Yorkshire, playing against Sussex at Bramall Lane and immediately impressed as a hard-hitting opening batsman. In 1878 he was credited with clearing the players' seats at Lord's, dropping the ball into the gravel behind the pavilion, a distance of 109 yards. In his early days Ulyett was also a goalkeeper for Sheffield Wednesday, thereby confirming his all-round sporting prowess. His opening partner at the time was Lewis Hall, renowned for his patience and immaculate defence, but he was a very slow scorer which was ideal for Jack's more flamboyant hitting and they complemented each other perfectly.

Not only was he a fine batsman, he was also a fast bowler, who moved the ball sharply back into the batsman. In 1873 he took his first five-wicket haul for Yorkshire, with 5 for 17 against Nottinghamshire at Huddersfield, and the following year he took the first of six seven-wicket hauls, with 7 for 82 against United South of England XI at Bradford Park Avenue, where he and Allen Hill bowled throughout both completed innings.

In the winter of 1877 he went on the tour to Australia with James Lillywhite's team and played in the inaugural Test match in Melbourne in 1877. He was the player who bowled the ball which damaged Charles Bannerman's finger and compelled the first centurion in Test cricket to retire. In all he toured Australia five times, and at Sydney in February 1882 he and R.G. Barlow shared the first century partnership in Test cricket. In the Melbourne Test during the series he scored 149, his only Test century and the first Test hundred for England in Australia. He was also the first Englishman to score two 50s in a Test match, with 52 and 63 at Melbourne in the second Test of 1877.

'Happy Jack' was also the first bowler to take four wickets in four balls in a first-class match in Australia (for Lord Harris's team against New South Wales in 1878–79). In his 25 Test matches he took 50 wickets at an average of only 20.40, with a best of 7 for 36 against Australia at Lord's in the second Test of the 1884 series, a match that England not only won by an innings and five runs, but which included a magnificent caught-and-bowled by Ulyett off the Australian big-hitting batsman George Bonnor, confirming his all-round ability in Test cricket.

In county cricket he continued to be a consistent performer both with bat and ball during the latter part of the 1870s and 1880s, and his best three seasons were in 1878 when he scored 1,083 runs, which included a top score of 109 against Gloucestershire, and took 7 for 30 against Surrey at Sheffield with the ball, his best first-class bowling figures; 1882, when he made 1,158 runs, his top score being 120 against Surrey; and 1887, when he scored 1,285 runs with a best of 199 not out, carrying his bat out of a total of 399 against Derbyshire, his highest score in first-class cricket. He also received a benefit that season which raised £1,000. With the ball he took 5 for 16 against Lancashire in the Roses Match of 1883, which included a hat-trick, while in 1889, also against Lancashire, he took a best analysis of 12 for 102, that included 7 for 50 and 5 for 52.

Altogether for the county he scored 14,157 runs at 24.11, which included 15 centuries, took 457 wickets at 17.90, with 21 five-wicket hauls, and held 235 catches.

On retirement he umpired for a time and then became landlord of the Vine Hotel in Brunswick Street, Pitsmoor, Sheffield. Unfortunately, his health had been failing him for some time, and he died at the age of 46 from pneumonia on 18 June 1898, a few days after watching his beloved Yorkshire play Kent at his home ground Bramall Lane, Sheffield.

Hedley Verity

RHB & SLA, 1930–39

Born: 18 May 1905, Headingley.
Died: 31 July 1943, Caserta, Italy.
Played for: Yorkshire.
Test Matches: (40) 1931–39 Cap No. 262
Batting Career for England

I	NO	HS	Runs
44	12	66*	669
AV	**100**	**50**	**Catches**
20.90	-	3	30

Bowling for England

Balls	Runs	Wkts	Av
11,173	3,510	144	24.37
Best	**5wl**	**10wl**	**Sr/Rate**
8–43	5	2	77.59

First-Class Career: (378 Matches) 1930–39
Batting

I	NO	HS	Runs
416	106	101	5,605
AV	**100**	**50**	**Catches**
18.08	1	13	269

Bowling

Balls	Runs	Wkts	Av
84,081	29,146	1,956	14.90
Best	**5wl**	**10wl**	**Sr/Rate**
10–10	164	54	42.98

Hedley Verity, the son of a coal merchant, was a pupil of Yeadon Secondary School and played his early cricket for Rawdon when he was only 15 years of age, moving to Horsforth Hall Park three years later. At that time he was an opening batsman and slow bowler and in his last season with them he took 62 wickets at nine runs apiece, in the process picking up the Yorkshire Council junior bowling prize. He was eventually offered a professional engagement at Accrington in the Lancashire League before moving to Central Lancashire League Club Middleton, where he played for three seasons.

Two years after an unsuccessful trial with Warwickshire in 1928, he made his debut for Yorkshire against Sussex and took over the position of slow left-arm bowler from Wilfred Rhodes. He was 25 years of age by then and in his first season collected 64 wickets at 12.42, which included 9 for 60 against Glamorgan at Swansea and 7 for 26 against Hampshire at Bournemouth. The following season, however, he rose to prominence with 188 first-class wickets at 13.52 (which included 169 for Yorkshire) and he finished second in the national bowling averages. His best return was all 10 wickets for 36 against Warwickshire at Headingley. He was only the second Yorkshire bowler to achieve this feat, Alonzo Drake being the first with 10 for 35 against Somerset in 1914. Verity also took seven wickets on four occasions and 8 for 33 against Glamorgan, once again at Swansea. In June 1931 he was awarded his county cap and it was no surprise when he was selected a month later for his Test debut against New Zealand at the Oval, where he took 4 for 85 in the match, while he was also selected as one of *Wisden's* Five Cricketers of the Year in 1932.

In 1932 he wrote his name in the annals of the game when he took 10 for 10 against Nottinghamshire at Leeds in the space of 52 balls, which included a hat-trick, but like his 10 wickets at Headingley against Warwickshire it was done without him bowling a single batsman. It still remains the best analysis in all first-class cricket. As a consequence he was chosen for the bodyline tour of 1932–33, and even in a pace dominated series he still took 11 wickets at only 24.63. In the summer of 1933 he took 17 wickets for 91 against Essex at Leyton (8 for 47 and 9 for 44), a record shared only by Colin Blyth of Kent and Tom Goddard of Gloucestershire. Twelve months later the MCC toured India for the first time and Verity was an automatic selection. He responded in his usual way by taking 23 wickets in the three-match series at only 16.82 runs per wicket, with a best of 11 for 153 at Madras (7 for 49 and 4 for 104). Two years later, however, in the 1934 series, on a drying pitch at Lord's he demolished the old enemy, taking 7 for 61 and 8 for 43 (his best Test figures) and 14 Australian wickets fell to him in just one day, which is still the most wickets taken against Australia in a day's play. He also dismissed Don Bradman eight times in Tests, which is more than any other bowler, while in Bradman's Best England XI he names Verity as the best English slow bowler he ever faced.

In the summers of 1935, 1936 and 1937 his bowling figures became legendary as he took over 200 first-class wickets in each, and in 1935 he took 199 at 13.87 for Yorkshire alone. He took 100 wickets in a season on nine occasions, and nine wickets seven times, eight wickets on 11 occasions and seven wickets 28 times.

Verity had wonderful control of spin and flight, and although he tended to push the ball through on wet wickets, he varied his pace to suit the conditions and occasionally looped the ball to great effect. He also had an uncanny ability to spot a batsman's weakness, and he was virtually unplayable on a drying wicket. He was a more than useful late-order batsman and scored one century for Yorkshire (101) against Jamaica in 1936 at Sabina Park, on Yorkshire's winter tour of 1935–36. In addition, he had a safe pair of hands at backward point, or anywhere close to the wicket.

In the last season before World War Two he took seven wickets for only nine runs against Sussex at Hove, and 14 wickets for 68 runs (7 for 48 and 7 for 20) against Leicestershire at Hull. In his last game in England that summer, while playing League cricket for Rawdon, he took 10 for 51.

On the outbreak of war he was commissioned in the Green Howards, but he was mortally wounded leading his company into battle at Sicily. He was taken to a hospital in an Italian POW camp in Caserta but died on 31 July 1943. It was a terrible loss not only to Yorkshire, but to English cricket in general.

For Yorkshire alone he took 1,558 wickets at 13.70, with 141 five-wicket hauls, scored 3,898 runs at 17.96 and took 191 catches.

Abraham Waddington

RHB & LFM, 1919–27

Born: 4 February 1893, Clayton, Bradford.
Died: 28 October 1959, Throxenby, Scarborough.
Played for: Yorkshire.
Test Matches: (2) 1920–21 Cap No. 184
Batting Career for England

I	NO	HS	Runs
4	0	7	16
AV	**100**	**50**	**Catches**
4.00	-	-	1

Bowling for England

Balls	Runs	Wkts	Av
276	119	1	119.00
Best	**5wl**	**10wl**	**Sr/Rate**
1–35	-	-	276.00

First-Class Career: (266 Matches) 1919–27
Batting

I	NO	HS	Runs
265	69	114	2,527
AV	**100**	**50**	**Catches**
12.89	1	4	232

Bowling

Balls	Runs	Wkts	Av
39,842	16,833	852	19.75
Best	**5wl**	**10wl**	**Sr/Rate**
8–34	51	10	46.76

A fine cricketer even as a young schoolboy, 'Abe' Waddington was playing West Bradford League cricket for Crossley Hall and Sandy Lane when he was not even a teenager. He moved to Lidgett Green and then Laisterdyke and was a member of their Bradford League Championship-winning team of 1913. In the last season before the war he took 98 wickets at 12 runs each for Wakefield, before joining up with the Bradford Pals and being wounded at Serre, France, in 1916.

The war stopped what could have been a blossoming early career in first-class cricket, for when it started again in 1919 Waddington was 26 years old. However, he began to make up for the lost years in earnest, taking 4 for 26 against Derbyshire at Chesterfield on his Yorkshire debut, and although he missed the next game he returned to take 9 for 65 in the match against Essex at Hull and then snared 12 for 126 (6 for 58 and 6 for 68) against Gloucestershire at Leeds. He retained his place for the remainder of the season and played a huge part in Yorkshire winning the Championship by taking 100 wickets at 18.74 each.

A native of Clayton, Bradford, he was a left-arm fast-medium bowler with a curved run and classical upright action. He could not only swing and seam the ball, but could extract considerable lift from the pitch, which caused discomfort for many of the leading batsmen of the day. He was also a useful late-order batsman and a good fielder, though he had a short fuse and his quick temper got him into trouble on more than one occasion.

In 1920 he took his best return for a season, 140 wickets at 16.67, which included 12 for 74 (5 for 49 and 7 for 25) against Leicestershire at Hull and 13 for 48 in 32.3 overs (6 for 30 and 7 for 18) against Northamptonshire at Northampton, as he and Emmott Robinson (6 for 34) bowled unchanged throughout the match, Northamptonshire making only 57 and 40.

As a consequence he was chosen for the winter tour to Australia but was only selected for two Test matches, the first at Sydney, where he took 1 for 35 and scored 7 in the first innings, both best figures in Test cricket, and the fourth at Melbourne where he was wicketless in five overs. Indeed, his best performance on what was a disappointing tour was against an Australian XI at Brisbane, where he and fellow Yorkshireman Rockley Wilson (56) shared a last-wicket partnership of 97, Waddington making 51 not out.

However, he was still an integral part of Yorkshire's attack and in 1921 and 1922 took in excess of 100 wickets in each season, with 132 at 15.83 in the latter, making him the county's top wicket-taker. Included in this season was 7 for 6 against Surrey at Hull, and three 'eight-fors': 8 for 35 against Hampshire at Bradford; 8 for 39 against Kent at Headingley; and then a career best of 8 for 34 against Northamptonshire, once again at Headingley.

In the following summer of 1923 he was well on target to reach the milestone again when, having taken 65 wickets at 17.92, he slipped on a wet outfield at Huddersfield, damaging his shoulder ligaments, and was out for the season.

Twelve months later his fiery temper flared up in the match against Middlesex at Bramall Lane, when the umpires reported him for his attitude towards their decisions, which had often led to a barracking from the player.

The season of 1925 was the last time he took 100 wickets (105 at 20.23), his powers declining somewhat in the following two seasons, obviously still troubled by his shoulder injury, but he did score his maiden first-class century in 1927 with a score of 114 against Worcestershire at Headingley. He refused Yorkshire's terms for 1928, preferring to play League cricket for Bradford, and so came to an end a fine, but often volatile, cricket career. Fittingly, Yorkshire granted him a benefit in 1928 which realised £1,000. For the county he played 255 matches, scored 2,396 runs at 12.95, took 835 wickets at 19.40 and held 222 catches.

An all-round sportsman, Waddington was also on the books of Bradford City as a goalkeeper, and in 1921 he played seven games for Halifax Town, as well as representing Yorkshire at golf.

He later went into business as the head of P. Waddington and Company, fat refiners in Bradford. He died in Scarborough at the age of 66 in 1959.

Edward Wainwright

RHB & ROB, 1888–1902

Born: 8 April 1865, Tinsley, Sheffield.
Died: 28 October 1919, Sheffield.
Played for: Yorkshire.
Test Matches: (5) 1893–98 Cap No. 85
Batting Career For England

I	NO	HS	Runs
9	0	49	132
AV	**100**	**50**	**Catches**
14.66	-	-	2

Bowling for England

Balls	Runs	Wkts	Av
127	73	0	-
Best	**5wl**	**10wl**	**Sr/Rate**
-	-	-	-

First-Class Career: (388 Matches) 1888–1902
Batting

I	NO	HS	Runs
603	32	228	12,475
AV	**100**	**50**	**Catches**
21.84	19	48	346

Bowling

Balls	Runs	Wkts	Av
45,986	19,331	1,062	18.20
Best	**5wl**	**10wl**	**Sr/Rate**
9–66	63	15	43.30

Born in Tinsley, Sheffield, Ted Wainwright was the elder brother of Walker Wainwright, who played 24 times for Yorkshire between 1903 and 1905 and was one of Yorkshire's best professional all-round cricketers in the period leading up to World War One.

He began his cricket career with Tinsley, and after a successful trial with the County Second XI he made his debut for Yorkshire against the MCC in 1888. In June of that year, against the Australians at Bradford, he scored his maiden first-class century (105) after being sent in to open the second innings.

Two years later he took all 10 wickets against Staffordshire at Sheffield, but the game was not recognised as first-class, and in 1891 he took 8 for 33 and 8 for 49 against Warwickshire and Middlesex respectively.

Ted was a true Yorkshire character, and although he had a dry sense of humour he could also be blunt at times. A tall and sound right-hand batsman, he could score quickly when required, but it was with his off-spin bowling on wet wickets that he first found fame. On dry pitches he was somewhat ordinary, but he was an outstanding slip fielder.

In 1892 he was the leading all-rounder in the Championship, scoring 641 runs at 27.86 and taking 77 wickets at 16.22. In the match at Bramall Lane against Middlesex he took 12 for 96 (4 for 47 and 8 for 49) and in the Sussex game, also at Sheffield, he scored 114 runs and took 11 for 123, thus completing 100 runs and 10 wickets in a match for the only time in his career. Only four other Yorkshire players, George Hirst (on three occasions), Emmott Robinson, Ray Illingworth and Gavin Hamilton have achieved that feat in county cricket.

The following year he took 114 wickets at 12.55, finishing second in the national bowling averages, and made his Test debut at Lord's against Australia, scoring 1 and 26.

In 1894 he proved what a magnificent bowler he was on wet wickets by taking 166 wickets at 12.73 (which included 97 at only 10.71 in the Championship). He was not only the leading bowler in the country, but his average of 10.71 was also the lowest of any bowler since the County Championship began in 1890. At Dewsbury he snared 13 wickets for only 38 runs against Sussex, including 6 for 18 and 7 for 20 with five wickets in seven balls, including a hat-trick. He also took a career best that year of 9 for 66 against Middlesex at Bramall Lane.

Three years later, in 1897, he achieved the double for the first and only time in his career with 1,612 runs at 35.82, which included 171 in four hours against Middlesex, and 101 wickets at 23.06. His performances earned him a trip to Australia under the leadership of Andrew Stoddart, and although he played in four of the five Tests he failed to take a wicket on the hard, dry surfaces, and is the only Yorkshire bowler not to take a wicket in his Test appearances. In the remaining first-class matches he opened the batting, and he scored his highest Test score of 49 in the final Test at Sydney. He also recorded 50 and 68 against New South Wales also at the SCG and his only century on tour, 105 against South Australia at Adelaide.

In the summer of 1898 he was given a Yorkshire benefit and a fixture against Lancashire, which raised the sum of £1,800. At New Road, Worcester, he scored what he always considered was his best innings, a magnificent 182 out of a total of 269, steering Yorkshire home by three wickets, with only three other batsmen reaching double figures in the innings.

The remaining three years of his career saw him register plenty of runs, and in 1899 he recorded his highest first-class score, 228 against Surrey at the Oval, sharing a still record partnership of 340 with George Hirst (186) in three and a half hours. Despite the emergence of Hirst and Rhodes, which restricted his bowling somewhat, he still managed to take 7 for 38 against Derbyshire at Derby.

Wainwright's last full season was two years later when he scored 1,086 runs, which included his last century, 112 against South Africa at Harrogate, and his best bowling return of 5 for 19 against Sussex at Bradford.

For the county he played 352 matches, scored 11,092 runs at 21.53, with 18 centuries, took 998 wickets at 17.77 and held 327 catches.

When he left Yorkshire in 1902 he played in the Bassetlaw League with Wiseton and Worksop Cricket Clubs, before being appointed coach at Shrewsbury School in Shropshire in 1913. His assistant there was Neville Cardus, who wrote about his days with Wainwright in his book *Close of Play*. Six years later he died in his native city after a long illness at the age of 54.

Albert Ward

RHB & OB, 1886–1904

Born: 21 November 1865, Waterloo, Leeds.
Died: 6 January 1939, Bolton, Lancashire.
Played for: Yorkshire and Lancashire.
Test Matches: (7) 1893–95 Cap No. 86
Batting Career for England

I	NO	HS	Runs
13	0	117	487
AV	**100**	**50**	**Ct/St**
37.46	1	3	1

First-Class Career: (385 Matches) 1886–1904
Batting

I	NO	HS	Runs
642	51	219	17,783
AV	**100**	**50**	**Ct/St**
30.08	29	87	168

Bowling

Balls	Runs	Wkts	Av
5,036	2,473	71	34.83
Best	**5wl**	**10wl**	**Sr/Rate**
6–29	4	-	70.92

Albert Ward learned his cricket with Hunslet Cricket Club before he had a four-game trial with Yorkshire as a 20-year-old in 1886. He made his first-class debut against Middlesex at Bradford, scoring 22, which was his highest score in seven innings, but he only averaged 6.83 and was not called upon again. He then took up an assistant teaching position at Leyland and became a professional at Darwen before he decided to qualify for Lancashire, making his debut against the MCC in 1889. He was impressive in the game, making the top score, and when he returned to Lord's to play against Middlesex he again top scored with 114 not out and finished second in the averages at 29.00. He was a valuable member of a team that finished level with Nottinghamshire and Surrey at the top of the County Championship. Indeed, when the season ended the magazine *Cricket* noted of Ward: 'There are few instances of such remarkable success as the outcome of a professional introduction to important matches. It is quite possible that that there may have been cases of similar fortune, but of late years we cannot recall to mind, one in which a young player has reached at the end of a season, such a high position in the batting averages of a leading county, as A. Ward can claim in this year of Grace 1889.'

In 1890 he scored 1,511 runs at 37.77, which included 145 against Kent, scored in 195 minutes. He also shared an eighth-wicket partnership of 150 with Charles Robert Hartley against

Leicestershire, a record which stood for 79 years. In passing 1,000 runs for the season he became the first Lancashire professional to do so and was named one of *Wisden's* Five Cricketers of the Year.

In the following summer he made his highest first-class score for Lancashire, 185 against Kent at Gravesend, and in 1893 he scored 1,035 runs at 38.33. When the Australians visited Old Trafford he carried his bat with 45 not out in a total of only 97, and the innings earned him an England call-up for the Oval Test. He batted soundly to make 55 and kept his place for the next Test at Old Trafford, which was drawn, and as expected he was selected for the tour to Australia in 1894–95.

In the first Test at Sydney he top scored in both innings with 75 and 117, England winning by 10 runs, while in the fifth and last Test at Melbourne, with the series tied at two Tests each, England were set 297 runs to win. Early wickets were lost, but Ward, defending for his life, scored a valuable 93 and added 210 with J.T. Brown (140), to give England victory by six wickets, thereby enabling them to retain the Ashes. He went on to top score in the series with 419 runs at 41.90, but inexplicably he was never selected for England again. On the tour he also recorded his highest first-class score, 219 against South Australia at Adelaide, and made the most runs on tour, 916 at an average of 41.

In 1895 he again carried his bat for Lancashire, making 75 not out in a total of 168 against Leicestershire and notched up 1,790 runs at an average of over 42.

While essentially a careful opening batsman, in 1897 against Derbyshire at Derby he went from 54 not out overnight to 162 before lunch on the second day of the match. Two years later he twice carried his bat, 109 out of 337 against Hampshire at Southampton and 83 not out (of 262) against Middlesex at Lord's. In the return game against Derbyshire at Old Trafford in 1899 he was dismissed in an unusual way; in playing a ball from Frank Davidson he broke his bat, whereupon a piece of the wood knocked off his bail and he was out for 72 hit wicket.

Although only an occasional bowler, he claimed Arthur Shrewsbury, George Hirst, Charles Fry and Charles Townsend among his first victims, while in 1899 he had his best bowling figures of 6 for 29 against Derbyshire at Glossop.

In 1902 he took a deserved benefit against Yorkshire at Old Trafford. Over 24,000 paid at the gate on the first day and the total amount realised at the game came to £1,739.

For Lancashire Ward scored 15,392 runs at 30.96, with 24 centuries and 65 wickets at 36.61. He played 330 matches between 1889 and 1904, scored 1,000 runs in a season on nine occasions and carried his bat five times.

John Henry Wardle

LHB & SLA, 1946–68

Born: 8 January 1923, Ardsley, Barnsley.
Died: 23 July 1985, Doncaster.
Played for: Yorkshire and Cambridgeshire.
Test Matches: (28) 1948–57 Cap No. 333

Batting Career for England

I	NO	HS	Runs
41	8	66	653
AV	**100**	**50**	**Catches**
19.78	-	2	12

Bowling for England

Balls	Runs	Wkts	Av
6,597	2,080	102	20.39
Best	**5wl**	**10wl**	**Sr/Rate**
7–36	5	1	64.68

First-Class Career: (412 Matches) 1946–68

Batting

I	NO	HS	Runs
527	71	79	7,333
AV	**100**	**50**	**Catches**
16.08	-	18	256

Bowling

Balls	Runs	Wkts	Av
102,367	35,027	1,846	18.97
Best	**5wl**	**10wl**	**Sr/Rate**
9–25	134	29	55.45

Born in Ardsley, near Barnsley, Johnny Wardle began working for the NCB when he left school as a colliery fitter, and he played his early League cricket for Denaby and Cortonwood.

He began his career at Yorkshire when they were looking for a replacement for Hedley Verity, who had been killed in action during the war. They had turned to Arthur Booth, but his illness in 1946 saw them give Wardle the opportunity to make his debut against Worcestershire at Headingley in the same year. Twelve months later, the young Wardle had cemented his place with 86 first-class wickets at 25.46, with a best of 7 for 66 against Middlesex at Headingley, and he was soon awarded his county cap.

Johnny was a unique slow left-arm bowler, who apart from his orthodox ball could bowl the chinaman and googly consistently and on a good length. He was also a useful late-order batsman who hit the ball hard and a brilliant close-to-the-wicket fielder.

His potential soon alerted the England selectors and he was selected for the tour to the West Indies with the MCC, playing in the Test at Port-of-Spain, Trinidad, but he was given only three overs by the skipper Gubby Allen.

In 1948 he took 150 wickets, which included a best of 8 for 87 against Derbyshire at Chesterfield, while he took 12 hauls of five wickets per inning or above. An injury restricted his appearances the following season, but he still took 103 first-class wickets at 22.65, with a best of 7 for 41 against Surrey at the Oval.

In 1950 he took 8 for 26 against Middlesex at Lord's, 7 for 65 against Worcestershire at Worcester and 172 wickets for Yorkshire at only 16.30. He bowled more balls that season (9,551) than any bowler since Tich Freeman in 1934, and his 741 maidens showed just how accurate a bowler he was.

He continued to take well in excess of 100 wickets per season, 127 in 1951 (this season also saw his highest batting score, 79 against Lancashire), 172 in 1952, 146 in 1953 and 155 in 1954, which included his best ever bowling figures when he routed Lancashire at Old Trafford and took 9 for 25 off 21.2 overs and 12 for 85 overall. This summer he also took 16 for 112 against Sussex at Anlaby Road, Hull, which included 9 for 48 in the first innings and 7 for 64 in the second.

In the Oval Test of 1954, when England were in trouble against Pakistan, he took 7 for 56 in the second innings to ease the pressure. His good form led to him being selected for the winter tour to Australia, where he earned his trip with 57 tour wickets at 20.45. In the second Test at Sydney, an attacking innings of 35 when he added 43 with Brian Statham for the 10th wicket was vital in an England win by only 38 runs. In the fifth and final drawn Test at Sydney he bamboozled the Aussies with his wrist-spin and took 5 for 79 and 3 for 51.

In the summer of 1955 he took 195 first-class wickets at 16.14, with 13 five-wicket hauls and two 10-wicket hauls. In three Tests against South Africa he took 15 wickets at 18.2 runs per wicket by bowling a mixture of orthodox left-arm spin and round the wicket wrist-spin with surprising accuracy.

Due to the Laker/Lock combination he was often overlooked for England, but in the 28 matches he did play he took 102 wickets at only 20.39, and only Bobby Peel (16.98), Johnny Briggs (17.74) and Colin Blyth (18.63) have better averages as England slow bowlers. Indeed, a renowned former England player, Trevor Bailey, remarked that had Wardle played in the Old Trafford Test of 1955 instead of Lock, Jim Laker would never have taken 19 of the 20 wickets to fall.

On the 1956–57 tour of South Africa, Wardle, bowling predominantly googlies and chinamen, took 26 wickets in the four Tests at 13.80, which included 12 for 89 at Cape Town, with a Test best of 7 for 36, and he took 90 wickets in total from all matches at 12.25 apiece.

After the tour, Wardle returned to find that Yorkshire had installed Ronnie Burnett, an amateur from the Bradford League, as captain to impose discipline on the senior professionals. A clash was inevitable, and Wardle openly criticised the committee in the way the club was being run. They responded by dropping him for the Bank Holiday match with Lancashire and then sacking him. When Wardle announced he would play for Nottinghamshire, who were struggling at the time, Yorkshire refused to allow a special registration. He was also dropped by the MCC from the forthcoming Ashes tour, but he went as a journalist instead. He then departed to Lancashire League cricket, playing first with Nelson, then Rishton and finally Cambridgeshire, where he played Minor County Championship cricket. However, he was still only 35 years of age, with much to offer, and it was one of Yorkshire's biggest ever mistakes that they let him go. Fortunately, the rift was healed and he was made a honorary life member of the county and became a bowling advisor, later helping Geoff Cope with his action. In total for Yorkshire alone he took 1,539 wickets at 18.13, with 117 five-wicket hauls, scored 5,765 runs at 15.96 and took 210 catches.

Without question Wardle will go down in the history of Yorkshire cricket as one of their greatest bowlers and perhaps, arguably, the best spin bowler ever on all types of wickets.

William Watson

LHB & RM, 1939–64

Born: 7 March 1920, Bolton-on-Dearne, Rotherham.

Died: 24 April 2004, Johannesburg, South Africa.

Played for: Yorkshire and Leicestershire.

Test Matches: (23) 1951–59 Cap No. 357

Batting Career for England

I	NO	HS	Runs
37	3	116	879
AV	**100**	**50**	**Ct/St**
25.85	2	3	8

First-Class Career: (468 Matches) 1939–64

Batting

I	NO	HS	Runs
753	109	257	25,670
AV	**100**	**50**	**Ct/St**
39..86	55	132	295

Bowling

Balls	Runs	Wkts	Av
194	127	-	-
Best	**5wl**	**10wl**	**Sr/Rate**
-	-	-	-

Although Willie Watson was born in Bolton-on-Dearne, he was educated at Royds Hall Grammar School and played cricket for Paddock in the Huddersfield League. He followed the usual pattern of Yorkshire cricketers, appearing first for the second XI before making his debut against Nottinghamshire at Bramall Lane in 1939, playing four games in his first season.

He took over from Maurice Leyland after World War Two and the stylish left-hander notched up his first century for the county against Surrey in 1947, making 153 not out. He also registered 1,331 runs at 31.69, and only Len Hutton scored more for Yorkshire that summer.

Over the next four years Watson scored 3,435 runs for the county at an impressive average of 43.98, which gained him Test selection against South Africa in 1951 at Trent Bridge. He made 57 on debut and played in all five Tests, scoring 240 runs at 34.28, thereby becoming one of the select few who have had the distinction of being a double international, having represented England in football.

Two years later at Lord's he carved his name into Test match history when, in a partnership with Trevor Bailey, he thwarted all attempts by the Australians to dislodge them on a thrilling last day. He

strode to the wicket with the score 12 for 3 and batted for 346 minutes for 109 runs, as Bailey made 71. The pair survived from 12.45pm to 5.50pm to steer England to safety, enabling England to win the series at the Oval and regain the Ashes. He was later named as one of *Wisden's* Five Cricketers of the Year.

Watson continued to play on and off for his country until the 1958–59 series against New Zealand, making 23 Test appearances and scoring 879 runs at 25.85 with just one more century, 116 against the West Indies at Kingston, Jamaica, in the 1953–54 series. His highest first-class score was also on this tour (257), when he shared a stand of 402 with Tom Graveney (231) against British Guiana at Georgetown.

However, he continued to score runs for Yorkshire, amassing over 1,000 runs per season, with the exception of 1950 when he notched up only 636 (but at a very high average of 70.66), which was due to limited appearances because of his football commitments.

He had a benefit season in 1956, which yielded £5,356. For the White Rose County he scored 13,953 runs at an average of 38.21 with 26 centuries and a highest score of 214 not out against Worcestershire at New Road in 1955. He also held 170 catches. And he left Yorkshire at the end of the 1957 season to join Leicestershire as assistant secretary and captain.

He showed excellent form in his first season at Grace Road, scoring 1,521 runs at 47.53, and he was second only to Peter May in the national averages. He again came second in 1959 with 2,212 runs at 55.30, which included seven centuries to equal the county best in a season.

In 1961 he notched up his highest first-class score in England, 217 not out, against Somerset at Taunton, when he shared a unbroken third-wicket partnership of 316 with Alan Wharton which remained a county record until 2003, when it was broken by Darren Maddy and Brad Hodge (436 unbroken) in a game agaist Loughborough University.

In addition to being a talented cricketer he was also a fine footballer, and he began his career at Huddersfield Town, making 11 appearances before the war. He signed for Sunderland in April 1946 and appeared in 223 League and Cup games during the next seven years, before departing to become player-manager of Halifax Town. Indeed, he had two spells as manager at the Shay (1954–1956 and 1964–1966), and he also managed Bradford City (1966–1968). An attacking right-half, he soon gained the attention of the England selectors, and he made his debut against Northern Ireland in 1949 in a 9–2 England win. Watson played in the following game against Italy (2–0), and in games against Wales (4–2) and Yugoslavia (2–2) in 1950. He was also a member of the 1950 World Cup squad in Brazil, but he did not play a game.

Watson was a Test selector for three years from 1962 to 1965 and ended his career at Grace Road in 1964. He emigrated to South Africa in 1968 to coach at the Wanderers club in Johannesburg, but he still continued to follow England's fortunes with interest. He died in Johannesburg in April 2004 at the age of 84.

Craig White

RHB & RFM, 1990–to date

Born: 16 December 1969, Morley, Bradford.
Played for: Yorkshire, Central Districts and Victoria.
Test Matches: (30) 1994–2002 Cap No. 567
Batting Career for England

I	NO	HS	Runs
50	7	121	1,052
AV	**100**	**50**	**Catches**
24.46	1	5	14

Bowling for England

Balls	Runs	Wkts	Av
3,959	2,220	59	37.62
Best	**5wl**	**10wl**	**Sr/Rate**
5–32	3	-	67.10

First-Class Career: (276 Matches) 1990 to date

Batting

I	NO	HS	Runs
438	57	186	12,395
AV	**100**	**50**	**Catches**
32.53	21	62	167

Bowling

Balls	Runs	Wkts	Av
21,286	11,260	395	28.50
Best	**5wl**	**10wl**	**Sr/Rate**
8–55	11	-	53.80

Although born in Yorkshire, Craig White was brought up in Australia in the Victoria town of Bendigo, where he attended Bendigo High School. He played cricket and Aussie rules football for his school, and later played for the Australia Under-17 and Under-19 cricket teams, mainly as batsman, but one who could keep wicket and bowl off-spin. He also played sub-district cricket for Bendigo United and grade cricket for Hawthorn in Melbourne.

In 1990 he arrived in England on a cricket scholarship and made his first-class debut against Northamptonshire at Headingley in the opening game of the season before he had even appeared for the second XI. He played eight first-class games that season without much success, but in the second team he notched up 469 runs at an average of 156.33, with a 209 not out and 115 not out against Worcestershire at New Road, plus 11 wickets at 21.36. Yorkshire signed him, but initially he had to do so as an overseas player. In the winter he briefly returned to Australia and played two matches for Victoria.

In his early 20s White changed from off-spin to bowling fast-medium after doubts had been raised as to his action as an off-spinner. During the season of 1993 he came of age as a Yorkshire cricketer, scoring 816 first-class runs, which included his first century (146) against Durham at Headingley, while he also topped the bowling averages with 12 wickets at 24.33. In the process he was awarded his county cap in August of that year.

When Raymond Illingworth became the new England boss the following year he decided he needed an all-rounder in the middle order and selected White for the first Test against New Zealand at Trent Bridge, but he did not do enough in his eight Tests and was dropped.

However, he became an integral part of the Yorkshire team, and in 1995 he scored three centuries for the county, 107 against Leicestershire, and 110 and 107 not out against Northamptonshire and Worcestershire respectively. The following summer he notched up 949 runs at 32.72, which included his highest first-class score (181) in the Roses match at Headingley, putting on 252 with wicket-keeper Richard Blakey (109 not out) for the sixth wicket.

His fast paced bowling was also having an impact, and between 1996 and 1999 he took 142 wickets at 25.18, which included a career best of 8 for 55 against Gloucestershire at the King's School Ground, Gloucester, which included a hat-trick as well. He was now firmly established as a top-six batsman and a first or second change bowler.

In the winter he went on the 1999–2000 tour to South Africa and Zimbabwe, taking a best of 5 for 21 against Zimbabwe at Bulawayo. Unfortunately, in 2000 he suffered a blackout and woke up in the streets of Scarborough. However, he recovered sufficiently to get a recall to the England team against the West Indies and grabbed his chance with both hands. Apart from useful runs, his reverse-swing bowling at a pace of up to 90 mph from around the wicket troubled all the opposition's batsmen. He took his first five-wicket haul in England's sensational two-day victory at Headingley, and he recorded his best figures in a Test with 5 for 32 in the final Test at the Oval and was one of 12 players to be awarded a central contract.

In the winter of 2000–01 he went to the subcontinent, scoring 93 against Pakistan at Lahore and scored his highest Test score, a brilliant 121 against India in the heat and dust of Ahmedabad for his only Test century.

Two years later he went on the tour to Australia, playing in the first four Tests and scoring a fine 85 not out at Melbourne, but a rib injury prevented him playing in England's only success on the tour, the fifth Test at Sydney. In the one-day series at the MCG he hit his highest score in one-day internationals, 57 not out.

He recovered from his injury in time to play in the 2003 World Cup, but that was the last of his England appearances. His back injuries were taking their toll and he decided to concentrate only on his batting, filling a gap in Yorkshire's top order by opening the innings. As a batsman he was always aggressive, looking to play his shots, and never afraid to thump the slow bowlers over the top.

In 2004 he was appointed Yorkshire captain and a year later led them to promotion from Division Two of the County Championship. He resigned as captain at the end of 2006 and is currently skipper of the second XI.

For Yorkshire he played 195 first-class games, scored 9,071 runs at 34.23, with 15 centuries, took 272 wickets at 27.80 and held 126 catches

John James Whitaker

RHB & RM, 1983–99

Born: 5 May 1962, Skipton.
Played for: Leicestershire.
Test Matches: (1) 1986 Cap No. 524
Batting Career for England

I	NO	HS	Runs
1	0	11	11
AV	100	50	Catches
11.00	-	-	1

First-Class Career: (315 Matches) 1983–99
Batting

I	NO	HS	Runs
497	51	218	17,198
AV	100	50	Catches
38.56	38	80	172

Bowling

Balls	Runs	Wkts	Ave
178	268	2	134.00
Best	5wl	10wl	Sr/Rate
1–29	-	-	89.00

Although born at Skipton, James Whitaker attended Uppingham School, playing for four years in the first XI, and was captain in 1980 and 1981, topping the batting averages in the latter season. He scored many runs for the Leicestershire Second XI during the summers of 1982 and 1983, and made his first-class debut for the county during 1983.

The following year he gained a regular first-team place and registered 1,097 runs at 36.57 with two centuries. His maiden century came in his first Championship match of the season against Somerset at Grace Road and was a superb innings. He had arrived at the crease to face a hat-trick ball from Ian Botham with Leicestershire at 30 for 4, but he survived and smashed 160, his century taking only 118 minutes. In the Natwest Trophy against Wiltshire he registered another big hundred, this time 155, which was a record at this time, but it lasted only a few weeks as David Gower beat it by one run in the next round against Derbyshire.

In 1985 he had a purple July, with centuries in three consecutive matches, and was quickly gaining a reputation as a hard-hitting batsman. His sharp eyesight enabled him to get away with shots that would have caused the downfall of a much less talented player. He also had the ability to make aggressive shots off both the front and back foot, with his runs came at a very high rate, and he deliberately attacked the bowling in the same manner, whether it was a first-class Championship match or a limited over one-day game.

The year of 1986 proved to be the most prolific of his career, as runs flowed from his bat to the tune of 1,526 at an average of 66.34, and he finished the year as the top English batsman in the first-class averages, second only to Hampshire's Gordon Greenidge. He also notched up his first double hundred with 200 not out against neighbours Nottinghamshire at Grace Road, which contained three sixes and 30 fours, sharing in a partnership of 244 with Peter Willey for the fourth wicket. Unfortunately for Whitaker, in the next match he had fingers broken in each of his hands by Malcolm Marshall when Hampshire were the visitors to Grace Road. Undeterred, however, he returned to the team a few weeks later to notch up 100 and 82, both unbeaten against his native county Yorkshire. Not surprisingly, his magnificent season not only gained him an award as one of *Wisden's* Five Cricketers of the Year, but also a trip to Australia for the Ashes series.

Despite a century against South Australia in his first game, his opportunities were few and, although an injury to Ian Botham gave him a chance to play his first Test at Adelaide, he made only 11, being caught at mid-off. Sadly for him, this proved to be his one and only innings at Test level. He did, however, play in two limited over internationals in the Sharjah Cup in April 1987, when he made 44 not out against India.

In 1990 Whitaker was appointed vice-captain of Leicestershire and he continued to score heavily at first-class level, with 1,767 runs at 45.30. He also scored his highest first-class score, 218 out of 681 for 7 against Yorkshire at Bradford. His innings came from 324 balls and included a partnership of 218 for the fourth wicket with Vince Wells. In the same season he scored another large hundred, 168 against Worcestershire, sharing a fifth-wicket stand of 320 with Aftab Habib.

In 1996 he was made captain and led the county to two County Championships in 1996 and 1998 and also managed to complete centuries in all the three major one-day competitions. In 1999 he suffered a bad leg injury which forced his retirement at the end of the summer, but he continued his association with the county until 2005, working first as general manager and then coach and director of cricket.

For Leicestershire, in 306 first-class matches, he scored 16,845 runs at 38.90, with 37 centuries, and took two wickets for 168 runs. In one-day cricket he notched up 7,602 runs at 32.90, with six tons.

In January 2008, when Geoff Miller became the England national selector, James joined a four-man panel which also included Peter Moores and Ashley Giles.

Revd Clement Eustace Marco Wilson

RHB & RFM/SLA, 1895–99

Born: 15 May 1875, Bolderstone, Stocksbridge.
Died: 8 February 1944, Calverhall, Shropshire.
Played for: Cambridge University and
Yorkshire.
Test Matches: (2) 1898–99 Cap No. 119
Batting Career for England

I	NO	HS	Runs
4	1	18	42
AV	**100**	**50**	**Ct/St**
14.00	-	-	-

First-Class Career: (51 Matches) 1895–99
Batting

I	NO	HS	Runs
78	10	115	1,632
AV	**100**	**50**	**Ct/St**
24.00	1	10	33

Bowling

Balls	Runs	Wkts	Av
5,719	2,283	121	18.86
Best	**5wl**	**10wl**	**Sr/Rate**
7–24	6	2	47.26

The Revd 'Clem' Wilson was born in Bolsterstone, a village near Stocksbridge, Sheffield, and was the eldest of five sons of William Reginald Wilson, the vicar of Bolsterstone. He was educated at Uppingham School in the county of Rutland and was an outstanding schoolboy cricketer. He learned much of his early cricket under the supervision of Heathfield (H.H.) Stephenson, who captained the first English side in Australia in 1861–62. In the summer of 1893 he scored 722 runs for the school, which included three consecutive centuries, 117, 145 and 183 not out against Repton School, when he carried his bat through the innings. He averaged 90.25 for the season and also headed the bowling averages.

A year later he went to Trinity College, Cambridge, where he gained his Blue as a freshman. In 1895 he made his first-class debut against Somerset at Fenners, taking a career best of 7 for 24 with the ball, and in three consecutive Varsity games against Oxford he scored 80, 77 and 115 (his highest first-class score) in 1898, his last year at university. He also represented Cambridge at hurling and in 1895 went on Mitchell's tour to South Africa.

Wilson was a sound, right-handed defensive batsman, who rarely hit the ball in the air and seldom threw his wicket away. He was also a very accurate right-arm medium-fast bowler, who once resorted to bowling left-arm slow against Surrey in 1895 while appearing for Cambridge, ending a partnership of 306 between Abel and Holland by holding a return catch off his own bowling.

In 1896 he made his debut for Yorkshire against Essex at Leyton, and, playing as an amateur, he made eight first-class appearances for the county between 1896 and 1899, hitting his top score for Yorkshire (91 not out) against Kent at Canterbury in 1897, the highest innings of the match. In the same year, while still at Cambridge, he played a vital part in posting a remarkable win over his native county, assisting Gilbert Jessop in scoring the 125 needed to win the match.

The following year he took 3 for 38 against Somerset, his best figures for Yorkshire, and in the winter of 1898 he toured South Africa under the leadership of Lord Hawke, playing in both Test matches at Johannesburg and Cape Town. He made his Test debut in the first match at the Old Wanderers Ground, Johannesburg, and scored 18 in the second innings, his best score in Test cricket.

In 1899 he retired from first-class cricket after playing eight matches for Yorkshire, scoring 256 runs at 25.60, taking 12 wickets at 21.41 and holding three catches.

It was then that he decided to follow his father William by entering the church, becoming the vicar of Sandhutton, near Thirsk, North Yorkshire. He was appointed rector of Eccleston in Cheshire in 1911, and from 1940 until his death at Calversham in Shropshire in 1944 he was prebendary of Bishopshull in Lichfield Cathedral.

He possessed a vast collection of cricket books and memorabilia, and his son D.C. Wilson played cricket for Cambridge in 1939. In the 1890s Clem also played for the Free Foresters and the Yorkshire Gentlemen in the 1920s.

Donald Wilson

LHB & SLA, 1957–74

Born: 7 August 1937, Settle.
Played for: Yorkshire.
Test Matches: (6) 1963–71 Cap No. 418
Batting Career for England

I	NO	HS	Runs
7	1	42	75
AV	**100**	**50**	**Catches**
12.50	-	-	1

Bowling for England

Balls	Runs	Wkts	Av
1,472	466	11	42.36
Best	**5wl**	**10wl**	**Sr/Rate**
2–17	-	-	133.81

First-Class Career: (422 Matches) 1957–74
Batting

I	NO	HS	Runs
533	91	112	6,230
AV	**100**	**50**	**Catches**
14.09	1	10	250

Bowling

Balls	Runs	Wkts	Av
69,724	24,977	1,189	21.00
Best	**5wl**	**10wl**	**Sr/Rate**
8–36	50	8	58.64

A native of North Yorkshire, Don Wilson first played cricket for his school Ingleton Secondary Modern, and then went on to play League cricket for Settle. He was recommended to Yorkshire by Len Hutton and made his first-class debut for the county against Scotland at Whitehaugh, Paisley, a match in which he snared three wickets for 28 runs off 26.4 overs.

A tall and wiry bowler, he used his height to full advantage and relied on flight and bounce, rather than vicious spin. He was generally an attacking slow bowler, who, similar to his predecessor Johnny Wardle, expected a wicket with every ball while still maintaining a good line and length. A late order batsman, he loved to attack the bowling, and he used his long reach to hit the ball over the top on many occasions, while as a fielder he was brilliant anywhere on the field.

In the summer of 1958 he was the leading wicket-taker in the second XI, with 61 wickets at 10.08, and he also took 17 first-class wickets at 17.17, with a best of 5 for 30 against Essex at Middlesbrough.

In 1959 he took over as the premier left-arm spin bowler due to the sacking of Johnny Wardle, and in the opening Championship match of the season he took a hat-trick against Nottinghamshire at Acklam Park, Middlesbrough. He snared 62 wickets in all first-class matches at 33.14, including 5 for 57 against Somerset at Bath.

In 1960 he took 83 wickets and scored 599 runs, and made his highest ever score for Yorkshire, notching up 83 against Surrey at Bramall Lane, Sheffield. As a consequence, he was awarded his county cap and was selected for the tour of New Zealand. Unfortunately, in the following summer he played only seven matches due to a fractured thumb he received in the Worcestershire game at New Road. However, it was still a memorable match for him, as, with Yorkshire requiring another 36 runs to win and only one wicket remaining, Wilson walked to the wicket with his left arm in plaster from elbow to hand. Batting one-handed, he scored 29 not out in a partnership with Bob Platt (7 not out), which brought off a remarkable win.

In 1963 he took 93 first-class wickets for Yorkshire with a best of 7 for 92 against the MCC at Scarborough, and made his debut for England against the West Indies at Old Trafford, taking 2 for 69 in the match. In the five-match series he took nine wickets at 36.18, and although dropped after the series he did tour India in the winter, where he scored his highest first-class score (112) against South Zone. He toured Sri Lanka in 1969–70 and played one further Test match against New Zealand in February 1971. His opportunities at international level were restricted by the presence of the legendary Derek Underwood, and at best he was only ever going to be used as a second spinner.

In 1966 he took 5 for 46 against Nottinghamshire at Worksop and 3 for 46 against Kent at Harrogate, on both occasions taking a hat-trick, thus becoming only the third bowler behind George Freeman (1868) and George Macaulay (1933) to take two hat-tricks in a season for Yorkshire. At Scarborough, in the last game of the season, he scored 30 runs off one over from Robin Hobbs.

Two years later he had his best season for Yorkshire, taking 107 wickets at 13.49, which included 13 for 52 against Worcestershire at Middlesbrough (6 for 31 and 7 for 21) and 7 for 50 against Somerset at Bath.

In 1969 he took his best bowling figures in first-class cricket, 7 for 19 against the MCC at Scarborough, and in 1972 he was awarded a benefit which realised £7,621.

For Yorkshire he took 1,104 wickets at 20.49, with 46 five-wicket hauls, scored 5,788 runs at 13.88 and held 235 catches.

He retired from the county in 1974 and played Minor County cricket for Lincolnshire from 1975 to 1977. He had a spell coaching in South Africa and then took up the role of indoor coach at Lord's in 1977. He stayed in that position until 1991, whereupon he returned to Yorkshire to become the director of sport at Ampleforth College.

Evelyn Rockley Wilson

RHB & SRA, 1899–1923

Born: 25 March 1879, Bolsterstone, Stocksbridge.
Died: 21 July 1957, Winchester, Hampshire.
Played for: Cambridge University and Yorkshire.
Test Matches: (1) 1921 Cap No. 189

Batting Career for England

I	NO	HS	Runs
2	0	5	10
AV	**100**	**50**	**Catches**
5.00	-	-	-

Bowling for England

Balls	Runs	Wkts	Av
123	36	3	12.00
Best	**5wl**	**10wl**	**Sr/Rate**
2–28	-	-	41.00

First-Class Career: (136 Matches) 1899–1923

Batting

I	NO	HS	Runs
190	28	142	3,565
AV	**100**	**50**	**Catches**
22.00	4	15	106

Bowling

Balls	Runs	Wkts	Av
23,840	8,234	467	17.63
Best	**5wl**	**10wl**	**Sr/Rate**
7–16	26	5	51.04

Evelyn Rockley Wilson, younger brother of Clem, was educated at Bilton Grange School, before he went on to Rugby where he was coached by Tom Emmett, the former Yorkshire cricketer. He spent three years at Rugby from 1895 to 1897, heading the batting and bowling averages, and as captain in 1897 he made a top score of 206 not out with an average of 51.11 and also took 31 wickets at 14.93. A dispute with authorities led to him leaving Rugby early, and like his brother Clem he went to Trinity College, Cambridge.

At Cambridge, he made his first-class debut against the university by appearing as a last-minute substitute for A.J. Webb's XI and scoring 117 not out and 70. He gained a Blue in the four years he spent at Cambridge and was captain in his final year. In 1901 he scored 118 and took 5 for 71 against

Oxford, thereby emulating his brother by scoring a century in the Varsity match, the only brothers to have done so for Cambridge, although H.K Foster and R.E. Foster had previously repeated the feat for Oxford.

The following year as captain he led the Light Blues to victory over their rivals by taking 8 for 89 in the match, and scored his highest first-class score (142) for the university against the MCC at Lord's, in addition to taking his best bowling figures of 7 for 16 for R.A. Bennett's XI against All West Indies at Georgetown. He had earlier toured the US in 1901, and was to tour Argentina and South America in 1911–12.

In 1899 he played his first game for Yorkshire against Somerset at Anlaby Road, Hull, making 55 on debut and adding 110 for the third wicket with David Denton (74). However, by the end of 1902 he had served the county on only nine occasions, before a teaching appointment at Winchester College took him away from Yorkshire until 1913. From 1903 to 1928 he was in charge of cricket at the college and one of his pupils was the future England captain Douglas Jardine. On the eve of the 1932–33 tour of Australia, a member of the press asked Wilson about England's chances under Jardine. 'He may win us the Ashes,' was Wilson's reply, 'but he might lose us a Dominion.'

He began playing for Yorkshire again in 1913, a year in which he scored his highest score for the county, 104 not out against Essex at Bradford, and he took 19 first-class wickets at 19.66, with a best of 6 for 89 against Warwickshire in his first match since 1902.

After World War One ended, Yorkshire was in need of his services, and though 40 years of age he was a welcome addition to the team and captured 36 wickets at 16.38.

He was a useful all-rounder, a right-hand, middle order batsman with a sound technique, who scored quickly, and a very accurate off-spin bowler, who could spin the ball both ways. In a whimsical remark, Wilson once said, 'My best ball is the one which breaks from the off, when I mean it to break from the leg.'

In 1920, even though he did not appear until August, he still finished seventh in the national averages with 49 wickets at 14.20, and was a surprise selection for Johnny Douglas's team to tour Australia. He made his only Test appearance in the fifth and final match at Sydney, scoring 5 runs in each innings and taking 2 for 28 and 1 for 8 with the ball. Indeed, his main impact on tour was to cable match reports back to the *Daily Express*, which prompted the board of control to make it a condition of selection that in future players would not make statements on a match that they were playing in until the end of the season.

The following season he topped the County Championship averages with 41 wickets at 11.34 (51 at 11.19 overall, his best for a season), and which included a Yorkshire best of 7 for 32 against Middlesex at Bramall Lane.

Twelve months later he captained the team in the Roses match at Old Trafford when Geoff Wilson was taken ill with appendicitis and took 23 wickets at 15.04 as Yorkshire won the Championship title for the first of four consecutive years.

His last season came in 1923, and he remained at Winchester coaching cricket and adding to his extensive collection of cricket books, part of which he bequeathed to the MCC on his death in 1957.

Arthur Wood

RHB & WK, 1927–46

Born: 25 August 1898, Fagley, Bradford.
Died: 1 April 1973, Middleton, Ilkley.
Played for: Yorkshire.
Test Matches: (4) 1938–39 Cap No. 304
Batting Career for England

I	NO	HS	Runs
5	1	53	80
AV	**100**	**50**	**Ct/St**
20.00	-	1	10/1

First-Class Career: (420 Matches) 1927–46
Batting

I	NO	HS	Runs
500	83	123*	8,842
AV	**100**	**50**	**Ct/St**
21.20	1	43	631/257

Bowling

Balls	Runs	Wkts	Av
30	33	1	33.00
Best	**5wl**	**10wl**	**Sr/Rate**
1–33	-	-	30.00

A native of Fagley, near Bradford, Arthur Wood was one of the most colourful characters in the history of Yorkshire County Cricket Club. He began his career with Eccleshill Parish Church, before moving on to play for Bradford Cricket Club and taking over the wicket-keeping gloves when Arthur Dolphin retired to become a first-class umpire. He made his debut for Yorkshire against Derbyshire at Chesterfield in 1927, and for the following 13 years, plus the first season after the war, he was the hub of the Yorkshire team that won eight County Championship titles.

Wood made wicket-keeping look easy with his superb handling skills, while his leg-side work and stumpings were a joy to watch. His batting was solid and dependable, and he was not only good enough to score a first-class century, but he also took part in several partnerships in excess of a hundred runs in every wicket from the sixth downwards.

During the 1930s he was unfortunate to have to compete with the likes of Les Ames in particular, who was not only a fine 'keeper but a good top-order batsman as well. During this period Wood featured in the top 'keepers lists in the County Championship, and in 1934 he was third with 75 dismissals (63 caught and 12 stumped), the following year he was fourth with 70 dismissals (43 caught and 17 stumped) and in 1939 he had 66 (39 caught and 27 stumped). Known as 'Mr Reliable' behind the timbers, he had a variety of bowling styles to handle, with Hedley Verity, George Macauley and Bill Bowes to name but three.

Between the years of 1927 and 1946, he played 225 consecutive matches (222 in the Championship), a record since beaten by Jimmy Binks, and he averaged in excess of 60 dismissals and 700 runs a season.

In 1935 he was the first Yorkshire wicket-keeper to score 1,000 runs for the season (1,249), which included his one and only century, 123 not out against Worcestershire at Bramall Lane, an innings in which he shared a sixth-wicket unbroken partnership of 217 with Herbert Sutcliffe (200 not out). It was the first century by a regular wicket-keeper in the history of the White Rose County. In the following summer, in a game against Somerset, also at Sheffield, he got to within three runs of another century, recording 97 in a stand of 180 with Cyril Turner for the seventh wicket.

In 1938, and only five days before his 40th birthday, he was summoned in an emergency to play his first Test match, the fifth and final game against Australia at the Oval, as a replacement for Fred Price of Middlesex. Wood had to make the dash from Nottingham to the Oval in a taxi, a journey that cost him £7 and 15 shillings. Apparently, when he was quoted this price he replied that he was only paying for the ride, not buying the taxi. When England batted he went to the wicket with the score at 770 for 6, and proceeded to hit 53 (his highest Test score) in a partnership of 106 with Joe Hardstaff Jnr (169 not out). He was caught and bowled off a full toss from Sidney Barnes, and when he returned to the pavilion he made the famous remark, 'Trust me to lose my head in a crisis'.

Another of his well documented remarks came when the great Hedley Verity was being treated rather harshly by the South African wicket-keeper batsman 'Jock' Cameron at Bramall Lane in 1935, as the South African took 30 runs off a Verity over. Wood reportedly said, 'Thas got him in two minds Hedley, he doesn't know whether to hit thee for four or six'.

The good humoured Wood, known as 'Rhubarb' or 'Sawdust', took a well deserved benefit in 1939 which realised the sum of £2,563, and he was fittingly selected as one of *Wisden's* Five Cricketers of the Year. He played a further three Tests against the West Indies during that season and played his last match for the county in 1946.

For Yorkshire he played 408 games, scored 8,579 runs at 21.39 and took 1 wicket for 33 against Jamaica at Sabina Park on the Yorkshire tour of 1935–36. He also took 855 dismissals behind the timbers (612 caught and 243 stumped).

On his retirement from the county he played for many seasons with Undercliffe in the Bradford League. He was a good billiards and snooker player, and he played golf to a single handicap. He died on 1 April 1973 at the age of 74 in Ilkey.

Barry Wood

RHB & RM, 1964–83

Born: 26 December 1942, Osset.
Played for: Yorkshire, Lancashire, Eastern
Province and Derbyshire.
Test Matches: (12) 1972–78 Cap No. 453
Batting Career for England

I	NO	HS	Runs
21	0	90	454
AV	**100**	**50**	**Catches**
21.61	-	2	6

Bowling for England

Balls	Runs	Wkts	Av
98	50	0	-
Best	**5wl**	**10wl**	**Sr/Rate**
-	-	-	-

First-Class Career: (357 Matches) 1964–83
Batting

I	NO	HS	Runs
591	75	198	17,453
AV	**100**	**50**	**Catches**
33.82	30	81	283

Bowling

Balls	Runs	Wkts	Av
21,571	9,160	298	30.73
Best	**5wl**	**10wl**	**Sr/Rate**
7–52	8	-	72.38

The Ossett-born Barry Wood was the eighth of 11 children and a younger brother of Ronald Wood, who played 22 matches for Yorkshire between 1952 and 1956. In his early career Barry played League cricket in the Central Yorkshire League with Hanging Heaton and Mirfield, before moving to Barnsley in the Yorkshire League in 1965.

After playing five games for the Yorkshire Second XI in 1963, he made his Championship debut a year later against Somerset at Middlesbrough. However, he decided that he was unlikely to become a regular with his native county and opted to move across the Pennines to join Lancashire after only five first-class matches, in which he scored 63 runs at 12.60 and held four catches.

Wood made his debut for Lancashire in 1966 against Essex at Castle Park, Colchester, but in 10 matches his highest innings was only 39. However, if nothing else he was a competitive cricketer and his determination to succeed finally paid off when in 1970 he was moved up the batting order to open the innings with David Lloyd. Later, that summer he had great success against his native Yorkshire, scoring 105 at Headingley and then 144 and 30 not out in the return match at Old Trafford.

As a batsman he had a compact defence, his best shots being the cut and pull, while he was also a brilliant fielder, particularly at gulley. His bowling was medium-paced, and adept at breaking partnerships, and in 1968 he took 7 for 52 against Middlesex at Old Trafford and was awarded his county cap that season. His all-round ability was ideally suited to one-day cricket, and he won 16 Man of the Match awards from 219 matches.

In 1971 he had his best season with the bat, recording 1,492 runs at 38.25 and he also had a (then) record fifth-wicket partnership of 249 with Andrew Kennedy against Warwickshire at Edgbaston.

In the winter of 1971–72 he travelled to South Africa to play for Eastern Province, and on his return he was selected for his first Test against Australia at the Oval, scoring 26 and then 90 in the second innings, which, incidentally, was his highest score in Test cricket. His display earned him a trip for the winter tour to India, but he had great difficulty in reading the Indian spinners and made only 101 runs at 16.83.

Altogether Wood played 12 Tests for England but only managed one more half-century, against Australia in the second Test at Lord's in 1975. In the same year he got into trouble with the Lancashire committee when he and his colleagues Frank Hayes and Peter Lever went on strike for more money on the morning of a county game. Hayes and Lever received a two-match suspension, while Wood got six, which suggests that they thought he was the ringleader.

In the winter he toured Rhodesia with the International Wanderers, and in the following summer he hit his highest first-class score, 198 against Glamorgan at Aigburth, Liverpool.

Although not successful at Test level, he nevertheless proved a more than useful one-day international cricketer, playing 13 matches between 1972 and 1982, scoring 314 runs at 31.40, with a top score of 78 not out, and 9 wickets at 24.88, with an economy rate of 3.20.

In the winter of 1979–80 he received a record benefit of £62,429 from Lancashire, but refused to sign for 1980 unless they increased their offer of £7,000. Lancashire declined and he signed for Derbyshire after having played 260 matches, scored 12,969 runs at 35.24, with 23 centuries, and taken 251 wickets at 27.5. He also held 200 catches.

Wood proceeded to play 63 matches for his new county between 1980 and 1983, and his best season came in 1981 when he scored 1,439 runs at an average of 46.00, with a top score of 153 against Worcestershire at Chesterfield, and he took a bowling best of 3 for 22 against Sussex at Derby. He also helped Derbyshire to win the 1981 Natwest Trophy, their first major honour since 1936.

Upon leaving Derbyshire he played Minor County cricket for Cheshire, and as late as 1988, at the ripe old age of 45, he assisted them to their giant-killing act over Northamptonshire in the 1988 Natwest Trophy.

Charles William Wright

RHB & WK, 1882–99

Born: 27 May 1863, Harewood, Leeds.
Died: 10 January 1936, Saxelby Park, Melton
  Mowbray.
Played for: Cambridge University and
  Nottinghamshire.
Test Matches: (3) 1895–96 Cap No. 101
Batting Career for England

I	NO	HS	Runs
4	0	71	125
AV	**100**	**50**	**Ct/St**
31.25	-	1	-

First-Class Career: (265 Matches) 1882–99
Batting

I	NO	HS	Runs
461	21	114	6,989
AV	**100**	**50**	**Ct/St**
15.88	2	30	195/41

Bowling

Balls	Runs	Wkts	Av
59	55	-	-
Best	**5wl**	**10wl**	**Sr/Rate**
-	-	-	-

Although born at Harewood in Leeds, Charles Wright attended Charterhouse School and followed a strong family cricketing tradition, his father William being a member of the Nottinghamshire Committee. Indeed, during his school holidays he practised with the Nottinghamshire players and received coaching from the professional coaches at Trent Bridge. He went to Cambridge in 1882 and was a Blue in each of the four years he spent at university. A strong defensive right-hand batsman, he was also a wicket-keeper and made his debut for Nottinghamshire while still at university. During the season he recorded his highest score for the county, 99 against Surrey at Hove, a match in which he opened the batting and was the last wicket to fall after having battled for 270 minutes.

The following year Wright was the outstanding player in the Varsity match against Oxford University and won a medal for his efforts. Opening the batting for Cambridge, he compiled a chanceless 102 (his maiden century in first-class cricket) out of a score of only 215. Oxford were bowled out for 55 and 215, leaving Cambridge needing 56 to win, of which Wright scored an unbeaten 29 to secure victory for the Light Blues by seven wickets.

Wright was one of the most difficult batsmen of his era to dismiss, and in 1891 he carried his bat for 7 not out in a total of 51 for Staffordshire against the Australians, having notched up 26 out of 60 in the first innings. In the same summer against the MCC at Lord's he opened the batting and was last out again, scoring 5 in the Nottinghamshire total of 21, and he made 39 out of total of 69 in the second innings. The match was over in a day.

Wright played many first-class games for the MCC and went on four overseas tours, in 1891 and 1894 to the United States and Canada, to India in 1892–93 and South Africa in 1895–96. It was on his last tour to South Africa in 1896 that he made his three England appearances, at Port Elizabeth, Johannesburg and Cape Town, scoring 125 runs with a top score of 71 in the second Test at Johannesburg.

A few months later in the summer of 1896 he made his highest first-class score, 114, playing for A.J. Webb's XI against Cambridge University at Fenners.

In 1890 he was the first captain to declare an innings closed. In the game against Kent at the Bat and Ball Ground in Gravesend, he declared Nottinghamshire's second innings closed on 157 for 5 to set Kent a target of 231 to win. However, his tactic did not succeed as the game was drawn with Kent on 98 for 9 and Notts had to settle for a draw. He was captain of Nottinghamshire on 26 occasions.

One other notable occurrence in his career came in 1893, when he was given out for handling the ball while removing it after it had lodged in his pad. He returned it to a fielder, but W.G. Grace appealed and he was given out. He therefore became the fourth batsman to be given out this way; the first three cases being James Grundy, also a Nottinghamshire player, playing for the MCC against Kent in 1857; George 'Farmer' Bennett for Kent against Sussex in 1872 and William Scotton, another Nottinghamshire player, who was playing for the Smokers versus the Non Smokers in 1886.

In 1904 Wright lost the sight of his right eye during a partridge shoot and retired from playing. However, he remained closely involved with the game, and with Nottinghamshire cricket in particular, first serving on the committee and then acting as honorary treasurer until his death in January 1936 at Saxelby Park, Melton Mowbray.

For the county he played 117 matches and scored 2,565 runs at 13.35.

Norman Walter Dransfield Yardley

RHB & RM, 1935–55

Born: 19 March 1915, Gawber, Barnsley.
Died: 4 October 1989, Lodge Moor,
    Sheffield.
Played for: Cambridge University and
    Yorkshire.
Test Matches: (20) 1938–50 Cap No. 307

Batting Career for England

I	NO	HS	Runs
34	2	99	812
AV	**100**	**50**	**Catches**
25.37	-	4	14

Bowling for England

Balls	Runs	Wkts	Av
1,662	707	21	33.66
Best	**5wl**	**10wl**	**Sr/Rate**
3–67	-	-	79.14

First-Class Career: (446 Matches) 1935–55

Batting

I	NO	HS	Runs
658	75	183*	18,173
AV	**100**	**50**	**Catches**
31.17	27	83	328

Bowling

Balls	Runs	Wkts	Av
21,220	8,506	279	30.48
Best	**5wl**	**10wl**	**Sr/Rate**
6–29	5	-	76.05

Norman Yardley was born in Barnsley and educated first at Wakefield Grammer School and then at St Peter's School in York, where he was cricket captain in 1933–34, before going on to Cambridge. In his four years at university he gained a Blue and was captain of the cricket team in 1938. In addition to cricket, he played rugby, gained a Blue for hockey and was a North of England squash champion on six occasions. At Cambridge he excelled in the varsity games of 1936 and 1937 against Oxford, scoring 90 and 101 respectively, and he notched up over 2,000 runs in his Cambridge career.

    Although he was a strong, hard-hitting batsman, he had a sound technique and was particularly strong on the leg-side. He was also a fine all-round fielder and a medium-pace seam bowler who was adept at breaking partnerships. He first appeared for the Yorkshire Second XI while still at St Peter's School and scored 189 for the Young Amateurs versus the Young Professionals at Lord's.

He made his first-class debut for Yorkshire in 1936 against Derbyshire at Bramall Lane, but it was three years later before he notched up his first century for the county, 101 against Surrey. Meanwhile, he was selected for the MCC tour to South Africa in the winter of 1938–39, making his debut at Johannesburg. On the same tour he scored 142 against Griqualand West at Kimberley in a record total of 676.

In the summer of 1939 he notched up 1,028 first-class runs for Yorkshire, which included three centuries, the highest of which was 140 not out against his old team, Cambridge University.

During the war he served in the Green Howards in the Middle East and Italy, and was wounded in the Western Desert. Immediately after the war he was selected for England's tour of Australia in 1946–47 and excelled himself in the third Test at Melbourne: not only did he score 61 and 53 not out, but he also snared the wicket of Don Bradman in both innings, while posting his best Test bowling figures of 3 for 67. In the last Test at Sydney he took over the captaincy from Wally Hammond and also led England in the five-match home series against South Africa the following summer.

It was a great summer for him, as not only did he hit his highest Test score of 99 against South Africa at Trent Bridge, but he also figured in a record fifth-wicket partnership of 237 with Denis Compton. In first-class cricket he amassed his most runs in a season, 1,904 with a top score of 177 against Derbyshire at Scarborough, which included four centuries. As a result he was named one of *Wisden's* Five Cricketers of the Year in 1948.

As a captain he was described as unflappable, and his cheerful nature made him popular with his players. However, it seemed that he lacked the personal strength to deal with some of the strong-willed characters, both for England and Yorkshire, and perhaps the tactical flair needed at the highest level. In 1948 he took over as captain of Yorkshire and was also the skipper in the disastrous home series against the 'invincible' Australians, probably the best team ever to visit these shores. He later became unavailable for England, but returned in 1950 as both player and captain for the last time for the first three Tests against the West Indies, ending his reign at Nottingham, where he scored 41 in his last Test innings.

While captain of Yorkshire he shared the Championship of 1949 with Middlesex, and two years later he notched up his highest first-class score, 183 not out Hampshire at Headingley. The following season he took a career best with the ball for Yorkshire, 6 for 106 against MCC at Scarborough, and played his last first-class game for the Gentlemen versus the Players, again at Scarborough in the last match of 1955.

In total he exceeded 1,000 runs a season on eight occasions, and for the White Rose County he played 302 matches, in which he scored 11,632 runs at 31.95, including 17 centuries, took 195 wickets at 29.83, with two five-wicket hauls, and held 220 catches.

Upon retirement he continued his business interests as a wine merchant, while at the same time staying involved in cricket. He was a Test selector from 1951 to 1954, including chairman for two years, and was president of Yorkshire County Cricket Club from 1981 to 1984. In addition he was a writer and broadcaster, appearing as a commentator for *Test Match Special* from 1956 to 1973.

STATISTICS *(ALL CORRECT AS AT END OF 2008)*

BATTING

Most Runs (Min 1,000 Runs)

	Tests	Inn	No	Runs	Avg	Hs	100s	50s
G. Boycott	108	193	23	8,114	47.72	246*	22	42
L. Hutton	79	138	15	6,971	56.67	364	19	33
H. Sutcliffe	54	84	9	4,555	60.73	194	16	23
M. Leyland	41	65	5	2,764	46.06	187	9	10
W. Rhodes	58	98	21	2,325	30.19	179	2	11
R. Illingworth	61	90	11	1,836	23.24	113	2	5
F.S. Jackson	20	33	4	1,415	48.79	144*	5	6
C. White	30	50	7	1,052	24.46	121	1	5

Highest Batting Averages (Min 35.00)

	Avg	Inn	No	Tests	Runs	Hs	100s	50s
H. Sutcliffe	60.73	84	9	54	4,555	194	16	23
L. Hutton	56.67	138	15	79	6,971	364	19	33
F.S. Jackson	48.79	33	4	20	1,415	144*	5	6
G. Boycott	47.72	193	23	108	8,114	246*	22	42
P.J. Sharpe	46.23	21	4	12	786	111	1	4
M. Leyland	46.06	65	5	41	2,764	187	9	10
P.A. Gibb	44.69	13	0	8	581	120	2	3
J.B. Bolus	41.33	12	0	7	496	88	0	4
A. Ward	37.46	13	0	7	487	117	1	3
J.T. Brown	36.15	16	3	8	470	140	1	1

Highest Individual Scores (Min 150 Runs)

L. Hutton	(364)	v	Australia	The Oval	1938
G. Boycott	(246*)	v	India	Headingley	1967
L. Hutton	(206)	v	New Zealand	The Oval	1949
L. Hutton	(205)	v	West Indies	Kingston	1954
L. Hutton	(202*)	v	West Indies	The Oval	1950
L. Hutton	(196)	v	West Indies	Lord's	1939
H. Sutcliffe	(194)	v	Australia	Sydney	1932
G. Boycott	(191‡)	v	Australia	Headingley	1977
M. Leyland	(187)	v	Australia	Headingley	1938
W. Rhodes	(179)	v	Australia	Melbourne	1912
H. Sutcliffe	(176)	v	Australia	Melbourne	1925
L. Hutton	(169)	v	West Indies	Georgetown	1954
L. Hutton	(165*)	v	West Indies	The Oval	1939
M. Leyland	(161)	v	South Africa	The Oval	1935
H. Sutcliffe	(161)	v	Australia	The Oval	1926

H. Sutcliffe	(161)	v	Australia	The Oval	1930
L. Hutton	(158)	v	South Africa	Johannesburg	1948
L. Hutton	(156*)	v	Australia	Adelaide	1951
G. Boycott	(155)	v	India	Edgbaston	1979
M. Leyland	(153)	v	Australia	Old Trafford	1934
W. Rhodes	(152)	v	South Africa	Johannesburg	1913
L. Hutton	(150)	v	India	Lord's	1952

‡ *100th first-class century*

Most Runs in a Series (Min 500 Runs)

	Opp	Season	Inn	No	Runs	Hs	Avg	100s	50s
H. Sutcliffe	Aus	1924–25	9	0	734	176	81.56	4	2
L. Hutton	W.I.	1953–54	8	1	677	205	96.71	2	3
G. Boycott	Aus	1970–71	10	3	657	142*	93.85	2	5
L. Hutton	S.A.	1948–49	9	0	577	158	64.11	2	2
L. Hutton	Aus	1950–51	10	4	533	156*	88.83	1	4
H. Sutcliffe	S.A.	1929	9	1	513	114	64.12	4	0

Most Runs in a Calendar Year (Min 700 Runs)

	Year	Inn	No	Runs	Hs	Avg	100s	50s
G. Boycott	1981	26	2	975	137	40.62	3	4
L. Hutton	1951	18	4	903	156*	64.50	2	6
L. Hutton	1954	17	1	825	205	51.56	2	3
L. Hutton	1949	12	0	800	206	66.66	3	3
G. Boycott	1971	11	4	766	142*	109.42	4	3
L. Hutton	1948	15	0	759	158	50.60	1	7
G. Boycott	1978	18	1	759	131	44.64	2	5
G. Boycott	1980	18	3	700	128*	46.66	1	4

Most Runs in a Day

L. Hutton	206	v	New Zealand	The Oval	1949

Most Runs in a Match

L. Hutton	364	(364 & DNB)	v	Australia	The Oval	1938
H. Sutcliffe	303	(176 & 127)	v	Australia	Melbourne	1925

Batsman Carrying His Bat Through a Completed Innings

L. Hutton	202*	(344)	v	West Indies	The Oval	1950
L. Hutton	156*	(272)	v	Australia	Adelaide	1951
G. Boycott	99*	(215)	v	Australia	Perth	1979

Most Centuries

G. Boycott	(22)	193 innings	1964–1982
L. Hutton	(19)	138 innings	1937–1955
H. Sutcliffe	(16)	84 innings	1924–1935
M. Leyland	(9)	65 innings	1928–1938
F.S. Jackson	(5)	3 innings	1893–1905

Most Centuries in a Series

| H. Sutcliffe (4) | v | Australia | 1924–1925 |
| H. Sutcliffe (4) | v | South Africa | 1929 |

Centuries in Consecutive Innings

H. Sutcliffe (3)	115	v	Australia	Sydney	1924
	176	v	Australia	Melbourne	1925
	127	v	Australia	Melbourne	1925
G. Boycott (3)	119*	v	Australia	Adelaide	1971
	121	v	Pakistan	Lord's	1971
	112	v	Pakistan	Headingley	1971

Centuries in Consecutive Matches

H. Sutcliffe (3)	161 & 54	v	Australia	The Oval	1930
	117	v	New Zealand	The Oval	1931
	109*	v	New Zealand	Old Trafford	1931
G. Boycott (3)	58 & 119*	v	Australia	Adelaide	1971
	121*	v	Pakistan	Lord's	1971
	112 & 13	v	Pakistan	Headingley	1971

Century in Each Innings

| H. Sutcliffe | 176 & 111 | v | Australia | Melbourne | 1925 |
| H. Sutcliffe | 104 & 109* | v South Africa | | The Oval | 1929 |

Century and Fifty in a Match

G. Ulyett	149 & 64	v	Australia	Melbourne	1882
A. Ward	75 & 117	v	Australia	Sydney	1894
J.W.H. Makepeace	117 & 54	v	Australia	Melbourne	1921
H. Sutcliffe	59 & 115	v	Australia	Sydney	1924
H. Sutcliffe	76 & 161	v	Australia	The Oval	1926
H. Sutcliffe	58 & 135	v	Australia	Melbourne	1928
M. Leyland	137 & 53*	v	Australia	Melbourne	1929
M. Leyland	73 & 102	v	South Africa	Lord's	1929
H. Sutcliffe	161 & 54	v	Australia	The Oval	1930
P.A. Gibb	93 & 106	v	South Africa	Johannesburg	1938
L. Hutton	73 & 165*	v	West Indies	The Oval	1939
G. Boycott	77 & 142*	v	Australia	Sydney	1971
G. Boycott	58 & 119	v	Australia	Adelaide	1971
G. Boycott	99 & 112	v	West Indies	Port-of-Spain	1974
G. Boycott	107 & 80*	v	Australia	Trent Bridge	1977
G. Boycott	79 & 100*	v	Pakistan	Hyderabad	1978
G. Boycott	62 & 128*	v	Australia	Lord's	1980

Fifty in Each Innings

| G. Ulyett | 52 & 63 | v | Australia | Melbourne | 1877 |
| W. Rhodes | 66 & 54 | v | Australia | The Oval | 1909 |

W. Rhodes	59 & 57*	v	Australia	Adelaide	1912
P. Holmes	70 & 56	v	South Africa	Durban	1928
H. Sutcliffe	63 & 69*	v	Australia	Old Trafford	1934
A. Mitchell	58 & 72	v	South Africa	Headingley	1935
N.W.D. Yardley	61 & 53*	v	Australia	Melbourne	1947
L. Hutton	94 & 76	v	Australia	Adelaide	1947
L. Hutton	56 & 60	v	West Indies	Kingston	1948
L. Hutton	81 & 57	v	Australia	Headingley	1948
L. Hutton	79 & 60*	v	Australia	Melbourne	1951
L. Hutton	72 & 77	v	West Indies	Bridgetown	1954
P.J. Sharpe	63 & 83	v	West Indies	The Oval	1963
G. Boycott	62 & 80*	v	West Indies	Port-of-Spain	1968
G. Boycott	70 & 50	v	Australia	Perth	1970
G. Boycott	61 & 92	v	New Zealand	Lord's	1973

Century on Debut

P.A. Gibb	93 & 106	v	South Africa	Johannesburg	1938
J.H. Hampshire	107 & 5	v	West Indies	Lord's	1969

Fastest Century

J.T. Brown   140 (100 in 95 minutes)   v   Australia Melbourne 1895

Fastest Fifty

J.T. Brown   140 (50 in 28 minutes)   v   Australia Melbourne 1895
(Still the second fastest fifty in minutes in Test cricket)

BOWLING

Leading Wickets-Takers (Min 50 Wickets)

	Tests	Wkts	Avg	Best	5 wkts	10 wkts	S/R
F.S. Trueman	67	307	21.57	8–31	17	3	49.43
M.J. Hoggard	67	248	30.50	7–61	7	1	56.08
D. Gough	58	229	28.39	6–42	9	0	51.61
J.C. Laker	46	193	21.24	10–53	9	3	62.31
H. Verity	40	144	24.37	8–43	5	2	77.59
C.M. Old	46	143	28.11	7–50	4	0	61.94
W. Rhodes	58	127	26.96	8–68	6	1	64.81
R. Ilingworth	61	122	31.20	6–29	3	0	97.81
R. Peel	20	102	16.81	7–31	6	2	51.13
J.H. Wardle	28	102	20.39	7–36	5	1	64.67
R.J. Sidebottom	18	76	25.68	7–47	5	1	56.20
W.E. Bowes	15	68	22.33	6–33	6	0	53.75
G.W. Hirst	24	59	30.00	5–48	3	0	67.23
C. White	30	59	37.62	5–32	3	0	67.10
W. Bates	15	50	16.42	7–28	4	1	47.28
G. Ulyett	25	50	20.40	7–36	1	0	52.54

Lowest Bowling Averages (Min Qualification 20 wickets and 30 average)

	Tests	Avg	Runs	Wkts
W. Bates	15	16.42	821	50
R. Peel	20	16.81	1,715	102
R. Appleyard	9	17.87	554	31
W.S. Lees	5	17.96	467	26
J.H. Wardle	28	20.39	2,080	102
G. Ulyett	25	20.40	1,020	50
J.C. Laker	46	21.24	4,101	193
F.S. Trueman	67	21.57	6,625	307
E. Peate	9	22.00	682	31
W.E. Bowes	15	22.33	1,519	68
H. Verity	40	24.37	3,510	144
R.J. Sidebottom	18	25.68	1,952	76
S. Haigh	11	25.91	622	24
W. Rhodes	58	26.96	3,425	127
G.G. Macaulay	8	27.58	662	24
C.M. Old	46	28.11	4,020	143

Lowest Strike Rates (Min Qualification 20 wickets and S/R 70)

	Tests	S/R	Balls	Wkts
W. Bates	15	47.28	2,364	50
W.S. Lees	5	48.30	1,256	26
F. S. Trueman	67	49.43	15,178	307
R. Peel	20	51.13	5,216	102
R. Appleyard	9	51.48	1,596	31
D. Gough	58	51.61	6,503	229
G. Ulyett	25	52.54	2,627	50
W.E. Bowes	15	53.75	3,655	68
S. Haigh	11	53.91	1,294	24
M.J. Hoggard	67	56.08	13,909	248
R.J. Sidebottom	18	56.20	4,272	76
C.M. Old	46	61.94	8,858	143
J.C. Laker	46	62.31	12,027	193
J.H. Wardle	28	64.67	6,597	102
W. Rhodes	58	64.81	8,225	127
C. White	30	67.10	3,959	59
G.H. Hirst	24	67.23	4,010	59

Best Bowling (Min 6 Wickets)

	Wickets	Opposition	Venue	Year
J.C. Laker	10–53	Australia	Old Trafford	1956
J.C. Laker	9–37	Australia	Old Trafford	1956
F.S. Trueman	8–31	India	Old Trafford	1952
H. Verity	8–43	Australia	Lord's	1934

W. Rhodes	8–68	Australia	Melbourne	1904
W. Rhodes	7–17	Australia	Edgbaston	1902
W. Bates	7–20	Australia	Melbourne	1883
R. Peel	7–31	Australia	Old Trafford	1888
G. Ulyett	7–36	Australia	Lord's	1884
J.H. Wardle	7–36	South Africa	Cape Town	1957
F.S. Trueman	7–44	West Indies	Edgbaston	1963
R.J. Sidebottom	7–47	New Zealand	Napier	2008
C.M. Old	7–50	Pakistan	Edgbaston	1978
W. Rhodes	7–56	Australia	Melbourne	1904
J.H. Wardle	7–56	Pakistan	The Oval	1954
M.J. Hoggard	7–61	South Africa	Johannesburg	2005
H. Verity	7–61	Australia	Lord's	1934
M.J. Hoggard	7–63	New Zealand	Canterbury	2002
T. Emmett	7–68	Australia	Melbourne	1879
W. Bates	7–74	Australia	Melbourne	1883
F.S. Trueman	7–75	New Zealand	Christchurch	1963
J.C. Laker	7–103	West Indies	Bridgetown	1948
S. Haigh	6–11	South Africa	Cape Town	1899
R. Peel	6–23	Australia	The Oval	1896
R. Illingworth	6–29	India	Lord's	1967
F.S. Trueman	6–30	Australia	Headingley	1961
F.S. Trueman	6–31	Pakistan	Lord's	1962
W.E. Bowes	6–33	West Indies	Old Trafford	1939
W.E. Bowes	6–34	New Zealand	Auckland	1933
D. Gough	6–42	South Africa	Headingley	1998
D. Gough	6–49	Australia	Sydney	1995
C.M. Old	6–54	New Zealand	Wellington	1978
J.C. Laker	6–55	South Africa	The Oval	1951
J.C. Laker	6–55	Australia	Headingley	1956
M.J. Hoggard	6–57	India	Nagpur	2006
R. Peel	6–67	Australia	Sydney	1894
W.S. Lees	6–78	South Africa	Johannesburg	1906
E. Peate	6–85	Australia	Lord's	1884
R. Illingworth	6–87	Australia	Headingley	1968
F.S. Trueman	6–100	West Indies	Lord's	1963
W.E. Bowes	6–142	Australia	Headingley	1934

Best Bowling In a Match (Min 10 Wickets)

J.C. Laker	19–90	(9–37 and 10–53)	Australia	Old Trafford	1955
H. Verity	15–104	(7–61 and 8–43)	Australia	Lord's	1934
W. Rhodes	15–124	(7–56 and 8–68)	Australia	Melbourne	1904
W. Bates	14–102 †	(7–28 and 7–74)	Australia	Melbourne	1883
J.H. Wardle	12–89	(5–53 and 7–36)	South Africa	Cape Town	1957
F.S. Trueman	12–119	(5–75 and 7–44)	West Indies	Edgbaston	1963

M.J. Hoggard	12–205	(7–61 and 5–141)	South Africa	Johannesburg	2005
R. Peel	11–68	(7–31 and 4–37)	Australia	Old Trafford	1888
F.S. Trueman	11–88	(5–58 and 6–30)	Australia	Headingley	1961
J.C. Laker	11–113	(5–58 and 6–55)	Australia	Headingley	1956
F.S. Trueman	11–152	(6–100 and 5–52)	West Indies	Lord's	1963
H. Verity	11–153	(7–49 and 4–104)	India	Madras	1934
R. Peel	10–58	(5–18 and 5–40)	Australia	Sydney	1888
J.C. Laker	10–119	(4–64 and 6–55)	South Africa	The Oval	1951
R.J. Sidebottom	10–139 †	(4–90 and 6–49)	New Zealand	Hamilton	2008

† *including hat-trick*

Most Wickets in a Series (Min 25 Wickets)

	Opp	Season	Wkts	Avg	5 wkts	10 wkts	Best
J.C. Laker	Aust	1956	46	9.60	4	2	10–53
F.S. Trueman	W.I.	1963	34	17.47	4	2	7–43
W. Rhodes	Aus	1903–04	31	15.74	3	1	8–68
F.S. Trueman	Ind	1952	29	13.31	2	0	8–31
R. Peel	Aust	1894–95	27	26.70	1	0	6–67
J.H. Wardle	S.A.	1956–57	26	13.70	3	1	7–36
W.S. Lees	S.A.	1905–06	26	17.96	2	0	6–78
M.J. Hoggard	S.A.	2004–05	26	25.50	2	1	7–61
F.S. Trueman	S.A.	1960	25	20.32	1	0	5–27
D. Gough	W.I.	2000	25	21.20	1	0	5–109

Most Wickets in a Calendar Year

	Year	Tests	Runs	Wkts	Avg	5wkts	10wkts	Best
F.S. Trueman	1963	11	1061	62	17.11	6	2	7–44
M.J. Hoggard	2005	13	1514	58	26.10	3	1	7–61

Hat-Tricks

W. Bates   v   Australia   Melbourne   1883
(P.S. McDonnell (bowled), G. Griffen (ct & b), G.J. Bonnar (ct Read))

D. Gough   v   Australia   Sydney   1999
(I. Healey (ct Hegg), S.C.G. MacGill (bowled), C.R. Miller (bowled))

M.J. Hoggard   v   West Indies   Bridgetown   2004
(R.R. Sarwan (ct Giles), S. Chanderpaul (lbw), R.O. Hinds (ct Flintoff))

R.J. Sidebottom   v   New Zealand   Hamilton   2008
(S.P. Fleming (ct Cook), M.S. Sinclair (ct Cook), J.D.P. Oram (lbw))

1,000 Runs and 100 Wickets

W. Rhodes	2,325 runs	(30.19)	and	127 wickets	(26.96)	1899–1930
R. Illingworth	1,836 runs	(23.24)	and	122 wickets	(31.20)	1958–73

1,000 Runs and 50 Wickets

C. White	1,052 runs	(24.46)	and	59 wickets	(37.62)	1994–2003

500 Runs and 100 Wickets

F.S. Trueman	981 runs	(13.81)	and	307 wickets	(21.57)	1952–65
D. Gough	855 runs	(12.57)	and	229 wickets	(28.39)	1994–2003
C.M. Old	845 runs	(14.82)	and	143 wickets	(28.11)	1972–81
J.C. Laker	676 runs	(14.08)	and	193 wickets	(21.24)	1948–59
H. Verity	669 runs	(20.90)	and	144 wickets	(24.37)	1931–39
J.H. Wardle	653 runs	(19.76)	and	102 wickets	(20.39)	1948–57

500 Runs and 50 Wickets

G.H. Hirst	790 runs	(22.57)	and	59 wickets	(30.00)	1897–1909
G. Ulyett	949 runs	(24.33)	and	50 wickets	(20.40)	1877–90
W. Bates	656 runs	(27.33)	and	50 wickets	(16.42)	1881–87

1,000 Runs, 100 wickets and 50 catches

W. Rhodes	2,325 runs (30.9)		and	127 wickets	(26.96)
60 catches	1899–1930				

50 and 10 Wickets in Same Match

W. Bates	55 runs and 7–28 and 7–74	v Australia	Melbourne	1883

50 and 5 Wickets in Same Match

D. Gough	65 runs and 4–47 and 2–105	v New Zealand	Old Trafford	1994
D. Gough	51 runs and 6–49 and 1–72	v Australia	Sydney	1995
G.H. Hirst	58* runs and 5–77 and 1–7	v Australia	The Oval	1902
F.S. Jackson	82* runs and 5–52 and 0–6	v Australia	Trent Bridge	1905
R. Kilner	74 runs and 3–29 and 2–41	v Australia	Melbourne	1925
P. Lever	88* runs and 5–70 and 0–14	v India	Old Trafford	1971
C.M. Old	52 runs and 2–37 and 3–38	v India	Calcutta	1977
R. Peel	53 runs and 1–21 and 4–77	v Australia	Melbourne	1894
H. Verity	55* runs and 4–64 and 4–76	v India	Calcutta	1934
H. Verity	66* runs and 4–41 and 1–66	v India	Old Trafford	1936
J.H. Wardle	54 runs and 4–19 and 1–9	v Pakistan	Old Trafford	1954
N.W.D. Yardley	61 & 53 runs and 2–50 and 3–67	v Australia	Melbourne	1947

FIELDING

Most Catches in a Test Career

F.S. Trueman	(64)	1952–65
W. Rhodes	(60)	1899–1930
L. Hutton	(57)	1937–55
R. Illingworth	(45)	1958–73
G. Boycott	(33)	1964–82
H. Verity	(30)	1931–39

Most Catches in a Calendar Year
F.S. Trueman   (12) 1959–67

Most Catches in a Series
W. Rhodes   (10)   v   South Africa   1910   South Africa

Most Catches in a Match
W. Rhodes   (5)   v   Australia   1905   Manchester

Most Catches in an Innings
W. Rhodes   (4)   v   Australia   1905   Manchester

Wicket-Keeping
Most Dismissals in a Career
H. Carter   (28)   44ct/21st   1907–08 – 1921–22
S.J. Rhodes   (49)   46ct/3st   1994–95
D.L. Bairstow   (13)   12ct/1st   1979–81
A. Wood   (11)   10ct/1st   1938–39

Most Dismissals in a Calender Year
S.J. Rhodes   (33)   30ct/3st   1994

Most Dismissals in a Series
S.J. Rhodes   (21)   20ct/1st v Australia   1994–95

Most Dismissals in a Match
S.J. Rhodes   (7)   v Australia, Adelaide   1995

Most Dismissals in an Innings
J.G. Binks   (5)   v India, Calcutta   1964

YORKSHIRE-BORN TEST PLAYERS

(Cap No. is Yorkshire Selection only)

	Tests	Runs	Avg	Wkts	Avg	Ct	St	Cap No.
R. Appleyard	9	51	17.00	31	17.87	4	-	57
T. Armitage	2	33	11.00	-	-	-	-	1
C.W.J. Athey	23	919	22.97	-	-	13	-	76
D.L. Bairstow	4	125	20.83	-	-	12	1	74
J.C. Balderstone	2	39	9.75	1	80.00	1	-	72
W. Barber	2	83	20.75	1	-	1	-	39
W. Bates	15	656	27.33	50	16.42	9	-	6
G.J. Batty	7	144	20.57	11	66.63	3	-	93
J.G. Binks	2	91	22.75	-	-	8	-	64
J. Birkenshaw	5	148	21.15	13	36.07	3	-	66
R.J. Blakey	2	7	1.75	-	-	2	-	84
J.B. Bolus	7	496	41.33	-	-	2	-	62
M.W. Booth	2	46	23.00	7	18.57	-	-	26
W.E. Bowes	15	28	4.66	68	22.33	2	-	37
G. Boycott	108	8114	47.72	7	54.57	33	-	65
D.V. Brennan	2	16	8.00	-	-	-	1	53
T.T. Bresnan	2	9	9.00	3	32.33	1	-	643
D. Brookes	1	17	8.50	-	-	1	-	45
J.T. Brown	8	470	36.15	-	-	7	-	13
H. Carter	28	873	22.97	-	-	44	21	25
D.B. Close	22	887	25.34	18	29.55	24	-	50
G. Cook	7	203	15.61	-	-	9	-	77
G.A. Cope	3	40	13.33	8	34.62	1	-	73
A. Coxon	1	19	9.50	3	57.33	-	-	49
W.R. Cuttell	2	65	16.25	6	12.16	2	-	17
R.K.J. Dawson	7	114	11.40	11	61.54	3	-	91
D. Denton	11	424	20.19	-	-	8	-	23
A. Dolphin	1	1	0.50	-	-	1	-	29
T. Emmett	7	160	13.33	9	31.55	9	-	2
P.A. Gibb	8	581	44.69	-	-	3	1	42
D. Gough	58	855	12.57	229	28.39	13	-	87
G.K. Glover	1	21	21.00	1	28.00	-	-	15
A. Greenwood	2	77	19.25	-	-	2	-	3
S. Haigh	11	113	7.53	24	25.91	8	-	18
J.H. Hampshire	8	403	26.86	-	-	9	-	67
A. Hill	2	101	50.50	7	18.57	1	-	4
G.H. Hirst	24	790	22.57	59	30.00	18	-	16
M.J. Hoggard	67	473	7.27	248	30.50	24	-	89
P. Holmes	7	357	27.46	-	-	3	-	31
J. Hunter	5	93	18.60	-	-	8	3	8
L. Hutton	79	6971	56.67	3	77.33	57	-	40
R.A. Hutton	5	219	36.50	9	28.55	9	-	69
R. Illingworth	61	1836	23.24	122	31.20	45	-	58
R.K. Illingworth	9	128	18.28	19	32.36	5	-	82
S.F. Jackson	20	1415	48.79	24	33.29	10	-	10
P.W. Jarvis	9	132	10.15	21	45.95	2	-	81
R. Kilner	9	233	33.28	24	30.58	6	-	33
J. Laker	46	676	14.08	193	21.24	12	-	46